Lecture Notes in Compu  71

Edited by G. Goos, J. Hartmanis an

Advisory Board: W. Brauer   D. Gries   J. Stoer

Springer

Berlin
Heidelberg
New York
Barcelona
Budapest
Hong Kong
London
Milan
Paris
Santa Clara
Singapore
Tokyo

Carol Small   Paul Douglas   Roger Johnson
Peter King   Nigel Martin (Eds.)

Advances in Databases

15th British National Conference
on Databases, BNCOD 15
London, United Kingdom, July 7-9, 1997
Proceedings

Springer

Series Editors

Gerhard Goos, Karlsruhe University, Germany

Juris Hartmanis, Cornell University, NY, USA

Jan van Leeuwen, Utrecht University, The Netherlands

Volume Editors

Carol Small
SCO
Hatters Lane, Watford WD1 8YN, UK

Paul Douglas
SCSISE, University of Westminster
115 New Cavendish Street, London W1M 8JS, UK

Roger Johnson
Peter King
Nigel Martin
Birbeck College, University of London, Department of Computer Science
Malet Street, London WC1E 7HX, UK

Cataloging-in-Publication data applied for

Die Deutsche Bibliothek - CIP-Einheitsaufnahme

Advances in databases : proceedings / 15th British National Conference on
Databases, BNCOD 15, London, United Kingdom, July 7 - 9, 1997. Carol Small ...
(ed.). - Berlin ; Heidelberg ; New York ; Barcelona ; Budapest ; Hong Kong ;
London ; Milan ; Paris ; Santa Clara ; Singapore ; Tokyo : Springer, 1997
  (Lecture notes in computer science ; Vol. 1271)
  ISBN 3-540-63263-8

CR Subject Classification (1991): H.2-5

ISSN 0302-9743
ISBN 3-540-63263-8 Springer-Verlag Berlin Heidelberg New York

© Springer-Verlag Berlin Heidelberg 1997
Printed in Germany

Typesetting: Camera-ready by author
SPIN 10548856   06/3142 – 5 4 3 2 1 0   Printed on acid-free paper

Foreword

This volume contains the proceedings of the 15th British National Conference on Databases held at Birkbeck College, London, in July 1997. The College has played a major role in database research since the early 1970s, and it is altogether fitting that the conference should at last be held at Birkbeck.

The changes in the area of databases that have occurred since the conference was first held in 1980 have been phenomenal. Databases are now ubiquitous, ranging from PC databases which sit atop almost every desktop, through data warehouses, to the vast, heterogeneous, unstructured "database" which comprises the Internet. One of the key unresolved questions is how the wealth of information within the Internet can be integrated and exploited. Our invited speaker, Larry Kerschberg, considers exactly this problem. In his keynote paper he proposes the use of co-operating intelligent agents called "knowledge rovers", which can be configured to seek out, retrieve and integrate data and knowledge that is specific to their mission.

The first conference session concerns a more traditional database area: Transaction Processing. The first two papers are written by researchers working on the ClustRa project. Bratsberg et al. show how high availability can be achieved in mission critical database applications, using data replication, takeover and takeback, and self-repair; and Grøvlen et al. examine the problem of running ad-hoc queries over TP systems, where long-lived transactions may acquire and hold locks for a long period. Ferreira Rezende et al., consider the detection and resolution of deadlock in nested transactions, and advocate storing additional information in a Wait-for Graph.

No matter how databases evolve one issue always remains important: performance. The second session contains papers spanning the entire spectrum of current research in this area, from relational, through to object and temporal databases. Bratsbergsengen and Nørvåg describe a buffer management strategy for relational systems which effectively doubles the average block size. Object databases are becoming increasingly commonplace, and yet the optimisation of Object Query Languages (OQLs) is still in its infancy: Grust et al. tackle this issue, translating OQL queries into a mix of monoid calculus and algebra, and rewriting this representation by converting some calculus expressions into algebraic terms and the remainder into "fold" operations. Finally, Zurek shows how the processing of temporal joins can be optimised by choosing appropriate partitions of the temporal data, guided by information collected about the temporal data which is stored in a new data structure called an IP-table.

The proceedings also contain the abstracts of the posters presented at the conference. The posters cover distributed, heterogeneous, deductive and active databases, through database interface design for both traditional tabular data and non-traditional data (such as images, and Web data), to database mining.

The fourth session covers object oriented databases and the relationship between databases and the Internet. Lam, Chau and Wong propose a "double signature" indexing scheme suitable for efficiently answering queries on relations among classes, and over objects whose roles change over time. Knafla presents a prefetching technique for page servers for object oriented databases, which obtains its prediction information from the structure of objects. Finally, Faulstich et al. describe WIND, a model for organising Internet data in a data warehouse, and its query language WINDsurf which provides an integrated method of accessing the diverse data formats the warehouse contains.

Our fifth session concerns database integration. Santoyridis et al. describe an object versioning system, which supports collaborative design in a concurrent environment, and sketch a prototype implementation. Conrad et al. survey the problem of integrating the schemata of heterogeneous databases, and propose the use of a Generic Integration Model. Finally, Xu and Poulovassilis consider the integration of both the extensional and intensional parts of a set of deductive databases. They use a semi-automatic approach to integrating the component schemas rules, using a binary relational ER model as their common data model. To many of us at Birkbeck it is comforting that the binary model is still with us – the one sure landmark on an ever-changing landscape.

Acknowledgements

We are very grateful to the members of the programme committee both for the work they undertook in reviewing the papers and for attending the committee meeting to ensure that each submitted paper was fully and fairly considered. We are also grateful to Alex Gray, chairman of the steering committee, who gave sound and timely advice on planning the conference, to Peter Barclay for providing us with information on the preparation of the proceedings, and to the two previous conference organisers, Jessie Kennedy and Carole Goble, for their wide-ranging advice. At Birkbeck College we owe a debt of gratitude to Betty Walters, Lorrie Jobarteh and Alex Powell for preparing publicity material, handling conference enquiries and looking after the general administration of the conference.

Finally, on behalf of the British database community as a whole, we would like to thank the Engineering and Physical Sciences Research Council, without whose financial support much of the work described in these proceedings would not have taken place.

Birkbeck College, London
May 1997

Carol Small
Paul Douglas
Roger Johnson
Peter King
Nigel Martin

Conference Committees

Program Committee

P.J.H. King (Chair)	Birkbeck College
D. Bell	Univerity of Ulster
D. Bowers	Surrey University
R. Cooper	Glasgow University
C. Goble	University of Manchester
W.A. Gray	Univ. College of Wales, Cardiff
M. Jackson	University of Wolverhampton
K.G. Jeffrey	DRAL
M. Kay	ICL
G. Kemp	Aberdeen University
Z. Kemp	University of Kent
J. Kennedy	Napier University
S. Lavington	Essex University
M. Levene	University College London
G. Loizou	Birkbeck College
R. Lucas	Keylink Computers
V.A.J. Maller	Loughborough University
D. McGregor	Strathclyde University
R. Morrison	St Andrews University
N.W. Paton	University of Manchester
A. Poulovassilis	King's College London
G. Ringwood	Queen Mary and Westfield College
G. Sharman	IBM
M. Shave	Liverpool University
C. Small	SCO
P. Thanisch	University of Edinburgh
S. Todd	IBM
M.H. Williams	Heriot-Watt University
M.F. Worboys	Keele University

Organising Committee

P. Douglas (Social)	Westminster University
R.G. Johnson (Chair)	Birkbeck College
N.J. Martin (Treasurer)	Birkbeck College
C. Small (Proceedings)	SCO

Steering Committee

D.S. Bowers	Surrey University
C. Goble	University of Manchester
P.M.D. Gray	University of Aberdeen
W.A. Gray (Chair)	Univ. College of Wales, Cardiff
J. Kennedy	Napier University
C. Small	Birkbeck College
M. Worboys	Keele University

Table of Contents

Invited Paper

The Role of Intelligent Software Agents in Advanced Information Systems ... 1
L. Kerschberg

Transaction Processing

Location and Replication Independent Recovery in a Highly Available
Database 23
S.E. Bratsberg, S.-O. Hvasshovd and Ø. Torbjørnsen

Compensation-Based Query Processing in On-Line Transaction Processing
Systems 38
Ø. Grøvlen, Ø. Torbjørnsen and S.-O. Hvasshovd

Detection Arcs for Deadlock Management in Nested Transactions and Their
Performance 54
F. de Ferreira Rezende, T. Härder, A. Gloeckner and J. Lutze

Optimisation

Improved and Optimized Partitioning Techniques in Database Query
Processing 69
K. Bratbergsengen and K. Nørvåg

Query Evaluation in CROQUE - Calculus and Algebra Coincide 84
T. Grust, J. Kröger, D. Gluche, A. Heuer and M.H. Scholl

Optimisation of Partitioned Temporal Joins 101
T. Zurek

Posters

Maintaining Library Catalogues with an RDBMS: A Performance Study ... 116
O. Balownew, T. Bode, A.B. Cremers, J. Kalinski, J.E. Wolff and H. Rottmann

Merging an Active Database and a Reflective System: Modelling a New
Several Active Meta-Levels Architecture 119
L. Berti

A Framework for Database Mining 121
H. Gupta, I. McLaren and A. Vella

Query Processing Techniques for Partly Inaccessible Distributed Databases 123
O. Haase and A. Henrich

Indexing Multi-Visual Features in Image Database 126
R. Lei, A.H.H. Ngu and J.J. Jin

Customisable Visual Query Interface to a Heterogeneous Database
Environment: A Meta-Programming Based Approach 129
A.P. Madurapperuma, W.A. Gray and N.J. Fiddian

Automatic Web Interfaces and Browsing for Object-Relational Databases .. 131
M. Papiani, A.N. Dunlop and A.J.G. Hey

A Mechanism for Automating Database Interface Design, Based on Extended
E-R Modelling 133
S.R. Rollinson and S.A. Roberts

Exploration of the Requirements in a Visual Interface to Tabular Data 135
I. Taylor and S. Benford

DOA - The Deductive Object-Oriented Approach to the Development of
Adaptive Natural Language Interfaces 137
W. Winiwarter and Y. Kambayashi

Object Orientation and the Internet

An Efficient Indexing Scheme for Objects with Roles 139
F.M. Lam, H.L. Chau and R.K. Wong

A Prefetching Technique for Object-Oriented Databases 154
N. Knafla

WIND: A Warehouse for Internet Data 169
L.C. Faulstich, M. Spiliopoulou and V. Linnemann

Database Integration

An Object Versioning System to Support Collaborative Design within a
Concurrent Engineering Context 184
I. Santoyridis, T.W. Carnduff, W.A. Gray and J.C. Miles

Schema Integration with Integrity Constraints 200
S. Conrad, M. Höding, G. Saake, I. Schmitt and C. Türker

A Method for Integrating Deductive Databases 215
L. Xu and A. Poulovassilis

Author Index.. 233

The Role of Intelligent Software Agents in Advanced Information Systems

Larry Kerschberg
Center for Information Systems Integration and Evolution
Department or Information and Software Systems Engineering
MSN 4A4, George Mason University, Fairfax, VA 22032-4444
email: kersch@gmu.edu

Abstract. The paper presents an information architecture consisting of the information interface, management and gathering layers. Intelligent active services are discussed for each layer, access scenarios are presented, and the role of knowledge rovers is discussed. Knowledge rovers represent a *family* of cooperating intelligent agents that may be configured to support enterprise tasks, scenarios, and decision-makers. These rovers play specific roles within an enterprise information architecture, supporting users, maintaining active views, mediating between users and heterogeneous data sources, refining data into knowledge, and roaming the Global Information Infrastructure seeking, locating, negotiating for and retrieving data and knowledge specific to their mission.

Keywords: Knowledge Rovers, Active Services, Active Databases, Intelligent Software Agents, Information Architectures.

1 Introduction

During the mid- to late-1980's, this author saw the need to promote the integration and interchange of research and development in a new field that integrated work in Artificial Intelligence, Logic Programming, Information Retrieval and Database Systems, calling it *Expert Database Systems* [31-34]. Since then, substantial progress has been made in making Database Management Systems more active and knowledgeable, while at the same time facilitating access to large databases by Expert Systems and other knowledge-based systems.

Recently, research has focused on the Intelligent Integration of Information (I*3) [73]. Here the problem is to *access* diverse data residing in multiple, autonomous, heterogeneous information sources, and to *integrate* or *fuse* that data into coherent information that can be used by decision makers. To make the problem even more challenging:

1) data may by *multimedia* (video, images, text, and sound);

2) sources may store the data in diverse formats (flat files, network, relational-, or object-oriented databases);

3) the meaning of data, i.e., *data semantics* may conflict across multiple sources;

4) the data may have differing temporal and spatial granularities;

5) much of the *interesting* and *valuable* data may reside outside the enterprise, in the open-source literature accessible via subscription services, broadcast services, and on the World Wide Web (WWW)[3]; and

6) the data may be of uncertain quality, and the reliability of the source may be questionable.

The I*3 research has been sponsored primarily by DARPA, the Defense Advanced Research Project Agency, and our group at George Mason University (GMU) has been funded under this program, and more recently by the DARPA Advanced Logistics Program. The work reported in this paper reflects our research in I*3 in which we proposed a *federated* approach to providing I*3 *services* to support information integration needs. These points will be elaborated later in the paper. We have extended these notions further by incorporating cooperating software agents into our work in the Advanced Logistics Program.

It is becoming increasingly apparent that one cannot expect to solve I*3 and other large-scale system problems with a *monolithic* and integrated solution. Rather, the system should be composed of smaller components, with each component having the requisite knowledge to perform its tasks within the larger problem-solving framework.

Thus, if we are to design and build advanced information systems for large-scale systems, we must focus on a modular, service-oriented approach that provides the desired information to decision-makers, while shielding them for the torrent of information available through the Global Information Infrastructure. Intelligent software agents are a key feature for building advanced information systems.

2 Enterprise Data and Information Requirements

In this section we address enterprise data and information requirements with emphasis on I*3 tasks. These requirements are general and apply to most enterprises that have legacy systems and also access information on the Internet. We discuss the notions of data pull and data push requirements, review important concepts of intelligent agents as they pertain to data and information architectures, and introduce the notion of active services that will be implemented through a family of configurable and cooperating agents.

2.1 Data Pull and Data Push Requirements

In our research in architectures for large-scale systems [27, 35, 42], inspired primarily by our participation in an Independent Architecture Study of NASA's Earth Observing System Data and Information System (EOSDIS), we have identified two types of data requirements and their associated scenarios: Data Pull and Data Push.

Data Pull denotes a user-initiated information request, for example, in accessing data from EOSDIS archives, or in creating a logistics plan and then accessing multiple databases to instantiate that plan with actual data.

Data Push corresponds to the continual updating of databases used by the enterprise. These updates are under the control of the organizations that designed, built, control, and maintain the databases. The organizations have *autonomy* over and *responsibility* for the data, ensure its quality, and share the data within a federation of information systems [35, 36, 39, 56, 62].

Thus, a system must support both data *pull* and data *push*, while providing reasonable service to all users. The approach proposed in this paper is a family of intelligent agents, called *knowledge rovers*, which provide services, such as, information access, query formulation, facilitation, brokerage, mediation, integration, and wrapping services, that enable the modern enterprise to realize its information management needs, while serving its users in a timely, efficient and cost-effective manner.

2.2 Intelligent Agents for the Enterprise

Bird [5] has proposed an agent taxonomy based on two client/server classes. They are *Mobile Agents* (Clients) for Content, Communications and Messaging Services and Static Agents (Servers).

We add third type of agent, the *Active View Agent*, which site between the mobile agents and the server agents, and supports active objects and views. Active view agents may act on behalf of users in *materializing* objects based on real-time events and conditions, as well as pre-defined rules provided by either users or other agents. In defining an active view, the user provides a specification of the "real-world" objects of interest, and how they are materialized by data items contained in multiple information sources. In addition, certain staleness conditions — distributed integrity constraints — are specified, with the proviso that the view should be refreshed when the staleness conditions are violated. Once the active view is refreshed, the view itself may take action by executing a set of rules. We will have more to say about active views later in the paper.

Bird notes that distributed intelligent systems share many of the same characteristics of multidatabase systems [62], in particular, distribution, heterogeneity, and autonomy. Knowledge and data may be *distributed* among various experts, knowledge bases and databases, respectively. Problem-solving should be a cooperative endeavor [15, 30]. Multiple copies of knowledge and data, possibly in differing formats, must be maintained by the system.

There are several facets to the *heterogeneity* of information in systems [5]: syntactic, control and semantic.

1) *Syntactic heterogeneity* refers to the myriad of knowledge representation formats [28], data definition formats to represent both knowledge and data.

2) *Control heterogeneity* arises from the many reasoning mechanisms for intelligent systems including induction, deduction, analogy, case-based reasoning, etc. [6, 15, 18, 22, 23, 30, 63, 64].

3) *Semantic heterogeneity* [10, 20, 30, 69, 70, 78, 79] arises from disagreement on the meaning, interpretation and intended use of related knowledge and data.

Table 1: Internet Three Layer Information Architecture

Information Layer	Layer Service
Information Interface Layer	Users perceive the available information at this layer and may query and browse the data. This layer must support scalable organizing, browsing and search.
Information Management Layer	Responsible for the replication, distribution, and caching of information.
Information Gathering Layer	Responsible for the collecting and correlating the information from many incomplete, inconsistent, and heterogeneous repositories.

A third characteristic of intelligent systems is that of *autonomy*. There are several aspects to autonomy; in the control structure of an agent, in the extent to which an agent shares information with other agents [22, 24], the manner in which an agent associates with other agents, and structural autonomy in the way an agent fits into an organization of agents for problem-solving [13, 21, 29, 36-39, 41, 55, 63].

2.3 Enterprise Information Architecture

Bowman et al [7, 8] describe a three-layer architecture for scalable Internet resource discovery, proposed by the Internet Research Task Group. Table 1 denotes the three-layer architecture which provides access to heterogeneous repositories, including those on the WWW.

Figure 1 depicts GMU approach to the three-layer architecture for the application domain of logistics; the architecture is general enough to apply to most enterprises. The information architecture incorporates the three information layers consisting of:

1) *Information interface layer* where users access the system, formulate queries, collaborate in problem-solving activities, initiate pull scenarios and receive information from push scenarios. Users have access to their local databases and work through local views. We assume that collaboration mechanisms and tools exist at this layer;

2) *Information management layer* where objects, mediated active views, and information in an Information Repository are integrated, managed, replicated, updated. This layer mediates between the information interface layer and the information gathering layer, allowing users to perceive an *integrated information space*, when in reality, data resides in multiple heterogeneous databases and information sources. A mediated view of data is provided at this layer and user views are materialized from the mediated view.

The Real-Time Information Processing and Filtering process constantly monitors the system for events of importance to enterprise activities, and informs users, the mediated view, and the Information Repository should these events occur.

The Information Repository contains meta-data and knowledge associated with enterprise resources. It is provided information by the Data/Knowledge Refinement, Fusion and Certification process, and constantly updates the repository. Here data from diverse, heterogeneous inter-networked information sources are mined, scrubbed, refined and evolved to produce high-quality information.

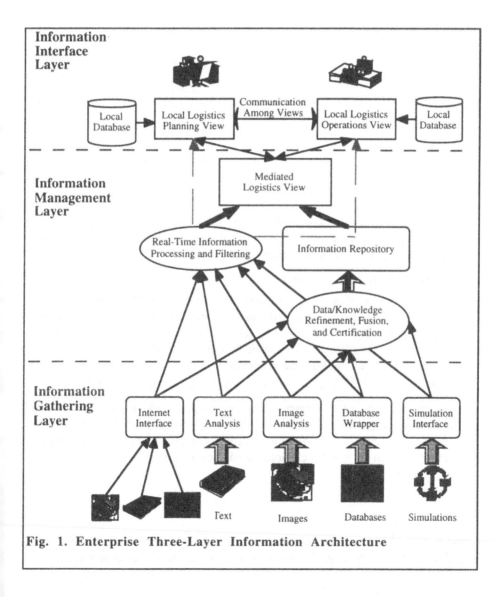

Fig. 1. Enterprise Three-Layer Information Architecture

Table 2: Enterprise Active Services

Information Layer	Layer Service	Active Services
Information Interface Layer	Users perceive the available information at this layer and may query and browse the data. This layer must support scalable organizing, browsing and search.	Thesaurus Services Federation Services Place your service here![1]
Information Management Layer	Responsible for the replication, distribution, and caching of information.	Mediation Services Active Views I*3 Services Place your service here!
Information Gathering Layer	Responsible for the collecting and correlating the information from many incomplete, inconsistent, and heterogeneous repositories.	Data Quality and Inconsistency Management Place your service here!

3) *Information gathering layer* where data from diverse, heterogeneous inter-networked information sources are accessed. Special rovers are used to perform the mediated access to local as well as internet resources.

2.4 Enterprise Active Services

Table 2 presents a collection of active services for the enterprise. These services reflect our I*3 research, particularly in mediated data access through brokerage, facilitation and wrapping services. The GMU research group has developed a federated service architecture that provides Federation Interface Managers (FIMs) as active wrappers for information sources, an intelligent thesaurus [69, 70], temporal mediation services [4, 66-68], active views [1, 57-61], and inconsistency management services [45-52].

Data mining and knowledge discovery techniques are applicable to the study of data quality, user usage patterns, automatic classification, schema evolution, and system evolution [43, 53, 54, 76-79]. We now present a synopsis of the various services. Readers may consult the relevant citations for additional details.

---

[1] This is an invitation to classify your services within the framework. Ideally they should be modular, serve a specific need, and be composable with other services.

2.4.1 Thesaurus Services

The *intelligent thesaurus* [35, 69, 70] is an *active* data/knowledge dictionary capable of supporting multiple ontologies and allowing users to formulate and reformulate requests for objects. The intelligent thesaurus is similar to the thesaurus found in a library; it assists users in identifying similar, broader or narrower terms related to a particular search term, thereby increasing the likelihood of obtaining the desired information from the information repository. In addition, active rules may be associated with object types as well as their attributes and functions.

2.4.2 Federation Services

At GMU we have developed an I*3 federated distributed client/server architecture [25] in which the constituent systems maintain authority and autonomy over their data which at the same time sharing certain information with the federation. Client software and/or server software is provided to members so that they can interface existing information systems with the federation. This was proposed in our Independent Architecture Study for the EOSDIS system [26, 35, 42], and some form of federation is planned for EOSDIS.

A Federation Interface Manager (FIM) is associated with each information system joining the federation. It is specialized into client and server FIMs. Each Client-Federation Interface Manager (FIM) consists of three subsystems, a Client Router, Client-to-Federal Translation Services, and Federal-to-Client Translation Services. The translation services map local data objects to the federal representation and vice-versa. The Client-FIM 1) accepts local transactions (including query requests) from local clients in the format used by the local information system, and 2) the router determines whether the transaction is for a local server or a remote server of the federation. If the destination is a valid server, the request is passed to the Client-to-Federal Translation Services so the request may be translated to standard federal transaction format prior to routing it to the appropriate server.

The Server-FIM consists of Federal-to-Server Translation Services, Server-to-Federation Translation Services, and the Server Router. When a transaction arrives at a destination, the Federal-to-Server Translation Services translates the federal transaction into the local transaction format of the server. After translation the transaction is sent to the server router. The router receives all transactions, both locally and remotely generated, and logs them. Transactions are then queued for processing. Once the server has processed the transaction, the server router sends the response, if necessary, to the Server-to-Federal Translation Services, for server to federal translation, and then routes the response to the appropriate Client-FIM, where the response is translated into the local format.

2.4.3 Mediation Services

Mediation refers to a broad class of services associated with I*3 [72-75]. At GMU we have focused on the mediation of temporal data of differing granularity. This is of particular importance in the context of multidimensional databases and data warehousing applications, where historical data is integrated and analyzed for patterns and interesting properties.

A *temporal mediator* [4, 67, 68] consists of three components: 1) a repository of *windowing functions* and *conversion functions*, 2) a time unit thesaurus, and 3) a query interpreter. There are two types of windowing functions: the first associates time points to sets of object instances, and the other associates object instances to sets of time points. A conversion function transforms information in terms of one time unit into that in terms of some other time unit. The time unit thesaurus stores the knowledge about time units (e.g., names of time units and relationships among them). The time-unit thesaurus stores concepts such as the seasons, fiscal year definitions, and calendars, and effects translation of these time units into others.

Users pose queries using the windowing functions and desired time units using a temporal relational algebra. To answer such a user query, the query interpreter first employs the windowing functions together with the time unit thesaurus to access the temporal data from the underlying databases and then uses the time unit thesaurus to select suitable conversion functions which convert the responses to the desired time units. Thus, a temporal mediator provides a simple, yet powerful, interface that supports multiple temporal representations in a federated environment. Temporal mediators may also be used to compare historical databases such as those needed for auditing and data warehousing purposes.

2.4.4 Active Views

Active views are motivated by the need to mediate between users and the plethora of enterprise data and information being generated. Active views can be used to define complex objects, events and conditions of interest.

Thus, active views mitigate the need for users to constantly issue queries to verify the existence of certain events or condition in the enterprise, or to be bombarded constantly with irrelevant information. The active view automates this task by compiling user object specifications into rules monitored by active databases [11, 16, 17, 71], or polling queries issued against traditional enterprise database systems. These rules can also be given rovers that comb the WWW seeking relevant information. Active views also provide active caching [1, 59] of materialized views so as to support subscription services, notification services, and to update user profiles. Further, materialized views can be updated automatically. Active views are discussed in more detail later in this paper.

2.4.5 Data Quality and Inconsistency Management

In any environment of multiple information resources one would expect that sources would overlap in providing similar but inconsistent data. Inconsistencies are detected during the process of integration, and *harmonization agents* are engaged to resolve them. The concept of the harmonization agent is incorporated in the Multiplex [46, 49] proof-of-concept system which considers the reliability and quality of the conflicting information sources, and resolves conflicts in a way that increases the overall value of the information[52].

3 Knowledge Rover Architecture

The concept of Knowledge Rovers serves as a metaphor for the family of cooperating intelligent agents that support the information architecture. The notion of a rover is that it can be configured automatically with appropriate knowledge bases (ontologies), task-specific information, negotiation and communication protocols for its mission into cyberspace. Figure 2 superimposes the various agents in the Knowledge Rover Family onto Figure 1, and roles are described below:

3.1 Knowledge Rover Types

Executive Agent — is a *coordinator* for a group of agents. It is informed of significant events. A significant event can lead to the activation of new agents. For example, if the enterprise is notified of disaster-relief request, then the executive agent would coordinate with other agents in implementing the relief scenario.

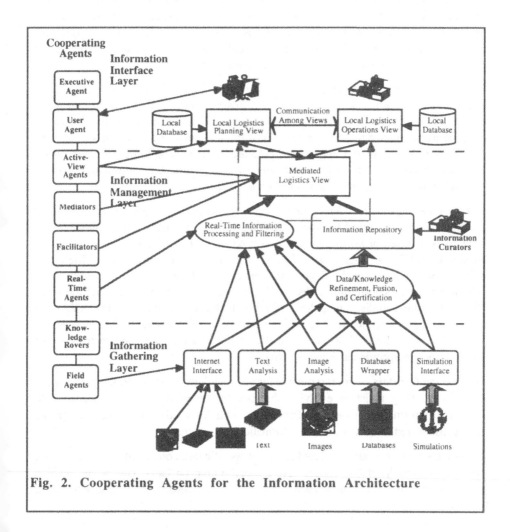

Fig. 2. Cooperating Agents for the Information Architecture

User Agents — acts on behalf of a user, and is responsible for assisting users: 1) in browsing catalogs and information holdings such as the information repository, 2) in the intelligent formulation of queries, and 3) in the planning of tasks within a mission-specific scenario such as provisioning logistic support for a disaster relief effort.

Real-time Agents — are mission-specific, defined and configured to process incoming data, and update the appropriate database or notify the appropriate users. The real-time agents are autonomous, communicate with each other using a pre-defined protocol. Real-time agents are responsible for monitoring the external environment, interacting with other systems, or acting on inputs from users. When an event is detected by a real-time agent, it is signaled to the relevant agents.

Facilitation Agents — provide intelligent dictionary and object location services. For example a facilitation agent [24] might accept a request from the Executive Agent to find all *external* providers of 'antibiotics,' and it might respond with the pharmaceutical producers and suppliers for the region in question. Other agents such as *knowledge rovers* (defined below) could then arrange for the items to be requisitioned, retrieved, and paid for. A knowledge rover could also post a request for bids, accept responses, make contracts, and provision the requested items.

Mediation Agents — are configured to assist in the integration of information from multiple data and information sources, having diverse data formats, different meanings, differing time units, and providing differing levels of information quality. Mediators [72, 73] are configured to accept queries from the Executive, translate the queries into the query language of the appropriate database system, accept the retrieved result, integrate it with results from other sources, and return the information to the Executive for presentation to the User Interface Agent.

Active View Agents (AVA) — are created to support user views specified over multiple, autonomous and heterogeneous data sources. In many cases, users do not have to be notified of all event occurrences; rather users, and their associated active views, are notified whenever *critical* events and object states are signaled. The active view agent is initially specified as a view materialized from multiple data sources. In addition, integrity constraints, called *staleness conditions*, are specified, and the AVA then transforms and distributes the constraints to local data sources. The AVAs and Real Time Agents cooperate in assessing when the significant events arise or staleness conditions are violated. The views are then materialized and appropriate triggers are invoked and pre-specified actions are taken.

Information Curators — are responsible for the quality of information the Information Repository. They assist in evolving the data and knowledge bases associated with enterprise information resources. They work with knowledge rovers to incorporate newly discovered resources into the information repositories.

Knowledge Rovers — are instructed carry out specific tasks on behalf of the executive, such as to identify which vendors have a specific item on hand. This would involve obtaining information from several vendors. The knowledge rover dispatches *field agents* to specific sites to get the relevant information. If the knowledge rover gets similar information from more than one source, it may ask a *mediator* such as Multiplex [49] to resolve the inconsistency. The knowledge rover reports back to the Executive Agent. The rovers are also responsible for Internet resource discovery. These new information sources and their data are analyzed to determine the adequacy, quality and reliability of retrieved information and whether it should be incorporated into the information repository.

Field Agents — are *specialized* rovers that have expertise in a certain domain, for example, pharmaceuticals, and knowledge about domain-specific information holdings at one or more sites. For example, a field agent could be tasked to monitor all aspects of a single item, say an 'antibiotic' produced by several manufactures and distributed by several vendors. They negotiate with the local systems through their *wrapper*, or Federation Interface Manager, retrieve appropriate data, and forward it to the appropriate requesting agent.

3.2 Scenarios for Knowledge Rover Family

This section presents examples of *push* and *pull* scenarios showing how the agent community would cooperate in providing information to logistics users. A pull scenario is one initiated by the user. A user agent acts on behalf of the user. We include in our pull scenario, access to commercial services available on the Internet [9, 14, 40, 65].

A push scenario is a pre-defined scenario, or pattern, in which incoming data is processed in real-time by real-time agents and passed onto active view agents to update the mediated and local logistics views shown in Figure 2. A push scenario defines a configuration of cooperating agents, the data to be collected in real-time from the external environment, the events to be monitored, and to whom they should be communicated.

3.2.1 Pull Scenario

In a pull scenario, the user would initiate a query or propose a set of tasks to be handled by the executive agent. For example, suppose the user notices that a convoy of ships suddenly has a *new* but unidentified object nearby. He works with the user agent to formulate a query [2, 4, 12, 19, 44, 69, 78, 79] which has both temporal and spatial conditions; the English version of the query might be as follows:

> Determine the identity and type of any objects X that are or have been near Convoy Y (using either radar or satellite imagery or contact reports or a combination of the three) during the last two hours. The search for information should be within 5 degrees latitude and longitude from the present position of X in the convoy.

Suppose the fleet is in the Equatorial Pacific and the ship in question is also in that area. Further suppose the Local Logistics View has an object representing the convoy and another representing the unknown vessel. The User Agent would translate the user's query into an object-relational query based on the object specifications supplied by the local logistics view agent, the thesaurus, and the Information Repository.

The query might have the form:

> FIND identity(X), type(X) FOR X NEAR Convoy Y
> WHERE TIME INTERVAL BETWEEN (NOW — Two Hours)
> AND REGION IS BETWEEN (-5 and +5 Degrees Latitude
> AND 120 and 130 Degrees West Longitude)

The following is a possible scenario involving the cooperation of several agents in processing the query:

1) The User Agent assists the user in formulating the query, most probably by means of a graphical user interface that allows the specification of geographical queries involving latitude and longitude specifications and with pop-up menus for the specification of temporal constraints.

2) The query is then handed over to the Executive who is responsible for decomposing it into subqueries for the appropriate agents to handle. The executive consults the Local Logistics View agent responsible for the objects specified in the query to determine which underlying databases containing the desired information.

3) The LLV agent, in turn, consults with the Mediated Logistics View Agents, and one or more facilitators, to determine which databases should be queried.

4) The LLV sends the Executive a list of databases to be queried, and also suggests consulting with Jane's Ships Encyclopedia on the Internet [9] for identification of the object in question.

5) After consulting the Military Satellite Imagery Field Agent, the LLV notes that there was a forty-five minute gap in military imagery over the Equatorial Pacific during the time period in question, and suggests going out to the Internet for commercially-available imagery. The Field Agent suggests using the GENIE Satellite Imagery Broker operated by Lockheed [40, 65].

6) The Executive configures a Knowledge Rover to negotiate with the GENIE broker to determine the availability, appropriateness and cost of the images. Also several lower-resolution quick-look samples are requested to determine if the object in question appears in some of the images.

7) The appropriate images are ordered, paid for, and retrieved using electronic commerce services provided by the Internet, and the knowledge rover asks a translator mediator to translate the images into the appropriate format, and an image understanding field agent begins the object classification and identification process.

8) Concurrent with steps 6 and 7, the executive tasks a field agent capable of understanding messages to review contact reports for the time-period in question. The executive also asks a field agent to review radar screens for the moment the object might have appeared on the radar screens.

The various agents complete their tasks and report back to the executive, who then asks several mediators to integrate the information from these multiple sources into a coherent object-oriented multimedia presentation which the user can review. The user or an agent can ascertain the moment the ship was first spotted on the radar or images.

3.2.2 Push Scenario

For a push scenario, the following agents would be involved: Executive, Real-time, Active View, MLV and LLV, Facilitation, Mediation, Knowledge Rovers, and possibly User Agents.

Consider the following scenario:

1) A real-time agent is processing incoming radar images. It signals an event when a certain object is detected.

2) The object-detected event is communicated to the relevant agents such as:
   - Active view agents, which are responsible for updating the views in the mediated and local logistics views,
   - User agents, who have specifically requested to be notified of this event,
   - An executive agent, as this event necessitates the coordination of other agents to act upon this event.

3) The executive agent selects a knowledge rover to initiate a search to identify the object, or if known, to confirm it.

4) The knowledge rover combs local and Internet sites for relevant information about this object, identifies the object, and then sends a message to the executive agent identifying the object.

5) The executive agent compares this result with that from the real-time agent, confirming the identity of the object, and sends a message to user agent informing it of the confirmation.

Once this event and the associated information were accepted by the user, the executive agent would communicate with the MLV agent and the Information Curator to incorporate the event and associated information into the information repository.

3.3 Active View Agents

The active view agent concept is based on the notion of *quasi-views* and implemented in the Mediator for Approximate Consistency (MAC) as described in [58-61]. Quasi-views in turn were motivated by the concept of quasi-copies introduced by Alonso [1].

An active view agent is responsible for maintaining a complex view composed of objects of interest to the decision maker, and these objects are materialized [57] from data in multiple autonomous, heterogeneous information sources. In order to *mediate* the data push resulting from real-time events and updates to local databases — those that would normally propagate to users — the active view agent provides a *mediation service* between users and local databases, by: 1) filtering the information according to quasi-view specifications, 2) presenting only significant events and critical conditions to users, 3) refreshing the view only when *staleness conditions* are violated, and 4) processing pre-defined rules in response to the updated view, and the significant events and conditions.

Note that once a collection of active views have been defined, they can be "reused" by various decision-makers; they may also be generalized or specialized by changing certain conditions in the view specification.

3.3.1 Active-Views

In our knowledge rover architecture, it is assumed that the decision-maker is not interested in every single update to a the Local Logistics Views (LLV), the Mediated Logistics View (MLV), the Information Repository, or the constituent databases. Rather, he wants to be notified *only when* certain *threshold events or conditions* warrant an updated situation assessment. With an active view the decision-maker can specify those variations of interest, based on the following types of *consistency* conditions: 1) the version of an update, 2) the time between refresh, 3) the percent deviation from an initial value, 4) attribute-value conditions, 5) refresh when an attribute value is a member of a list of values, and 6) general relational operations among attribute values.

These are termed staleness conditions, because the decision-maker or other agents are interested in updating cached objects in their views when they become stale as per the view specification.

Figure 3 illustrates a specification, in an extended version of SQL, for an active view class called *FriendlyTrack*, which provides position and other information on military ships and planes from selected friendly countries. FriendlyTrack has attributes ID, Velocity, Location, Home-port, Image, Flag, and Force-magnitude, and it has one superclass, InterestingEntity. A more detailed discussion of quasi-view specifications can be found in [58].

The "select always" statement means that an instance of FriendlyTrack should be created whenever there is an instance of Track with Flag equal to either "US", "UK", or "DE". Had "always" been omitted, the active view would contain only those instances of Track satisfying the predicate at active view initialization time; the server would not continue to monitor for new Track instances meeting the predicate.

Following the keyword "always" is a list of derivations of attributes of FriendlyTrack. These derivations are illustrated in Figure 4. ID, Image, and Flag are derived trivially from Track.ID, Track.Image, and Track.Flag respectively. Location is derived by applying the function *list* to the arguments Track.Latitude and Track.Longitude. The derivation of Home-port illustrates the resolution of structural heterogeneity; it is derived by applying the *name* function to the value of Track.Home-Facility, whose domain consists of instances of the class Facility. More complex forms of heterogeneity could be resolved similarly using arbitrary functions (nested as required) in derivations. No derivation is specified for the attribute force-magnitude, because it is a non-persistent attribute meaningful only within the application program.

create active view FriendlyTrack
> (ID, Velocity, Location, Home-port, Image, Flag, Force-magnitude)
> **under** InterestingEntity **as**
> **select always** ID, Speed, List(Latitude, Longitude),
>> Name(Home-facility), Image, Flag
>> **from** Track
>> **where** Flag in ("US", "UK", "DE")
>
> **with   staleness-conditions**
>> **percent** Speed 50,
>> **version** 5,
>> **any change to** Image,
>> **user-defined-delta**
>>> > (delta (Latitude, Longitude), 20))
>>> **with delta-function** Distance-using-lat-long
>
> **with   hints**
>> **refresh-strategy** eager **except** Image

Fig. 3. Example Active View Specification

The *staleness conditions* describe the conditions under which the active view no longer meets the user's specified coherency requirements. This occurs when Track.Speed varies by more than 50 percent from the value of Velocity for a corresponding active copy, whenever a cached instance of Track is updated 5 or more times since the last refresh, or whenever Track.Image is updated.

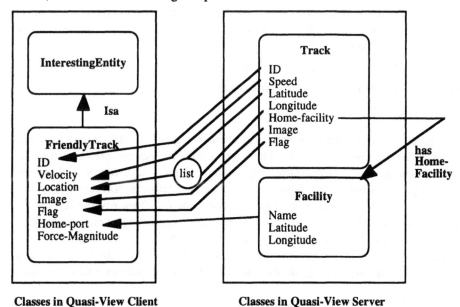

Classes in Quasi-View Client   Classes in Quasi-View Server

Fig. 4. Attribute Derivation for FriendlyTrack Example.

The last staleness condition is a *user-defined-delta*, used to describe data changes in the server that cause quasi-copies to become stale when those conditions depend upon changes to multiple attributes or to non-atomic or non-numeric attributes. The example illustrates how a user-defined-delta can track the magnitude of changes in Location, which is represented as a pair of complex attributes. The interpretation of the last staleness condition is this: an active copy becomes stale when the change in <Latitude, Longitude> exceeds 20, where the delta is measured by invoking the function Distance-using-lat-long with the arguments Latitude, Longitude, Cached-value-for-Latitude, and Cached-value-for-Longitude.

One implementation hint is specified in Figure 3: that the refresh strategy is "eager except Image." This indicates that quasi-copies should be refreshed as soon as they become stale, except for the attribute Image, which is refreshed only when it is accessed.

An implementation of the quasi-view concept is part of the Mediator for Approximate Consistency (MAC) [61] which has been implemented in Common Lisp and the ITASCA object-oriented database system.

We now extending the notion of quasi-views to active views and are investigating a number of issues including the following:

1) decomposition of active view staleness conditions into integrity constraints to be maintained and signaled by the local information sources,

2) strategies for monitoring of local constraints so as to satisfy global active view constraints,

3) performance models and quality-of-service tradeoffs as a function of maintaining refreshed and consistent active views in the face of increasing message traffic from local sources, and

4) the coordination of agents to support active views in information systems.

We hope to report on results in these areas in the future papers.

4 Conclusions

This paper has an information architecture consisting of the information interface, management and gathering layers. Intelligent active services are presented for each layer, access scenarios are presented, and the role of knowledge rovers is discussed. Knowledge rovers represent a *family* of cooperating intelligent software agents that may be configured to support enterprise tasks and scenarios. These rovers play specific roles within an enterprise information architecture, supporting users, maintaining active views, mediating between users and autonomous, heterogeneous data sources, refining data into knowledge, and roaming the Global Information Infrastructure seeking, locating, negotiating for and retrieving data and knowledge specific to their mission.

This paper represents the current architectural *vision* for our research activities, and we continue to work toward that vision.

5 Acknowledgments

I would like to acknowledge discussions and joint work with my co-Principal Investigators on the Knowledge Rover and I*3 research projects: Hassan Gomaa, Sushil Jajodia and Ami Motro. My doctoral students, past and present, through joint collaborations, have also influenced this work: Dr. Len Seligman, Dr. Doyle Weishar, Professor Jong Pil Yoon, Mr. Wiput Phijaisanit, Ms. Sonali Banerjee, Mr. Samuel Varas, Ms. Willa Pickering, and Mr. Anthony Scime.

This research is sponsored by DARPA grants N0060-96-D-3202 for Knowledge Rovers and N00014-92-J-4038, administered by the Office of Naval Research, for the I*3 research.

6 References

1. R. Alonso, D. Barbara, and H. Garcia-Molina, "Data Caching Issues in an Information Retrieval System," *ACM Transactions on Database Systems*, vol. 15, 1990.

2. Y. Arens, C. A. Knowblock, and W.-M. Shen, "Query Reformulation for Dynamic Information Integration," *Journal of Intelligent Information Systems*, vol. 6, 2/3, pp. 99-130, 1996.

3. T. Berners-Lee, R. Cailliau, A. Loutonen, H. F. Nielsen, and A. Secret, "The World-Wide Web," *Communications of the ACM*, vol. 37, pp. 76—82, 1994.

4. C. Bettini, X. S. Wang, E. Bertino, and S. Jajodia, "Semantic Assumptions and Query Evaluation in Temporal Databases," ACM SIGMOD International Conference on Management of Data, San Jose, CA, 1995.

5. S. D. Bird, "Toward a taxonomy of multi-agent systems," *International Journal of Man-Machine Studies*, vol. 39, pp. 689-704, 1993.

6. A. Bond and L. Gasser, "Readings in Distributed Artificial Intelligence," . San Mateo, CA: Morgan Kaufmann Publishers, Inc., 1988.

7. C. M. Bowman, P. B. Danzig, D. R. Hardy, U. Manber, M. F. Schwartz, and D. P. Wessels, "Harvest: A Scalable, Customizable Discovery and Access System," University of Colorado, Boulder, Technical Report CU-CS-732-94, March 1995.

8. C. M. Bowman, P. B. Danzig, U. Manber, and M. F. Schwartz, "Scalable Internet Resource Discovery: Research Problems and Approaches," *Communications of the ACM*, vol. 37, pp. 98—107, 1994.

9. BTG and Janes, *Jane's Electronic Information System*: http://www.btg.com/janes/, 1996.

10. S. Ceri and J. Widom, "Managing Semantic Heterogeneity with Production Rules and Persistent Queues," IBM Research Laboratory, San Jose, CA, Technical Report RJ9064 (80754), October 1992.

11. S. Chakravarthy and J. Widom, "Foreword to Special Issue on Active Database Systems," *Journal of Intelligent Information Systems*, vol. 7, pp. 64, 1996.

12. W. W. Chu, H. Yang, K. Chiang, M. Minock, G. Chow, and C. Larson, "CoBase: A Scalable and Extensible Cooperative Information System," *Journal of Intelligent Information Systems*, vol. 6, 2/3, pp. 223-259, June, 1996.

13. M. Cutkosky, R. Englemore, R. Fikes, M. Genesereth, T. Gruber, W. S. Mark, J. Tenenbaum, and J. Weber, "PACT: An Experiment in Integrating Concurrent Engineering Systems," In *IEEE Computer*, vol. 26, 1993, pp. 28-37.

14. S. Dao and B. Perry, "Information Mediation in Cyberspace: Scalable Methods for Declarative Information Networks," *Journal of Intelligent Information Systems*, vol. 6, 2/3, pp. 131-150, 1996.

15. R. Davis and R. Smith, "Negotiation as a Metaphor for Distributed Problem Solving," *Artificial Intelligence*, vol. 20, pp. 63-109, 1983.

16. U. Dayal, B. Blaustein, A. Buchmann, U. Chakravarthy, R. L. M. Hsu, D. McCarthy, A. Rosenthal, S. Sarin, M. J. Carey, M. Livny, and R. Jauhari, "The HiPAC Project: Combining Active Databases and Timing Constraints," *ACM SIGMOD Record*, vol. 17, pp. 51-70, 1988.

17. U. Dayal, A. P. Buchmann, and D. R. McCarthy, "Rules Are Objects Too: A Knowledge Model For An Active, Object-Oriented Database System," Proc. of 2nd Int'l Workshop on Object-Oriented Database Systems, Bad Munster am Stein-Ebernberg, Germany, 1988.

18. R. Engelmore and T. Morgan, "Blackboard Systems," In *The Insight Series in Artificial Intelligence*, T. Morgan, Ed.: Addison-Wesley Publishing Company, 1988, pp. 602.

19. C. Faloutsos, R. Barber, M. Flickner, J. L. Hafner, W. Niblack, D. Petovic, and W. Equitz, "Efficient and Effective Querying by Image Content," *Journal of Intelligent Information Systems*, vol. 3, pp. 231-262, 1994.

20. A. Farquhar, R. Fikes, W. Pratt, and J. Rice, "Collaborative Ontology Construction for Information Integration," Knowledge Systems Lab, Computer Science Department, Stanford University, Palo Alto, CA, KSL-95-63, August 1995.

21. T. Finin, "CIKM '94 Workshop on Intelligent Information Agents," , T. Finin, Ed. Baltimore, MD, 1994.

22. R. Fritzen, T. Finin, D. McKay, and R. McEntire, "KQML — A Language and Protocol for Knowledge and Information Exchange," International Distributed Artificial Intelligence Workshop, Seattle, WA, 1994.

23. L. Gasser and M. N. Huhns, "Distributed Artificial Intelligence," In *Research Notes in Artificial Intelligence*, vol. II. London and San Mateo: Pitman; Morgan Kaufmann Publishers, Inc., 1989, pp. 519.

24. M. Genesereth and S. P. Ketchpel, "Software Agents," *Communications of the ACM*, vol. 37, pp. 48-53, 1994.

25. H. Gomaa and G. K. Farrukh, "An Approach for Configuring Distributed Applications from Reusable Architectures," IEEE International Conference on Engineering of Complex Computer Systems, Montreal, Canada, 1996.

26. H. Gomaa, D. Menascé, and L. Kerschberg, "A Software Architectural Design Method for Large-Scale Distributed Information Systems," *Journal of Distributed Systems Engineering*, vol. September, 1996.

27. H. Gomaa, D. A. Menascé, and L. Kerschberg, "A Software Architectural Design Method for Large-Scale Distributed Data Intensive Information Systems," *Journal of Distributed Systems Engineering*, To appear.

28. T. Gruber, "A Translation Approach to Portable Ontology Specifications," *Knowledge Acquisition*, vol. 5, pp. 199-220, 1993.

29. R. V. Guha and D. B. Lenat, "Enabling Agents to Work Together," *Communications of the ACM*, vol. 37, pp. 126-142, 1994.

30. C. Hewitt, "Open Information Systems Semantics for Distributed Artificial Intelligence," *Artificial Intelligence*, vol. 47, pp. 79-106, 1991.

31. L. Kerschberg, "Expert Database Systems: Proceedings from the First International Workshop," . Menlo Park, CA: Benjamin/Cummings, 1986, pp. 701.

32. L. Kerschberg, "Expert Database Systems: Proceedings from the First International Conference," . Menlo Park, CA: Benjamin/Cummings, 1987, pp. 501.

33. L. Kerschberg, "Expert Database Systems: Proceedings from the Second International Conference," . Redwood City, CA: Benjamin/Cummings, 1988, pp. 777.

34. L. Kerschberg, "Expert Database Systems: Knowledge/Data Management Environments for Intelligent Information Systems," *Information Systems*, vol. 15, pp. 151-160, 1990.

35. L. Kerschberg, H. Gomaa, D. A. Menascé, and J. P. Yoon, "Data and Information Architectures for Large-Scale Distributed Data Intensive Information Systems," Proc. of the Eighth IEEE International Conference on Scientific and Statistical Database Management, Stockholm, Sweden, 1996.

36. M. Klusch, "Using a Cooperative Agent System FCSI for a Context-Based Recognition of Interdatabase Dependencies," Workshop on Intelligent Information Agents, CKIM Conference, Gaithersburg, MD, 1994.

37. M. Klusch, "Utilitarian Coalition Formation Between Information Agents," In *Cooperative Knowledge Processing*, S. Kirn and G. O'Hare, Eds. London: Springer-Verlag, 1996.

38. M. Klusch and O. Shehory, "Coalition Formation Among Rational Information Agents," Seventh European Workshop on Modelling Autonomous Agents in a Multi-Agent World (MAAMAW-96), Eindhoven, Netherlands, 1996.

39. M. Klusch and O. Shehory, "A Polynomial Kernel-Oriented Coalition Algorithm for Rational Information Agents," Second International Conference on Multi-Agent Systems, Kyoto, Japan, 1996.

40. D. Kuokka and L. Harada, "Integrating Information via Matchmaking," *Journal of Intelligent Information Systems*, vol. 6, 2/3, pp. 261-279, 1996.

41. P. Maes, "Designing Autonomous Agents: Theory and Practice from Biology to Engineering and Back," In *Special Issues of Robotics and Autonomous Systems*. Cambridge, MA, London, England: The MIT Press, 1990, pp. 194.

42. D. A. Menascé, H. Gomaa, and L. Kerschberg, "A Performance-Oriented Design Methodology for Large-Scale Distributed Data Intensive Information Systems," First IEEE International Conference on Engineering of Complex Computer Systems, Florida, 1995.

43. R. S. Michalski, L. Kerschberg, K. Kaufman, and J. Ribeiro, "Mining for Knowledge in Databases: The INLEN Architecture, Initial Implementation and First Results," *Journal of Intelligent Information Systems*, vol. 1, pp. 85-113, 1992.

44. A. Motro, "FLEX: A Tolerant and Cooperative User Interface to Databases," *IEEE Transactions on Knowledge and Data Engineering*, vol. 2, pp. 231-246, 1990.

45. A. Motro, "Accommodating Imprecision in Database Systems: Issues and Solutions," In *Multidatabase Systems: An Advanced Solution to Global Information Sharing*, A. R. Hurson, M. W. Bright, and S. Pakzad, Eds.: IEEE Computer Society Press, 1993, pp. 381-386.

46. A. Motro, "A Formal Framework for Integrating Inconsistent Answers from Multiple Information Sources," Department of Information and Software Systems Engineering, George Mason University, Fairfax, VA, Technical Report ISSE-TR-93-106, October 1993.

47. A. Motro, "Intensional Answers to Database Queries," *IEEE Transactions on Knowledge and Data Engineering*, vol. 6, pp. 444-454, 1994.

48. A. Motro, "Management of Uncertainty in Database Systems," In *Modern Database Systems: The Object Model, Interoperability and Beyond*, W. Kim, Ed.: Addison-Wesley Publishing Company/ACM Press, 1994.

49. A. Motro, "Multiplex: A Formal Model for Multidatabases and Its Implementation," ISSE Department, George Mason University, Fairfax, VA, Technical Report ISSE-TR-95-10, 1995.

50. A. Motro, "Responding with Knowledge," In *Advances in Databases and Artificial Intelligence, Vol. 1: The Landscape of Intelligence in Database and Information Systems*, vol. 1, L. Delcambre and F. Petry, Eds.: JAI Press, 1995.

51. A. Motro, D. Marks, and S. Jajodia, "Aggregation in Relational Databases: Controlled Disclosure of Sensitive Information," European Symposium on Research in Computer Security, 1994.

52. A. Motro and P. Smets, "Uncertainty Management in Information Systems: from Needs to Solutions," . Norwall, MA: Kluwer Academic Publishers, 1996, pp. 480.

53. G. Piatetsky-Shapiro and W. J. Frawley, "Knowledge Discovery in Databases," . Menlo Park, CA: AAAI Press/MIT Press, 1991.

54. J. Ribeiro, K. Kaufman, and L. Kerschberg, "Knowledge Discovery in Multiple Databases," ISMM International Conference on Intelligent Information Management Systems, Washington D.C., 1995.

55. D. Riecken, "M: An Architecture of Integrated Agents," *Communications of the ACM*, vol. 37, pp. 106-116, 1994.

56. M. Rusinkiewicz and others, "OMNIBASE: Design and Implementation of a Multidatabase System," *Newsletter of the Computer Society of the IEEE Technical Committee on Distributed Processing*, vol. 10, pp. 20--28, 1988.

57. A. Segev and J. Park, "Updating Distributed Materialized Views," *IEEE Transactions on Knowledge and Data Engineering*, vol. 1, pp. 173-184, 1989.

58. L. Seligman, "A Mediated Approach to Consistency Management Among Distributed, Heterogeneous Information Systems," In *Information and Software Systems Engineering*. Fairfax: George Mason University, 1994.

59. L. Seligman and L. Kerschberg, "An Active Database Approach to Consistency Management in Heterogeneous Data- and Knowledge-based Systems," *International Journal of Cooperative and Intelligent Systems*, vol. 2, 1993.

60. L. Seligman and L. Kerschberg, "Knowledge-base/Database Consistency in a Federated Multidatabase Environment," IEEE RIDE — Interoperability in Multidatabase Systems, Vienna, Austria, 1993.

61. L. Seligman and L. Kerschberg, "Federated Knowledge and Database Systems: A New Architecture for Integrating of AI and Database Systems," In *Advances in Databases and Artificial Intelligence, Vol. 1: The Landscape of Intelligence in Database and Information Systems*, vol. 1, L. Delcambre and F. Petry, Eds.: JAI Press, 1995.

62. A. Sheth and J. Larson, "Federated Database Systems for Managing Distributed, Heterogeneous, and Autonomous Databases," *ACM Computing Surveys*, vol. 22, pp. 183-236, 1990.

63. M. Tambe, W. L. Johnson, R. M. Jones, F. Koss, J. E. Laird, P. S. Rosenbloom, and K. Schwamb, "Intelligent Agents for Interactive Simulation Experiments," In *AI Magazine*, vol. 16, 1995, pp. 15-39.

64. M. Tambe and P. S. Rosenbloom, "Event Tracking in a Dynamic Multi-Agent Environment," USC — Information Sciences Institute, Technical Report ISI-RR-393, September 11, 1994.

65. C. Toomey and others, "Software Agents for Dissemination of Remote Terrestrial Sensing Data," i-SAIRAS 94, Pasadena, CA, 1994.

66. X. S. Wang, C. Bettini, A. Brodsky, and S. Jajodia, "Logical Design for Temporal Databases with Multiple Granularities," *ACM Transactions on Database Systems*, To appear.

67. X. S. Wang, S. Jajodia, and V. S. Subrahmanian, "Temporal Modules: An Approach Toward Federated Temporal Databases," ACM SIGMOD International Conference on Management of Data, Washington, D.C., 1993.

68. X. S. Wang, S. Jajodia, and V. S. Subrahmanian, "Temporal Modules: An Approach toward Federated Temporal Databases," *Information Sciences*, vol. 82, pp. 103-128, 1995.

69. D. Weishar, "A Knowledge-Based Architecture for Query Formulation and Processing in Federated Heterogeneous Databases," In *Information and Software Systems Engineering*. Fairfax, VA: George Mason University, 1993, pp. 230.

70. D. Weishar and L. Kerschberg, "Data/Knowledge Packets as a Means of Supporting Semantic Heterogeneity in Multidatabase Systems," In *ACM SIGMOD Record*, 1991.

71. J. Widom and S. Ceri, "Active Database Systems: Triggers and Rules for Advanced Database Processing," : Morgan Kaufmann Publishers, Inc., 1995.

72. G. Wiederhold, "The Roles of Artificial Intelligence in Information Systems," *Journal of Intelligent Information Systems*, vol. 1, pp. 35-56, 1992.

73. G. Wiederhold, "Foreword to Special Issue on the Intelligent Integration of Information," *Journal of Intelligent Information Systems*, vol. 6, 2/3, pp. 93-97, 1996.

74. G. Wiederhold, S. Jajodia, and W. Litwin, "Dealing with Granularity of Time in Temporal Databases," In *Lecture Notes in Computer Science*, vol. 498, R. Anderson and others, Eds.: Springer-Verlag, 1991, pp. 124-140.

75. G. Wiederhold, S. Jajodia, and W. Litwin, "Integrating Temporal Data in a Heterogeneous Environment," In *Temporal Databases: Theory, Design, and Implementation*, A. U. Tansel, S. Jajodia, and others, Eds.: Benjamin/Cummings, 1993, pp. 563-579.

76. J. P. Yoon and L. Kerschberg, "A Framework for Constraint Management in Object-Oriented Databases," International Conference on Information and Knowledge Management, Baltimore, MD, 1992.

77. J. P. Yoon and L. Kerschberg, "A Framework for Knowledge Discovery and Evolution in Databases," *IEEE Transactions on Knowledge and Data Engineering*, 1993.

78. J. P. Yoon and L. Kerschberg, "Semantic Query Reformulation in Object-Oriented Systems," In *International Conference on Deductive and Object-Oriented Databases*, vol. 760. Phoenix, AZ: Springer-Verlag, 1993.

79. J. P. Yoon and L. Kerschberg, "Semantic Update Optimization in Active Databases," Proceedings IFIP WG2.6 Working Conference on Database Semantics (DS-6), Atlanta, 1995.

Location and Replication Independent Recovery in a Highly Available Database

Svein Erik Bratsberg, Svein-Olaf Hvasshovd, Øystein Torbjørnsen

Telenor R&D
N-7005 Trondheim, Norway

Abstract. An increasing number of database applications demand high availability combined with scalable throughput and load balancing. We present a logging and recovery method which meets these goals by utilizing the log as a replication means from primaries to hot standbys. To be both scalable and highly available, recovery is performed independently of the location and replica of the original operations. The recovery method is designed to allow for load balancing in all situations of a highly available database, during normal processing, takeover and online self-repair. Logical tuple access is used both for redo and undo, and together with state identifiers connected to tuples this is the basis for the replication and location independent recovery. Unlike existing replication methods, this logging and recovery method allows for scalable replication by facilitating asynchronous parallel streams of log records from primaries to hot standbys. To provide high availability we also need fast takeover and takeback.

1 Introduction

This work is done as a part of the ClustRa project [9], which builds a database system focusing on the demanding requirements from open telecommunication applications. The driving requirements on availability and scalability are the following: Firstly, the traditional very high availability requirement for mission critical telecommunication equipment must be met. No more than two minutes unavailability at transaction service level is accepted per year. Secondly, the database must be able to scale to at least 1000 TPC-B like [4] transactions per second.

To achieve high availability we rely on data replication, fast takeover and takeback, and automatic self-repair. Data replication is maintained by redoing log records shipped from primaries to hot standbys. Takeback is done by recovering a failed node and letting it be caught up with the rest of the system. If the failed node does not recover, a new replica of the data and log at the failed node is produced, either by using several nodes having spare capacity (*distributed spare*), or by producing a complete replica at a spare node (*dedicated spare*).

The replication systems used by current products are limited to *physical replication* of blocks. This restrains the declustering and self-repair strategies, and load balancing is harder to achieve especially during and after failures. ClustRa's replication system is *logical* and allows the load to be balanced in all situations of a highly available database. During normal operations the load is balanced by horizontally fragmenting data to multiple nodes. At takeover, the load is balanced by having a declustering strategy allowing for parallel takeover at multiple hot standby nodes. Load balancing at self-repair is done by allowing for multiple senders and receivers in the fuzzy replica production. Load balancing is obtained due to the location and replication independent recovery method.

Commercial replication systems only allow for a single primary to hot standby log stream, which does not scale well. We allow for fully scalable replication by letting each primary/hot standby fragment replica pair have its own log stream. Most commercial replication systems are built on top of existing disk-based database systems. They are tuned for transaction throughput by buffering log records into batches either at primary or hot standby nodes. This results in takeover times, at best in order of seconds, which give an availability not tolerated by our target applications.

The organization of the paper is as follows: Section 2 reviews existing recovery and replication methods. Section 3 describes the declustering and online self-repair strategies used to achieve high availability. The principles of the location and replication independent recovery, which is necessary to support the declustering and online self-repair strategies, is explained in Section 4. The scalable replication method is presented in Section 5. Section 6 shows how access methods are logged and recovered. Fast takeover is presented in Section 7. Catchup and takeback is explained in Section 8. Section 9 presents synchronization of hot standby replicas at failures. Section 10 concludes the paper.

2 Related Work

2.1 Traditional Recovery Methods as a Basis for Replication

Most replication systems rely on shipping a copy of the log records produced at the primary over to the hot standby. They can be grouped into two main classes depending on the logged data unit [8]. The oldest method is *block-oriented*, i.e., concurrency control and recovery are both done in terms of blocks. Replication based on block logging demands that the replication is physical, i.e., that each primary block has its matching hot standby block replica.

The second class of recovery methods is *tuple-oriented*, because it relies on logging tuples. It can be combined with a physiological identification policy [5], compensation oriented logging [14], and a block state identifier policy. The physiological identification policy relates a redo log record part to a particular block. Hence, when using the log as the basis for replication, each primary block must have its corresponding hot standby block.

The physical level of replication resulting from both the block and the tuple-oriented recovery methods restrains the possible declustering schemes, i.e. fragmentation and replication. To avoid inconsistencies caused by overflow of hot standby blocks, a hot standby block must be equal to or greater than its corresponding primary replica of a block. If a hot standby replica of a fragment is subfragmented, a low fill level may be the result, because each subfragment replica will have the same number of blocks as the original primary replica. The hot standby blocks must still be of the same size as the primary blocks, because a full primary block may map all its tuples to the same hot standby block.

If the replication is not synchronized at the physical level, online non-blocking production of a new subfragmented replica of a fragment can not be allowed in combination with block state identifiers [8]. The tuple-oriented recovery method may support online non-blocking replication, but without subfragmentation. To minimize the need for subfragmentation during repair, each table can originally be fragmented into a large number of fragments [17].

2.2 Replication Methods used by Commercial Systems

Some commercial solutions use intra-site redundancy (e.g. RAIDs and disk mirroring) to mask single component failures. These solutions will not be treated further here, because their intra-site orientation does not allow masking of site failures. Other systems use inter-site redundancy by replicating sites for disaster recovery purposes. These are mostly primary/hot standby using a shared-nothing architecture. They use the tuple-oriented recovery method, e.g., the IBM Remote Site Recovery [2], Tandem Remote Duplicate Database Facility [6], Sybase Replication Server [7], Oracle7 Symmetric Replication Facility [16] and Informix-OnLine Dynamic Server [11]. The replication is either based on the database internal log or on a special replication log generated through the application of triggers. When the replication is based on the internal log, execution at the hot standbys can either be in redo mode directly from the log, or it can be based on new operations produced from the log. If an externally generated log is used, the only option available is generation of new operations.

These replication systems use different policies for log buffering at primary and hot standby nodes. Some buffer log records at primary nodes, so that log records are not shipped before a transaction commits. This reduces the shipped log volume, since no before images and compensation log records are sent. Others are shipping log records when a log block is flushed to disk. Some methods buffer log records at hot standby nodes. They do redo when all log records belonging to a transaction have been received and are stably stored. This avoids undo processing entirely at the hot standby during recovery processing. The disadvantage of the buffering policies is the delays they introduce. The delay typically causes takeover in the range of minutes. The delay is further extended if the log is only received and not executed at hot standby nodes before a takeover occurs. This may cause takeovers in the range of hours.

Log records can be shipped from primary to hot standby nodes as a single or multiple log streams. A single log stream may for large multi-node sites represent a bottleneck since it does not scale with the number of nodes. A single log stream may also increase the shipping latency. All commercial systems we have studied use a single log stream. Even when they have multiple nodes at the primary site, they concatenate the logs into a single log before it is shipped. Polyzois and Garcia-Molina [15] present a research system utilizing multiple log streams, but it replicates data in batches called *epochs*, which are geared towards throughput and network utilization, and not towards short takeover intervals.

3 Declustering and Self-Repair Strategies

3.1 Declustering Strategies

The data placement involved in fragmentation and replication constitute a *declustering strategy*. The main goal of our declustering strategy is to achieve high availability, scalability and load balancing, both during normal processing and upon failures. It is desirable to minimize the storage redundancy by keeping the number of replicas to a minimum, e.g., two replicas will often be enough. For high availability, the declustering strategy must ensure the replicas of a fragment to reside at different sites. To facilitate load balancing, fragment replicas must be evenly distributed over the nodes. Furthermore, all nodes must store both primary and hot standby fragment replicas. Primary fragment replicas will give higher load since read operations only affect them.

A straight forward declustering strategy is *multi-site mirrored declustering* [3, 17]. Pairs of nodes (one node from each site) store replicas of the same fragment. The nodes in the pair divide the primary and hot standby tasks between them to balance the load. A more flexible declustering scheme is *Q-rot declustering* [17], which is illustrated by a simple example in Figure 1. Each site has three nodes and 8 fragment replicas. At each site there are two active nodes and one spare node. Each active node has two primary and two hot standby fragment replica. Upon a uniform access pattern, this should give a balanced load over these nodes. The fragment replicas stored at one node at one site have corresponding fragment replicas distributed over multiple nodes at the other site. E.g., the primary fragment replicas at node 0, 1000-p and 1004-p, have hot standby fragment replicas located at node 10 and node 11 at the other site.

3.2 Takeover and Takeback

When a node has failed, a *takeover* takes place, i.e., the nodes holding the hot standby fragment replicas for the failed node take over as primaries. Q-rot declustering minimizes the takeover time, because the takeover is performed in parallel at multiple nodes. This is important since during the takeover parts of the database are temporarily unavailable. Unlike mirrored declustering, Q-rot declustering ensures the increased load for the nodes involved in the takeover to be spread over multiple nodes. E.g., if node 0 in Figure 1 failed, node 10 and 11 at site B will take over the primary responsibility for fragment replica 1000 and 1004, respectively.

After the takeover, the system is providing service as normal, but with a reduced fault tolerance level. To reestablish this, recovery at the failed node is started. If the recovery is successful, a *takeback* takes place, i.e. the recovered node achieves the same responsibility for primary and hot standby fragment replicas as before the crash.

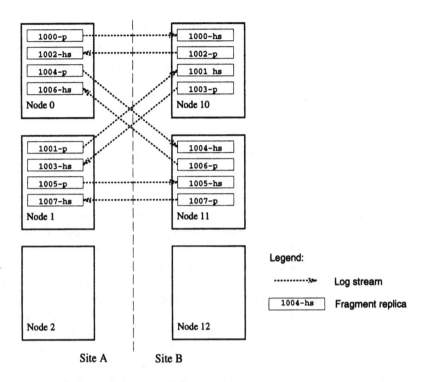

Fig. 1. Fragment replicas at two sites with three nodes each. -p means primary, -hs means hot standby.

3.3 Self-Repair

When a failed node does not recover within a certain time frame, a new copy of the lost replicas is automatically produced without waiting for manual intervention. This is done to reestablish the fault tolerance level prior to the crash.

One self-repair approach is to use *dedicated spares*. When the lost fragment replicas have been completely reconstructed at a spare node, it becomes an active node. The failed node after being replaced, will become a spare node. In Figure 1, node 2 will replace node 0 in self-repair by copying the fragment replicas 1000, 1002, 1004 and 1006 from the nodes at site B. Q-rot declustering allows this copying to be done in parallel from all active (sender) nodes at site B. Thus, the self-repair time may be reduced and there is a small increased load at the sender nodes while the self-repair takes place. The main problem with dedicated spares is that it is possible to run out of spare nodes. Adding nodes to the system makes it more expensive, and they are not useful during normal operation.

Q-rot declustering also allows for a *distributed spare strategy*. In this case, the fragment replicas created in the self-repair are distributed over multiple (receiver) nodes with spare capacity. An advantage of the distributed spare strategy is that the parallel copying is received by multiple nodes.

It is also possible to let the new fragment replicas be divided into smaller *subfragments*. To let the system scale with the data, subfragmentation is also used to distribute load over nodes in an environment where a table grows. As a table grows, it can be subfragmented over more nodes [8, 17].

4 Location and Replication Independent Recovery

Q-rot declustering allows high availability combined with scalability, load balancing and resource utilization. To achieve this, we cannot impose any restriction on the physical allocation and representation of data inside a node. Therefore, the tuples and tuple log records must be location transparent.

The fragment replicas consist of both the tuples themselves and the associated tuple log records. Log records are generated at the primary replica and sent to the hot standbys. Any log replica can be applied to any of their corresponding fragment replicas. Log records are *logical*, i.e., both undo and redo log records use primary-key based tuple access. Compared with physiological identification [5], logical identification imposes some overhead on redo and undo processing, because access methods must be used. However, it gives considerable flexibility with respect to the declustering and online self-repair strategy. An additional advantage of logical undo log records is that they are used internally at a node to allow a locked tuple to be moved between blocks when some transaction causes the block it resides in to be split. Thus, logical undo logging may avoid hot spot bottlenecks.

The location and replication independence improves availability by allowing for fast takeover and fast self-repair. Takeover is performed in parallel and new replicas may be produced in parallel and shipped to different nodes having spare capacity. To be able to do this, the scope of the *state identifier* (log sequence number, LSN) must be equal or less than the scope of the unit of distribution [8]. Thus, state identifiers are connected to tuples. The traditional method of connecting state identifiers to blocks would have implied that blocks were the atomic unit of replication, meaning that other declustering strategies than mirroring would be cumbersome.

Availability is also improved due to a greater encapsulation of implementation details at each node. The location and replication independent recovery allows different nodes to use different block sizes and different access methods, since log records do not refer to such details. This allows for heterogeneity and system change, because new system components may differ. Most software failures are caused by erroneous internal state at a node, e.g., counters that flip around, pointer or indexing errors. By making the nodes holding the different replicas physically dislike, there is less chance for a software fault to cause double failures. In a study done by Lee and Iyer [12], a process pair solution tolerated 75% of the software faults that result in processor failures.

5 Asynchronous Parallel Log Streams

A *log stream* is responsible for shipping log records from one primary fragment replica to the corresponding hot standby fragment replicas. Log records are sent as asynchronous parallel streams from primary fragment replicas to the hot standby replicas. One node will therefore host the same number of log streams as primary fragment replicas. Since the state identifiers are generated and maintained per fragment, parallel log streams become possible. This ensures that the log transport capability will scale linearly with the number of nodes. Node 0 in Figure 1 has two parallel outgoing log streams, one to node 10 and one to node 11 at site B.

Log records are sent in their LSN order per fragment to each hot standby fragment replica. If the hot standby replica is subfragmented, each subfragmented hot standby replica will receive log records in increasing LSN order, but not necessarily in monotonous order since log records may have been shipped to other subfragments replicas as well. The log stream received per subfragment reflects the record operation order per tuple, which is required to obtain a consistent hot standby replica. After a takeover, the subfragments will become primary and generate LSNs. The same LSN value may then be generated to two different subfragment replicas. This will not cause any inconsistencies because the subfragments are autonomous after a takeover with respect to LSN generation.

Subfragmentation creates a need for merging of subfragments into one consolidated fragment replica. This type of operation is needed when restarting a crashed node with a fragment replica having a subfragmented hot standby. The operation may also be done when a new node is included and some subfragmented fragments are to be gathered and merged at this node. The log stream from each subfragment will be kept separate. After a following takeover, all new log records are entered into a separate log and they are given LSNs that are higher than the LSNs in all the subfragment logs. The subfragment logs will be removed as part of the checkpointing policy [8].

6 Logging and Recovery of Access Methods

The replication and location independent logging and recovery method is logical. Thus, there is a need to solve the problems of *partial actions* and *action consistency* [5] for access methods.

Operations for access methods, e.g., block splits and index record inserts in B-trees, are logged internally at a node, and they are not replicated to any other node. These operations are organized in *node-internal transactions*. State identifiers reflecting the node-internal operations are connected to blocks and a traditional write-ahead logging method is used. However, committing a node-internal transaction *does not* involve any force-log-to-disk, since durability of *user transactions* is ensured by replicating the tuple log. Consider a node crash where the data and log in main-memory for a committed node-internal transaction were lost. At recovery time of this node, an equivalent, but not necessarily equal node-internal transaction will be regenerated by redoing the logical tuple log sent from other nodes.

The node-internal transactions are similar to the *nested top actions* of ARIES [14], but they differ because in ARIES there may be tuple log records later which are dependent on the effect of the nested top action, since the log records may refer to blocks generated by the nested top action. The purpose of our node-internal transactions and recovery of these is to establish an action-consistent node, i.e., a state where each tuple operation is fully reflected or not reflected at all.

Figure 2 shows the log records involved in a block split in a B^{link}-tree access method [13] with links in both directions. The figure shows links to previous log records in the same transaction. A block split creates three node-internal

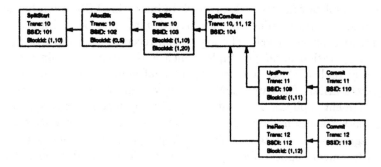

Fig. 2. Node-internal log records involved in a block split.

transactions which are chained together. The first transaction allocates a new block, updates the next links in the split block and the new block, and moves tuples to the new block. A sequence is imposed on writing blocks to disk to avoid logging tuples moved in a block split. The two other transactions may be delayed and may be run concurrently. One of them updates the previous link of the next block, and the other inserts the index tuple in the B-tree.

If during node-internal recovery only log records from the first transaction are found, the chained transaction may be rolled forward, because the first transaction has enough information to generate the two others. This forward rolling will "pre-split" the B-tree and make it consistent, and some time later, the tuple operation that originally caused the split will be redone or undone. An undo of the tuple operation does not cause an undo of the split.

Figure 3 and 4 show two states of a simple B-tree. These figures illustrate how the log records in Figure 2 are used in *main memory recovery* [9], which is important because it makes node crash recovery fast. Upon main memory-based recovery, block (1,10) is by checksums found to be corrupted. Figure 3 shows the B-tree after reading block (1,10) from disk and before redoing the node-internal log records to this block. Figure 4 shows the B-tree after redoing the node-internal log to this block. Each block has a *block state identifier* (BSID)

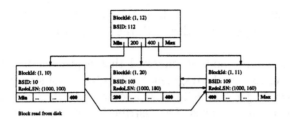

Fig. 3. B^{link}-tree before node-internal single block recovery.

which tells which node-internal log record was the last to be reflected to this block. Each block also has a *lower* and an *upper key limit* to determine which logical tuple log records to redo. For the image of block (1,10) read from disk the lower key is Min, the minimum key possible, and the higher key is 400. The node-internal log records 101 and 103 will be redone to this block. These two operations redo the split to this block, which also result in the next link and higher key to be updated. Tuples with keys between 200 and 400 will be removed from this block, since they have been moved to the next block.

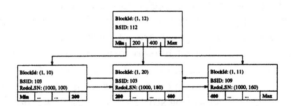

Fig. 4. B^{link}-tree after node-internal single block recovery.

After completing the node-internal recovery, as shown in Figure 4, the logical tuple log records with keys between Min and 200 will be redone to this block. This redo starts at the block's **RedoLSN**, which is the highest log sequence number for any tuple operations reflected in this block. However, state identifiers for the logical tuple log records are still contained within the tuples. **RedoLSN** shows the redo starting point in the logical tuple log without examining each tuple contained within the block, and it allows for representation of LSNs for deleted tuples.

7 Takeover Actions and Replication of Locks

Fast takeover is necessary to support high availability. We use two techniques to achieve fast takeover. Firstly, log records are sent across to hot standby nodes as soon as they are generated, and they are redone eagerly at the hot standby. Secondly, locks are shipped together with the log records.

When a hot standby node is informed that a primary node has failed, it will start activities to turn the fragment replicas being hot standby for the failed node into primary. In general, there may be several hot standby fragment replicas for one primary fragment replica. The distribution dictionary decides which hot standby fragment replica should become the new primary replica.

Fragment shield locks covering whole fragment replicas are used on hot standby fragment replicas, because during takeover new transactions should wait some time. During normal transaction processing, tuple locks are shipped together with the log records to the hot standby nodes and they are registered, but not effective. This means that all locks set at primaries become effective at hot standbys when they take over as primaries.

At takeover, first, the next LSN to be allocated for the fragment replicas turning primary will be increased by a certain interval. The resulting set of unused LSN values caused by this increase may be needed by the recovering node and the other hot standby nodes to produce undo log records for log records not being present at the current primary node (see Section 9). Second, the fragment shield locks for the actual fragment replicas are unlocked, and thus they become primary. At this point in time the tuple locks shipped with the log records become effective. As soon as the locks are set, new transactions may be served. Thus, by shipping locks together with log records, the period where the fragment is unavailable during takeover is minimized. New transactions may be served concurrently with the redo and undo resulting from the takeover. Third, for each failed node a redo phase will be started. The task of a redo phase is to redo all pending log records from the failed node and to close the log stream. Fourth, undo recovery of "failed" transactions will be done by an undo thread.

Transactions are coordinated through a two-phase commit protocol extended with a hot standby transaction controller [9]. All non-ready transactions where the primary transaction controller crashed will be aborted. Non-ready transaction slaves that acted as primaries at the crashed node will be aborted, and the abort decision will be distributed to all participants from the transaction controller. Non-ready transaction slaves for which the controllers are not known will also be aborted. These transactions appeared through receiving log records via the log stream prior to receiving the command from the transaction controller.

The aborted transactions are handled by an *undo thread*, which goes backwards in the tuple log and undoes log records. The undo thread will generate compensating log records (CLRs) for non-CLRs belonging to fragment replicas being primary at this node, including those fragment replicas that just became primary. For the other non-CLRs belonging to the aborted transactions, CLRs will arrive from the nodes currently being primaries for the fragments.

8 Catchup and Takeback

The purpose of node crash recovery is to bring a failed node back into the system in the same role as prior to the crash. Figure 5 shows the phases involved in node crash recovery of fragment replica 1000 at node 0 (from Figure 1). The upper line illustrates the primary and hot standby role of node 10 which took over for node 0 for fragment 1000. The lower line illustrates the roles of node 0. The shaded boxes show the two periods, takeover and takeback, when fragment 1000 is unavailable. The recovering node goes through several phases before it regains its role as a primary. First, a node-internal recovery makes node 0 action-consistent. Second, node 0 is *caught up* by using the replicated tuple log sent from node 10. Third, it is made hot standby for all its fragment replicas. Fourth, it regains the primary role as prior to the crash, the *takeback*.

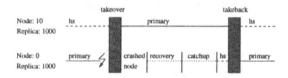

Fig. 5. The phases involved in recovery of a fragment replica 1000 at the crashed node 0.

To achieve a takeback, the recovering and the current primary nodes interoperate closely. When node 0 has finished the node internal recovery, it announces to all nodes that it is recovering. The primary nodes 10 and 11, send fragment shield locks for fragment 1000, 1002, 1004 and 1006 to node 0. Node 0 responds for each fragment replica with the largest LSN it knows. This information is found in the latest checkpoint log record, and is made up-to-crash consistent during a forward log scan. The primary nodes then know where to start the catchup log sending. When they have shipped all log records, they tell node 0 that they are done with catchup. When node 0 has received catch up from all relevant primary nodes, it announces that it has achieved hot standby responsibility for the fragments. This causes the transaction controllers to involve node 0 in the two-phase commit processing.

After a short period, node 0 announces that it supports a primary kernel service. This triggers an immediate takeback for fragment replicas 1000 and 1004. A takeback is a takeover, but it is triggered by completion of the catchup, and not by a node failure. Thus, at takeback there is a short period when all replicas of a fragment are unavailable. After the announcement of the primary responsibility, node 0 sends fragment shield locks to the nodes 10 and 11. This means that node 10 and 11 may have produced log records for fragment replicas 1000 and 1004 which did not arrive in node 0 before the takeback.

9   Synchronization of Hot Standby Replicas at Failures

It is the node holding the primary replica of a fragment that has the responsibility for synchronizing all replicas by producing log records and shipping them for redo execution at the hot standbys. Due to the asynchronous parallel streams of log records from the primary to the hot standbys, a takeover may result in different states at the different replicas.

node	replica	LSNs		
0	1000-p	101	102	103
10	1000-hs	101		
20	1000-hs	101	102	

Fig. 6. Log records for different replicas of a fragment at crash time of node 0.

Consider Figure 6 which illustrates at crash time of node 0 three replicas of a fragment, and the LSNs of log records for this fragment at the different nodes. The primary fragment replica, 1000-p, was located at node 0, which produced and shipped the log records. When node 0 crashed, the two hot standby replicas had received different numbers of log records. In particular, the new primary replica at node 10 received less log records than the other hot standby replica. The replica at node 0 will at recovery time have two log records which the new primary never got. Thus, the log records with LSNs 102 and 103 must be undone.

When a node takes over the primary responsibility for a fragment, it takes over the responsibility for LSN allocation as well. The takeover of LSN allocation responsibility is called a *bumpup*, because the LSN is increased by an interval. A *bumpup log record* is produced for each fragment replica a node took over for at takeover, and this log record registers the old and new LSN allocation information. Figure 7 shows the bumpup log record produced for replica 1000 at node 10, and which is shipped to node 2 at takeover time, and to node 0 during catchup. The bumpup log record says that this replica received 101 as the last log record, and the next log record to be allocated is 121.

The purpose of the bumpup log record is to synchronize the replicas of a fragment at takeover and at catchup. In Figure 7, we have shown the undo of the log records 102 and 103 at the different hot standby replicas. Node 10 produces the bumpup log record B[101–121] and ships it. This means that the next log record to be produced should have LSN 121. This interval is needed for the undo. Node 10 does not have any log records to undo, so it continues with the production of the next log record 121. Node 20 must undo 102. This undo will be done in parallel by the hot standby nodes without knowledge about the undo at other nodes. To let the different hot standby replicas produce the same LSNs for corresponding log records, the LSNs are produced according to

node replica	LSNs					
0 1000-hs	101	102 103	B[101–121]	119[103]	120[102]	121
10 1000-p	101		B[101–121]			121
20 1000-hs	101	102	B[101–121]		120[102]	121

Fig. 7. Synchronization of replicas of a fragment by bumpup log records.

the following rule:

$$N = H - (O - L)$$

N is the LSN for the CLR. O is the LSN for the non-CLR being compensated for. L is the low and H the high LSN in the bumpup log record. Thus, $N = 120$, is the CLR for $O = 102$, where $L = 101$ and $H = 121$.

Node 0 produces the undo log records at catchup time. Thus, when node 0 receives the bumpup log record from node 10, it must produce the undo log records for 102 and 103, before it continues with the catchup. There is a small subtility right here. If log record 103 was an undo log record produced by node 0 before the crash, this undo must be undone. The undo of the undo simply produces a new non-CLR with no references to the CLR.

Note that the undo in question here is due to synchronization of hot standby replicas with respect to the primary replica. It is the nodes holding primary replicas that have the responsibility to produce undo log records to make the system transaction consistent.

10   Conclusions and Further Work

This work has been implemented as a part of the ClustRa project. ClustRa has reached its goals with respect to response time and throughput [10]. For high availability we have measured the takeover time for a node failure to be in average approximately 1/3 of a second. Main-memory recovery with takeback where the failed node has been down for a few seconds, has been measured to take about five to ten seconds. The time of online self-repair is very dependent on the data volume, and is currently limited by the capacity of the network [1]. Further work includes estimation of long term availability by accelerated testing. This includes failure rate prediction and fault injection to estimate the error handling coverage.

There has been a growing interest in inter-site replication by industrial vendors, which have built the replication on top of existing database systems. Our work shows a system designed to support replication for high availability together with scalable throughput and load balancing. To reach these goals, the recovery method must be designed to support flexible declustering and self-repair strategies. This is achieved by having a location and replication independent recovery method, which is possible by having logical redo and undo log access together with state identifiers connected to tuples. To allow for scalable throughput, we allow for multiple parallel log streams. We have also presented many details necessary to support high availability, like fast takeover and takeback, and synchronization of multiple hot standby replicas at failures.

References

1. Svein Erik Bratsberg, Øystein Grøvlen, Svein-Olaf Hvasshovd, Bjørn P. Munch, and Øystein Torbjørnsen. Providing a highly available database by replication and online self-repair. *International Journal of Engineering Intelligent Systems for Electrical Engineering and Communications, Special issue on Databases and Telecommunications*, 4(3):131–139, September 1996.
2. D. L. Burkes and R. K. Treiber. Design approaches for real-time transaction processing remote site recovery. In *The 35th IEEE Computer Society International Conference COMPCON 90*, pages 568–572, February 1990.
3. George Copeland and Tom Keller. A comparison of high-availability media recovery techniques. In *Proceedings of the ACM SIGMOD Conference*, pages 98–109, June 1989.
4. Jim Gray, editor. *The Benchmark Handbook for database and transaction processing systems*. Morgan Kaufmann Publishers, 334 p., 1991.
5. Jim Gray and Andreas Reuter. *Transaction Processing: Concepts and Techniques*. Morgan Kaufmann Publishers, 1070 p., 1992.
6. Jorge Guerrero. RDF: An overview. *Tandem Systems Review*, 7(2), 1991.
7. Stephen Huang. The Sybase replication server. In *David B. Lomet (editor), Foundations of Data Organization and Algorithms, 4th International Conference, FODO '93, Chicago, Illinois, USA, October 13-15, Proceedings. Springer-Verlag LNCS*, pages 265–270, 1993.
8. Svein-Olaf Hvasshovd. *Recovery in Parallel Database Systems*. Verlag Vieweg, Wiesbaden, Germany, 1996.
9. Svein-Olaf Hvasshovd, Øystein Torbjørnsen, Svein Erik Bratsberg, and Per Holager. The ClustRa telecom database: High availability, high throughput, and real-time response. In *Proceedings of the 21st International Conference on Very Large Databases, Zurich, Switzerland (VLDB '95)*, pages 469–477, September 1995.
10. Svein-Olaf Hvasshovd, Øystein Torbjørnsen, Svein Erik Bratsberg, and Per Holager. A highly available, real-time database system for telecom applications. In *Information Network and Data Communication*, pages 234–245. Chapman and Hall ltd, June 1996.
11. Informix. INFORMIX-OnLine dynamic server, database server, administrator's guide, volume 1, version 7.1. Product documentation Part No. 000-7778, Informix Software, Inc., 4100 Bohannon Drive, Menlo Park, CA, USA, December 1994.
12. Inhwan Lee and Ravishankar K. Iyer. Software dependability in the Tandem GUARDIAN system. *IEEE Transactions on Software Engineering*, 21(5):455–467, May 1995.
13. Philip L. Lehman and S. Bing Yao. Efficient locking for concurrent operations on b-trees. *ACM Transactions on Database Systems*, 6(4):650–670, December 1981.
14. C. Mohan, Don Haderle, Bruce Lindsay, Hamid Pirahesh, and Peter Schwarz. ARIES: A transaction recovery method supporting fine-granularity locking and partial rollbacks using write-ahead locking. *ACM Transactions on Database Systems*, 17(1):94–162, March 1992.

15. Christos A. Polyzois and Hector Garcia-Molina. Evaluation of remote backup algorithms for transaction-processing systems. *ACM Transactions on Database Systems*, 19(3):423–449, September 1994.

16. M. Pratt et al. Oracle7 server distributed systems: Replicated data, release 7.1. Product documentation Part No. A21903-2, ORACLE Corporation, 500 Oracle Parkway, Redwood City, CA, USA, 1995.

17. Øystein Torbjørnsen. *Multi-Site Declustering Strategies for Very High Database Service Availability*. PhD thesis, The Norwegian Institute of Technology, University of Trondheim, January 1995. 186 p., ISBN 82-7119-759-2.

Compensation-Based Query Processing in On-Line Transaction Processing Systems

Øystein Grøvlen[1]*, Øystein Torbjørnsen[2], and Svein-Olaf Hvasshovd[2]

[1] Department of Computer and Information Sciences, Norwegian University of Science and Technology, N-7034 TRONDHEIM, Norway
[2] Telenor R&D, N-7005 Trondheim, Norway

Abstract. One of the problems associated with running ad-hoc queries in an OLTP system is lock contention. Compensation-based query processing has been proposed as a solution to this problem. In this paper, undo/no-redo compensation is used to bring inconsistent copies of the base relations into a transaction-consistent state. Queries process the database internal log to obtain information on updates made by concurrent transactions. A performance analysis of the algorithm shows that it can be executed efficiently in an OLTP system with low to medium system utilization.

1 Introduction

On-line transaction processing (OLTP) systems are used in many business-critical applications. In recent years, the ability to run ad-hoc queries on such systems has become increasingly important. However, introducing ad-hoc queries in OLTP systems presents several unsolved problems. One problem is that long-lived transactions tend to acquire many locks and hold them for a relatively long time. This prevents concurrent updates of data by simple on-line transactions [3].

In order to avoid that ad-hoc queries slow down OLTP transactions, many organizations keep two separate copies of the database, one for OLTP and one (e.g., a data warehouse) for queries.[1] One problem with this approach is the extra resources needed for the replication. In addition, the ad-hoc queried database, will usually not be up-to-date. The maintenance of the copy will have to be done during low-activity hours (e.g., each night) in order to avoid lock contention with queries [11]. However, due to increased globalization, many organizations have no off-peak hours.

Another approach is to run the ad-hoc queries with reduced degree of consistency. One example is cursor stability [5], where queries only hold locks a tuple while it is actually being read. This will, however, not give satisfying accuracy for all applications.

---

* Supported by a grant from the Norwegian Research Council.
  Email: oysteing@idi.ntnu.no.
[1] The term *query* will be used to denote read-only transactions. Transactions that update the database will be just called *transactions*.

In this paper, a method for running transaction-consistent queries in an OLTP system without delaying the OLTP transactions is proposed.

1.1 Related Work

One approach to avoid data contention when running queries in an OLTP system, is *transient versioning* [2,10,13]. In transient versioning algorithms, transactions create a new version of a data item when performing an update. Queries may access an older version in order to get a transaction-consistent view.

Another approach, *compensation-based query processing*, has been proposed by Srinivasan and Carey [12]. In the first phase of this two-phased approach, queries scan the base relations using cursor-stability locking, and a set of temporary relations is created. Concurrently, transactions that update the relations being scanned, append a compensation record for each update to an *update-list*. In the second phase, the compensation records are applied to the temporary relations making the final result reflect updates made by concurrent transactions. The information entered in the update-list can be tailored to each specific query.

The method proposed by Srinivasan has some disadvantages:

- Extra work is required of transactions in order to maintain the update-list.
- Temporary relations are needed to store the result of the first phase.
- The two-phased approach prevents efficient pipelining of relational algebra operations. Tuples could not be emitted from the query before the entire base relations have been scanned.
- The query process must either execute under cursor stability or wait for the termination of all transactions that have updated the update-list. This may significantly increase the response time of queries.
- Consistent handling of aborting transactions requires that either transactions wait until commit time to insert their entries into the update-list, or the query process must eliminate updates of all but committed transactions from the update-list before applying it to the temporary relations.
- The method is not applicable to transaction-consistent execution of read-only transactions that consist of several queries [1].

This paper presents an alternative method for compensation-based query processing. In Sect. 2, it is described how the query can use the log to obtain information about concurrent updates. Section 3 presents the new method for compensation-based query processing, and Sect. 4 explains how this method can support different types of queries. The performance of the algorithm is evaluated in Sect. 5. Conclusions and plans for further work are presented in Sect. 6.

2 Log-Oriented Compensation-Based Query Processing

Compensation-based query processing reduces the lock contention between a query and concurrent transactions without reducing the degree of consistency. A query reads inconsistent versions of its base relations, but returns a transaction-consistent result by compensating for updates made by concurrent transactions.

The compensation-based query-processing method presented in this paper, bases its compensation on the database internal log. In this way, very little extra work is required by transactions to inform queries about concurrent updates. In order to achieve non-blocking execution of queries with respect to transactions, queries will not set any locks on the tuples they access. This will, however, give the query an inconsistent view of the database, and the log will be used to bring the result of the query into a transaction-consistent state. This is done by redoing and undoing operations recorded in the log.

The query process performs three main operations: It scans the base relation(s) of the query, processes the log and extracts relevant log records, and performs the necessary undo/redo-operations before emitting the tuples.

The scan is performed by the *scan thread* which scans the relations tuple-by-tuple without setting any read locks. Thus, it will not have to wait for transactions to commit before reading a tuple, and transactions will not have to wait for the query to finish before updating a tuple. The equivalent of a latch will be set on each tuple only while it is being read to protect the read operation from other operations. The scan does not necessarily need to be a simple file-scan; other efficient access methods (e.g., an index) may be used.

Concurrently with the scan thread, transactions that update the relations being queried will have entered their updates into the log. The *log processing thread* will be extracting relevant information from these log records.

When compensating for a transaction that is active during the scan, the transaction may be rolled either back or forward. When rolling a transaction back, all operations performed by the transaction on a tuple *before* it was read by the scan thread should be undone. When rolling a transaction forward, all the operations performed on a tuple *after* it was read by the scan thread should be redone. One of the following three strategies for compensation could be chosen:

Undo/No-Redo All transactions that are active during the scan are rolled back. Thus, the query's view of the database will only include updates of transactions that committed before start of the query.

No-Undo/Redo All transactions that are active during the scan, and all later transactions that commit before any of these, are rolled forward. Thus, the query's view will be more up-to-date than for undo/no-redo compensation. However, the query process will have to wait for all transactions that are active during the scan to terminate. The compensation-based method proposed by Srinivasan and Carey [12] uses this approach.

Undo/Redo Some transactions are rolled back while others are rolled forward. In order to get a transaction-consistent view, none of the transactions that are rolled forward must be dependent on any of the transactions that are rolled back. One way to ensure this is to roll forward all transactions that have committed before a certain point in time, while all transactions committed after that point are rolled back.

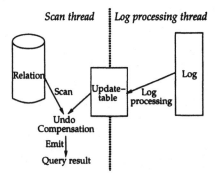

Fig. 1. Undo/no-redo compensation.

In this paper, we present an algorithm for transaction-consistent execution of queries using undo/no-redo compensation. It is assumed that transactions execute using strict two-phase locking (2PL) [4], and log their write operations using a tuple logging policy [7]. That is, all log records contain the primary key and the relation identifier of the corresponding tuple. This is necessary in order to be able to relate the log records to the tuples read by the scan thread. Also, compensation oriented logging is assumed (i.e., undo operations are logged using compensation log records). Both partial and complete tuple logging may be used, however, where not otherwise stated, partial tuple logging can be assumed. It is also assumed that each data block have a state identifier that contains the log sequence number (LSN) of the log record for the most recent update to the block. Each tuple may also have its own state identifier.

3 Undo/No-Redo Compensation

One of the main advantages of undo/no-redo compensation is that all log records needed for performing the compensation on a tuple is already available when the tuple is read by the scan thread. For each tuple being read by the scan thread, the log records for this tuple can be fetched and the operations undone before the next tuple is read. By interleaving scanning and compensation in such a manner, intermediate storage of the scanned tuples, possibly on disk, is avoided.

This interleaved execution requires direct access to the corresponding log records. The log processing thread will enter the relevant information found in the log in an *update-table* for later use by the scan thread (Fig. 1). This update-table supports direct access (hash-based) on primary key, and it is assumed that it can be entirely stored in main memory.

The undo/no-redo compensation algorithm divides the set of all transactions into two disjoint subsets, the BEFORE set and the AFTER set. The query result will reflect all updates made by transactions in the BEFORE set and no updates made by transactions in the AFTER set. All transactions active

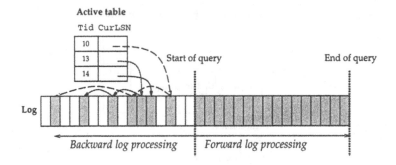

Fig. 2. Backward and forward log processing.

when or after the query is started will be members of the query's AFTER set, while all other transactions are members of the BEFORE set. This guarantees transaction-consistent execution of queries when transactions are executed using strict 2PL.

3.1 The Log Processing Thread

The log processing thread should process all log records[2] produced by transactions in the AFTER set before the end of the scan. When the query starts, the log processing thread will start processing all new log records produced. This part of the log processing is called *forward log processing* (FLP). In order to avoid reading the log records from disk, the FLP should process log records before they are removed from main memory.

The log records produced by members of the AFTER set before the start of the query, must also be processed. At the start of the query, *backward log processing* (BLP) will insert all transactions listed as active in the transaction table into its AFTER set. Then, it will go backwards in the log processing all log records created by members of this set. The shaded log records in Fig. 2 represents the records that are processed by the log processing thread.

When the log processing thread processes a log record, it hashes into the update-table on the primary key found in the log record. During BLP, the before-images of all attributes found in the log record will be entered into the update-table, substituting possible previous values. During FLP, a before-image will only be entered into the update-table if no value already exists for this attribute. BLP and FLP will be done concurrently. When BLP is finished, the update-table will contain the committed values at the start of the query for all attributes that so far have been changed by concurrent transactions.

The entries in the update-table could be of three different types: *update*, *insert*, or *delete*. Update entries only contains before-images of attributes that

---

[2] By all log records is meant all log records referring to relations that are scanned by the query process.

have been changed by members of the AFTER set. For delete entries, the before-images of all relevant attributes of the deleted tuple are included in the entry. Insert entries contain no before-images.

3.2 The Scan Thread

When the log processing thread has finished BLP, the scan thread can start scanning the base relation(s) of the query. How the scan thread is executed will depend on the operations of the query. When producing a snapshot of a relation, the scan thread scans the entire relation, performing the following operations for each tuple:

1. Read the next tuple. If the state identifier of the tuple/block[3] is smaller than the LSN of the oldest log record processed during backward log processing, the tuple can be emitted without performing the steps below.
2. If not all the necessary log records have been processed, wait for the log processing thread to process more log records.
3. Hash into the update-table on the primary key of the current tuple. If an insert entry is found, the tuple is not emitted. If an update or delete entry is found, the values of each attribute found in the update-table are substituted for the attribute values of the tuple. If no entry is found, the tuple is emitted in the form it was read.

When the entire relation has been read by the scan thread, the result will include all tuples of a transaction-consistent snapshot, except for some tuples that have been deleted during the scan. These tuples could be emitted at the end of the scan by searching the update-table for delete entries of tuples that have not been visited by the scan thread. However, query evaluation algorithms often exploit that the scan sequence is sorted on a combination of attributes, the *sort key*. In order to preserve the scan order, the log processing thread will when processing a log record for a deletion, in addition to entering the tuple in the update-table, insert the sort key and the primary key of deleted tuples into a priority queue. The scan thread will then, check the priority queue for tuples that should be emitted before the current tuple. These tuples can be found in the update-table by using the primary key stored in the priority queue. If it is not necessary to maintain the scan sequence, tuples in the queue could be emitted at any time during the scan.

3.3 Synchronizing the Scan Thread and the Log Processing Thread

Before the scan thread performs compensation, all log records of operations that are reflected in the current tuple must have been processed by the log processing

---

[3] If each tuple has its own state identifier, this will be used.

thread. If that is not the case, the scan thread will wait for the log processing thread to process more log records.[4]

One way to ensure that sufficient log has been processed, is to process all new log before compensation is performed. However, a less eager strategy can be used by taking advantage of the state identifiers included in each tuple/block. If the state identifier of the current tuple/block is smaller than the LSN of the last log record processed by the log processing thread, all operations needed for doing the compensation is already entered in the update-table. Thus, no more log records need to be processed before the compensation is performed. Otherwise, the scan thread is suspended until more log records have been processed.

If one wants to maintain the scan sequence, the state identifiers of the blocks can be used to check whether all possible deletions of tuples with a smaller sort key than the current tuple have been entered in the update-table.[5]

3.4 Space Optimization of the Update-Table

In order to minimize memory usage, the update-table should be kept as small as possible. The following optimizations will reduce the size of the update-table:

- Only before-images of relevant attributes are entered into the update-table.
- If the scan sequence is sorted, the log processing thread should, if possible, check whether the tuple referred in the current log record has already been read by the scan thread. If so, the log processing thread need not enter information from this log record into the update-table.
- When the scan thread has finished processing a tuple, the entry for this tuple in the update-table can be removed. However, if the log processing thread is not able to decide whether the tuple of a later log record lies behind or ahead of the scan thread, it may enter information on this tuple again. In order to avoid this, only the attribute values are deleted, while the primary key is kept and the entry marked *processed*.

3.5 Complete Tuple Logging

So far it has been assumed that partial tuple logging is used. If complete tuple logging is used, the before-image of the entire tuple is stored in the log record. In addition, at least the after-images of all attributes changed by the operation are stored. With complete tuple logging, the log processing thread will have access to all attributes of the tuple, and as will be shown below, this can be exploited to optimize query execution.

---

[4] Note that if before-images of all relevant attributes are available in the update-table, the compensation can be made without synchronizing with the log processing thread. Processing more log records will in this case never change the entry in the update-table.

[5] If the relations is scanned using a secondary index, the state identifiers of the index blocks must be used.

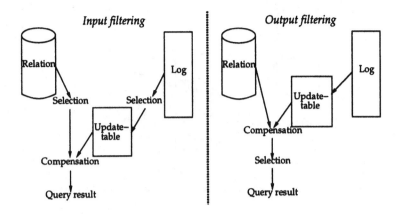

Fig. 3. Selection queries by input and output filtering.

Complete tuple logging also simplifies the update of the update-table. All relevant attributes of a tuple will be encountered in the first log record processed by the log processing thread, and no more log records for this tuple need to be processed during FLP. Also, if complete tuple logging is used, the log processing thread will always be able to decide whether the tuple of the current log record lies behind or ahead of the scan thread.

4 Query Execution

A query could be executed by obtaining a transaction-consistent copy of the base relations and then run the query on the copy. However, this simplistic two-phased approach may result in a potentially large overhead with respect to storage, disk accesses and other resources. Below, it is briefly discussed how queries can be efficiently executed when applying compensation-based query processing. For a more in depth discussion, see [6].

Selection queries can be executed by filtering either on the inputs to the scan thread and the log processing thread or on the output from the compensation (Fig. 3). Output filtering is just selection performed on the transaction-consistent relation produced by the compensation.

While performing input filtering, only tuples that satisfy the selection predicate will be compensated for by the scan thread. The log processing thread will evaluate the predicate on the before-images of log records. If the before-image evaluates to true, a delete entry is entered into the update-table. If it evaluates to false, an insert entry is entered into the update-table. Thus, the scan thread can do compensation as described above, ignoring tuples with insert entries and adding tuples with delete entries.

In order to perform the filtering, the log processing thread will need access to all attributes needed for evaluation of the selection predicate. This is not guaranteed when using partial tuple logging. However, input and output filtering

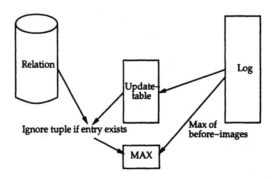

Fig. 4. Efficient evaluation of the **MAX** aggregate operator.

can be combined such that the log processing thread filters as much as possible, leaving the rest until after the compensation.

For aggregate queries it is possible to use an approach similar to the output filter approach for selection queries. However, the amount of compensation can be significantly reduced by using input filtering. As an example, consider the **MAX** operation (Fig. 4). The log processing thread will, in addition to entering entries in the update-table for updates to the aggregated attribute, compute the maximum over the before images. The scan thread will compute the maximum over the tuples not changed by concurrent updates, and need only check the update-table for tuples with a greater value than the current maximum. If an entry is found the value will be ignored. Algorithms for other aggregate operations, both scalar and functional, can be found in [6]. Some of these algorithms are variations of algorithms proposed by Srinivasan and Carey [12].

For join queries compensation will be done on the input relations. Several of the existing join algorithms [9] could directly be used for joining transaction-consistent outputs of selections. Hash join is especially well suited since the same buffer area could be used both for the update-table and the hash table of the inner relation.

5   Performance Analysis

In this section, a simple performance model for the compensation-based query processing algorithm is presented. The analysis will not give an exact prediction of the performance characteristics of the algorithm. However, it will be used to show that the algorithm could be executed efficiently in an OLTP system by comparing the query execution times to that of GO-processing.[6]

---

[6] GO-processing means that the query reads the base relations without acquiring or waiting for locks.

5.1 System load and capacity

Compared to running queries using GO-processing, all extra work added by the algorithm presented in this paper is CPU-based. Because of this, the performance analysis will be mainly based on the CPU load of an OLTP system. A prerequisite for on-line query processing is that the OLTP system has free capacity that can be used for running queries.

Let L denote the processing load of a system. This load is an abstraction of the CPU load, and the capacity of the system is set to 1.0. The overall load, L, of a system is the sum of the load contributed by each of the various tasks that must be served concurrently. For on-line query processing, the load be divided into four main components:

L_{oltp} : Load caused by normal OLTP. This is assumed to be constant during the execution of the query.
L_q : Query processing load when running a query without setting any locks and without compensating (GO processing).
L_{lp} : Load caused by the log processing thread.
L_c : Load caused by the compensation part of the scan thread.

At any time in a system running OLTP transactions and queries concurrently, we have that:
$$L = L_{oltp} + L_q + L_{lp} + L_c \leq 1.0 \ . \tag{1}$$

The performance of a query will also be limited by the disk capacity (bandwidth) of the system. Let D denote the total disk load in the system, and let the capacity be set to d, the number of disks in the system. The disk load consists of the bandwidth used by the OLTP transactions, D_{oltp}, and the bandwidth used by the query, D_q, and
$$D = D_{oltp} + D_q \leq d \tag{2}$$
must hold at any time.

5.2 Performance Analysis of Producing a Snapshot of a Relation

Let the database consist of a single relation with n tuples. Concurrently with OLTP transactions, a single query makes a transaction-consistent copy of the relation. To simplify the analysis it is assumed that no OLTP transactions are active at the start of the query (no backward log processing), and that complete tuple logging is used. It is also assumed that the update-table will be stored in the temporary buffer used by the query process. Thus, the buffer hit rate for OLTP-transactions will not be affected by the size of the update-table. Table 1 lists the parameters used for the performance analysis. The settings used for these parameters are based on measurements made on a single-node version of the ClustRa DBMS [8].[7]

---

[7] The settings for the different CPU operations is given in number of instructions. The actual values used for the constants will be the given number of instructions divided by the CPU rate, r_{CPU}.

Table 1. Parameters used in the performance analysis.

Parameter	Meaning	Setting
W_t	Cost of starting and committing a transaction	80000 instr.
W_{rr}	Cost of performing a read operation to a random tuple in the buffer	40000 instr.
W_{rw}	Cost of performing a write operation to a random tuple in the buffer (not including logging)	50000 instr.
W_s	Cost of sequential access to one tuple	8000 instr.
W_{io}	Cost of transferring a page between memory and disk	50000 instr.
W_{clog}	Cost of creating a log record	7000 instr.
W_{plog}	Cost of processing a log record	1400 instr.
W_{hash}	Cost for a hash lookup into the update-table	1000 instr.
W_{ins}	Cost of inserting an entry into the update table	7500 instr.
B_r	Disk bandwidth used for random access to a disk block	0.012
B_s	Disk bandwidth used for sequential access to a disk block	0.001
r_{CPU}	Instruction rate of CPU	300 MIPS
n_r	Number of read operations in each transaction	2
n_w	Number of write operations in each transaction	4
n_p	Number of tuples in one page	30
h	Database buffer hit rate	0.9
t_{ckpt}	Time interval between checkpoints	300 s
t_{grp}	Time interval between group commits	0.5 s
d	Number of disks in the system	4
n	Number of tuples in the database	10^6
α_t	Arrival rate of transactions	300 per sec.

The main components of the OLTP load is executing transactions and their database operations, fetching blocks from disk into the database buffer, logging of operations to disk, and writing dirty pages to disk during checkpoint. Let $\alpha_r = n_r\alpha_t$ and $\alpha_w = n_w\alpha_t$ be the access rate of read and write operations, respectively, to the database. Then the following equation approximates the OLTP load of the system:

$$L_{oltp} = \alpha_t W_t + \alpha_r \left(W_{rr} + (1-h)W_{io}\right) +$$
$$\alpha_w \left(W_{rw} + (1-h)W_{io} + W_{clog} + \frac{W_{io}}{n_{log}}\right) + \frac{n_{bw}W_{io}}{t_{ckpt}}, \qquad (3)$$

where n_{log} is the average number of log records in a log page, and n_{bw} is the average number of pages updated during one checkpoint interval. It is assumed that group commit is used, and that transactions are delayed a maximum of t_{grp} seconds. Assuming that $n_p/2$ log records fit in one page this gives $n_{log} = \min(n_p/2, \alpha_w t_{grp})$.

Assuming a uniform access pattern among n data objects, the probability that a specific data object has been updated after x write operations will be $1 - (1 - 1/n)^x$. Thus, the probability that a page is written to disk during a checkpoint interval is, assuming uniform distribution of access, $1 - (1 -$

$1/(n/n_{\rm p}))^{\alpha_{\rm w}t_{\rm ckpt}}$. Assuming a 20/80 access pattern[8] gives:

$$
n_{\rm bw} = \frac{0.2n}{n_{\rm p}} \left(1 - \left(1 - \frac{n_{\rm p}}{0.2n}\right)^{0.8\alpha_{\rm w}t_{\rm ckpt}}\right) + \frac{0.8n}{n_{\rm p}} \left(1 - \left(1 - \frac{n_{\rm p}}{0.8n}\right)^{0.2\alpha_{\rm w}t_{\rm ckpt}}\right) .
$$

The disk bandwidth used by OLTP transactions corresponds to the I/O part of (3). It will be assumed that the log, indexes, and temporary data are placed on separate disks that have sufficient bandwidth for supporting both the OLTP transactions and the query. Thus, only the disks used for storing the relation will be modeled:

$$
D_{\rm oltp} = \alpha_{\rm r} (1 - h) B_{\rm r} + \alpha_{\rm w} (1 - h) B_{\rm r} + \frac{n_{\rm bw} B_{\rm s}}{t_{\rm ckpt}} , \tag{4}
$$

assuming that the checkpoint algorithm writes the dirty pages in physical order.

The work done by the log processing thread has three main components: The work associated with reading a log record from the log and extracting the primary key, the work associated with hashing into the update-table to see if there is an entry for this primary key, and the work associated with extracting the relevant information from the log record and inserting it into the update-table. Since complete tuple logging is used, the last operation will only be done if an entry is not found in the update-table. Let $f(t)$ be the probability that an entry for a given tuple already exists in the update-table at time t after the start of the query. Assuming a 20/80 tuple access pattern gives:

$$
f(t) = 0.2 \left(1 - \left(1 - \frac{1}{0.2n}\right)^{0.8\alpha_{\rm w}t}\right) + 0.8 \left(1 - \left(1 - \frac{1}{0.8n}\right)^{0.2\alpha_{\rm w}t}\right) .
$$

The load caused by the log processing thread can now be modeled as:

$$
L_{\rm lp}(t) = \alpha_{\rm w}(W_{\rm plog} + W_{\rm hash} + (1 - f(t))W_{\rm ins}) . \tag{5}
$$

When executing the query, it is assumed that the entire relation is read from disk and the output written to a temporary relation on disk. The load caused by the query if executed using GO processing will be:

$$
L_{\rm q}(t) = \alpha_{\rm q}(t) \left(\frac{W_{\rm io}}{n_{\rm p}} + W_{\rm s} + \frac{W_{\rm io}}{n_{\rm p}}\right) , \tag{6}
$$

where $\alpha_{\rm q}(t)$ is the rate at which the query is processed at time t. The definition of $\alpha_{\rm q}(t)$ implies:

$$
\int_0^{\tau_{\rm q}} \alpha_{\rm q}(t)dt = n , \tag{7}
$$

where $\tau_{\rm q}$ is the time it takes to process the query.

The extra work done by the scan thread when doing compensation is to check the update-table. In other words:

$$
L_{\rm c}(t) = \alpha_{\rm q}(t) W_{\rm hash} . \tag{8}
$$

---

[8] 80% of the accesses goes to 20% of the pages, and vice versa.

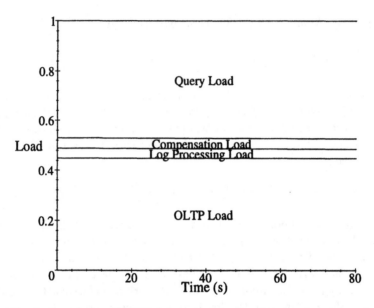

Fig. 5. Cumulative CPU load for compensation-based query processing.

This is an overestimate since by checking the state identifiers, the scan thread will avoid accessing the update-table for some tuples. The disk bandwidth used by the query will be:

$$D_q(t) = \frac{\alpha_q(t) B_s}{n_p} \ . \tag{9}$$

The rate at which the query is processed, $\alpha_q(t)$, is limited by both the CPU capacity and the disk capacity (bandwidth). The maximum processing rate at any time t will be the maximum value which can be chosen for $\alpha_q(t)$ such that both (1) and (2) hold.[9] Having computed $\alpha_q(t)$, (7) can be solved for τ_q in order to compute the query response time.

Figure 5 shows the CPU load when executing the query with the parameter settings given in Tab. 1. The extra work required by the compensation-based algorithm uses about 10% of the CPU. The query uses 80.2s to process the 1 million tuples. This is 17% longer than for GO-processing. 8.3% of the tuples were entered in the update-table at the end of the query.

As shown by Fig. 6, query performance decreases with increasing OLTP load. The relative difference between the execution times for GO-processing and compensation-based processing also increases as long as the query-processing is CPU-bound (Fig. 7). With no OLTP load, the compensation gives a 8% over-

---

[9] This assumes that the query will read all disks in parallel. If the query reads one disk at the time then $D_{oltp}/d + D_q \le 1$.

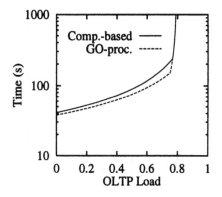
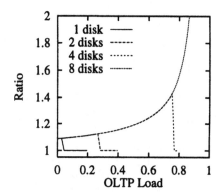

Fig. 6. Query execution times when varying OLTP load. (Logarithmic scale on the vertical axis.)

Fig. 7. Relative query performance compared to GO-processing when varying the number of disks in the system.

head[10] that increases to 20% at $L_{oltp} = 0.50$. When increasing the OLTP load to the point when GO-processing becomes disk-bound, only a little extra increase in the load will also make compensation-based query processing disk-bound. This can be seen from the sharp drops in the performance ratios in Fig. 7. When both approaches are disk-bound, the performance of the compensation-based algorithm will be equal to that of GO-processing.

The size of the update-table will also increase when increasing the OLTP load (Fig. 8). Increasing the load means both increased update rates and longer execution times, both of which leads to an increase in the total number of concurrent updates. For low OLTP loads, the number of the entries in the update-table is relatively small. However, at $L_{oltp} = 0.7$, 27.5% of the tuples will have entries in the update-table. Even when using the space optimization techniques presented in Sec. 3.4, the size of the update-table will probably require too much resources at such high loads.

When increasing the size of the base relation, the relative overhead in execution time compared to GO-processing slightly increases (Fig. 9). This is because the OLTP load of the system increases due to more work associated with checkpoints.

This performance analysis assumes that the base relation is the only relation in the database. If this is not the case, the log processing thread does not have to process all log records. In this case, both the compensation overhead and the size of the update-table will be smaller. On the other hand, if partial tuple logging is used, more work has to be done by the log processing thread. However, the size of the update-table will probably decrease as not all relevant attributes of a tuple will have been updated. If the update-table is stored in the database buffer,

---

[10] This is because the model assumes that the scan thread checks the update-table for all tuples. By checking the state identifier of the tuples most of this overhead is avoided.

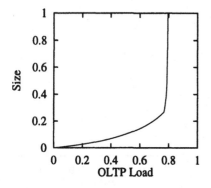

Fig. 8. Relative size of the update-table when varying OLTP load.

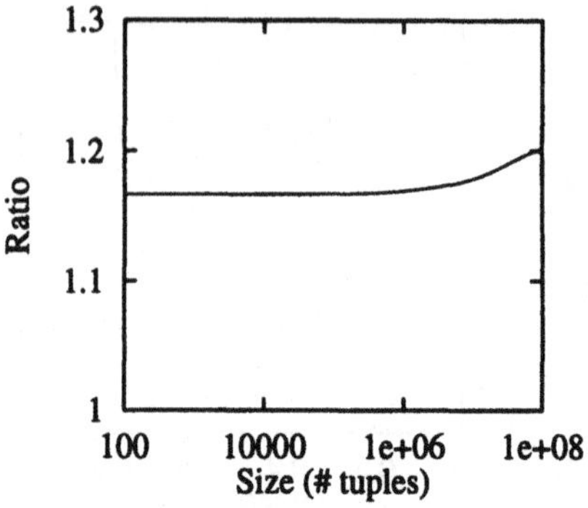

Fig. 9. Relative query performance compared GO-processing when varying the size of the base relation. (Logarithmic scale on the horizontal axis.)

the hit rate for OLTP transactions will decrease, resulting in longer response times for these transactions. A more detailed model will be developed in order to investigate these aspects.

The model above assumes that the throughput of transactions are not affected by concurrent queries. Experience show that this is a fair assumption as long as there is some spare capacity in the system. The capacity-based model above can not be used to analyze how response times of transactions are affected by concurrent queries. For that purpose a queuing model or simulations are needed.

6   Conclusions and Further Work

In this paper, we have presented a method for compensation-based query processing that overcomes most of the disadvantages of the method presented by Srinivasan and Carey [12]. Most importantly, by communicating updates through the log, little extra load is put on updating transactions. This means that all the work related to the compensation-based execution of a query could be done by a separate query process. By giving higher priority to OLTP transactions than that given to query processes, the execution of queries should not significantly affect the performance of the OLTP system.

Moreover, a two-phase approach is avoided by using undo/no-redo compensation. Thus, there is no need for temporary storage of the base relations. In addition, queries can emit tuples at once they are read, making it possible to exploit efficient pipelining of operations. Also, several queries can be run in the same transaction-consistent view by using the same update-table for all queries.

Our performance analysis shows that compensation-based query processing can be efficiently performed in OLTP systems with low to medium system utilization. In the future, the analytical model will be extended to be able to give a more precise analysis of the performance characteristics. Our plans for further work also includes verifying the analytical model through simulation. The simulation study will also compare our algorithm to other algorithms for on-line query processing.

Work has already been done on extending the method to parallel and distributed execution of queries. The plan is to implement the distributed algorithms in the ClustRa DBMS.

Acknowledgments

We would like to thank Rune Humborstad for several fruitful discussions.

References

1. P. M. Bober. *Towards Practical Multiversion Locking Techniques for On-Line Query Processing*. PhD thesis, University of Wisconsin - Madison, 1993.
2. P. M. Bober and M. J. Carey. On mixing queries and transactions via multiversion locking. In *Proc. Int. Conf. Data. Eng.*, pages 535–545, Tempe, AZ, Feb. 1992.
3. D. DeWitt and J. Gray. Parallel database systems: The future of high performance database systems. *Commun. ACM*, 35(6):85–98, June 1992.
4. K. P. Eswaran, J. N. Gray, R. A. Lorie, and I. L. Traiger. The notions of consistency and predicate locks in a database system. *Commun. ACM*, 19(11):624–633, Nov. 1976.
5. J. Gray and A. Reuter. *Transaction Processing: Concepts and Techniques*. Morgan Kaufmann, San Mateo, CA, 1993.
6. Ø. Grøvlen, S.-O. Hvasshovd, and Ø. Torbjørnsen. On-line query processing through undo/no-redo compensation. In *Proc. Int. Workshop on Advanced Transaction Models and Architectures*, Goa, India, Sept. 1996. Available at http://www.idt.unit.no/~oysteing/papers/atma.ps.
7. S.-O. Hvasshovd. *Recovery in Parallel Database Systems*. VieWeg, Wiesbaden, Germany, 1996.
8. S.-O. Hvasshovd, Ø. Torbjørnsen, S. E. Bratsberg, and P. Holager. The ClustRa telecom database: High availability, high throughput, and real-time response. In *Proc. Int. Conf. VLDB*, pages 469–477, Zurich, Switzerland, Sept. 1995.
9. P. Mishra and M. H. Eich. Join processing in relational databases. *ACM Comput. Surv.*, 24(1):63–113, Mar. 1992.
10. C. Mohan, H. Pirahesh, and R. Lorie. Efficient and flexible methods for transient versioning of records to avoid locking by read-only transactions. In *Proc. ACM SIGMOD*, pages 124–133, San Diego, CA, June 1992.
11. D. Quass and J. Widom. On-line warehouse view maintenace. In *Proc. ACM SIGMOD*, Tucson, AZ, May 1997.
12. V. Srinivasan and M. J. Carey. Compensation-based on-line query processing. In *Proc. ACM SIGMOD*, pages 331–340, San Diego, CA, June 1992.
13. K.-L. Wu, P. S. Yu, and M.-S. Chen. Dynamic finite versioning: An effective versioning approach to concurrent transaction and query processing. In *Proc. Int. Conf. Data. Eng.*, pages 577–586, Vienna, Austria, Apr. 1993.

Detection Arcs for Deadlock Management in Nested Transactions and their Performance

Fernando de Ferreira Rezende, Theo Härder, Andreas Gloeckner, and Jörg Lutze

Dept. of Computer Science - University of Kaiserslautern
67653 Kaiserslautern - Germany
E-Mail: {rezendelhaerderlgloecknellutze}@informatik.uni-kl.de

Abstract - In this paper, we address deadlock management in nested transactions. In our strategy, deadlocks are detected through the occurrence of cycles in a waits-for graph (WFG). However, the process of looking for cycles in the WFG considering all its nodes and edges can be very time-consuming. To accelerate this process, we propose the detection arcs. In essence, a detection arc represents a higher level abstraction embodying a hidden waiting relation between two transactions that is caused by a lock wait. Thus, the deadlock detection process needs to traverse only a minimal subset of the WFG's edges when it is started, the set of detection arcs. Therefore, the overall performance of deadlock management is improved, as confirmed by our performance measurements.

1 Introduction

When objects are to be accessed in a database (DB) system, transactions require locks on those in order to avoid consistency anomalies due to concurrent accesses. By requiring locks on objects, transactions may sometimes have to wait for other transactions. At this time, there may appear a cyclical sequence of transactions (T) each waiting for the next to release a lock it must acquire (T1 $\rightarrow$ T2 $\rightarrow$ ... $\rightarrow$ T1), and hence no one in the cycle can make any progress. These situations characterize *deadlocks*. To detect and, above all, to resolve such situations are the main tasks of a *deadlock manager*.

There are a lot of strategies to detect deadlocks. One of them is *timeout*, whereby the system, finding that a transaction is waiting too long for a lock, just guesses that there may be a deadlock involving this transaction. It then simply aborts it and restarts it again later. Although this strategy is imprecise in the detection of deadlocks, it does work. Particularly, we feel that timeout does not always offer an optimal solution to deadlocks. Although being very easy to implement, the number of transactions that may be unnecessarily aborted and restarted again may be unacceptably high due to the impreciseness of this technique.

Waits-for graph (WFG) [7] is another strategy, whereby the system maintains a directed graph showing which transactions are waiting for other ones. *Nodes* in this graph are labelled with transaction identifiers whereas the *edges* represent waiting situations. There is an edge from node Ti to node Tj if and only if transaction Ti is waiting for transaction Tj to release some lock. In such a strategy, deadlock detection is realized by means of searching for cycles in the WFG: When a cycle is found in this graph, it precisely means that the transactions in the cycle are deadlocked. The system then chooses one of them as a *victim*, aborts it, obliterating its effects from the DB, and restarts it again later. It is a fact that the waits-for graph strategy shows a very good precision for all kinds of transactions, independent of their duration.

Detection of deadlocks in nested transactions is more complicated and expensive than in flat transactions. The deadlock manager must be aware of the transactions nesting, since deadlocks may occur among transactions belonging to various transaction hierarchies and even among subtransactions within a single transaction hierarchy. In contrast to single-level transactions where *direct-waits-for-lock* relations are sufficient to search for waiting cycles among transactions, detection of all deadlocks in nested transactions further requires the maintenance of *waits-for-commit* relations. If deadlocks are frequently anticipated, opening-up deadlocks, which may span transaction trees, should be detected as early as possible to save transaction work [9]. For this purpose, our deadlock manager maintains further information (*indirect-waits-for-lock* relations). Finally, our strategy additionally represents in the waits-for graph *detection arcs*, which are a very efficient means to determine cycles in the graph. They represent an abstraction of other waiting relations, and their only purpose is to effectively detect the occurrences of deadlocks. Hence, they alleviate the process of searching for cycles, since it is no longer necessary to analyze all waiting relations in the graph every time a waiting situation occurs.

This paper is organized as follows. In Sect. 2, we briefly introduce the model of nested transactions and the terminology used throughout this paper. In Sect. 3, we discuss deadlock detection in nested transactions by presenting several kinds of possible deadlocks in nested transactions and by introducing the different waiting relations that are necessary to detect any of them. Thereafter, in Sect. 4 we enter the field of deadlock resolution and briefly discuss the many issues involved in choosing the lowest-cost victim for abortion. In Sect. 5, we show the most important performance measurements that we have realized, which confirm the feasibility of our strategy. Finally, in Sect. 6 we summarize the main points considered in this paper.

2 A Model of Nested Transactions

We basically follow Moss's terminology [13]. A transaction may contain any number of *subtransactions*, which again may be composed of any number of subtransactions – conceivably resulting in an arbitrarily deep hierarchy of nested transactions. The root transaction which is not enclosed in any transaction is called the *top-level transaction* (TL-transaction). Transactions having subtransactions are called *parents*, and the subtransactions are their *children*. We also speak of *ancestors* and *descendants*. The ancestor (descendant) relation is the reflexive transitive closure of the parent (child) relation. We use the term *superior* (*inferior*) for the non-reflexive version of the ancestor (descendant). The set of descendants of a transaction together with their parent/ child relationships is called the transaction's *hierarchy*. In the following, unless otherwise noted, we use the term *transaction* to denote both TL-transactions and subtransactions in general.

Notwithstanding, in contrast to Moss's nested transaction model [13], where only leaf transactions are supposed to lock objects, we assume a model of nested transactions where every transaction can acquire locks on objects. Thus, deadlocks may occur among transactions belonging to various TL-transactions and even among subtransactions within a single transaction hierarchy. Furthermore, we allow for parent/child as well as sibling parallelism in our model, that is, a parent transaction can concurrently proceed with all its inferiors (non-strict execution). However, it cannot commit before all its inferiors have committed (or aborted).

3 Deadlock Detection in Nested Transactions

Deadlocks in nested transactions can be managed by the concepts known for single-level transactions extended by some mechanisms tailored to the properties of the nested transactions [13, 19, 9]. To detect the occurrence of the different kinds of deadlocks, several waiting relations with different meanings must be represented in the WFG.

3.1 Direct-Wait Deadlocks

When a transaction requires a lock on an object which is incompatible with a lock held by another concurrent transaction, the requesting transaction is deactivated, and as a consequence a direct wait for the lock holder occurs. All direct waits are represented by *direct-waits-for-lock relations* in the WFG. Using these relations, deadlock detection can be performed immediately when a transaction is blocked or after some elapsed time. A deadlock exists if and only if a cycle is found in the direct-waits-for-lock relations. In the scenario of Fig. 1, a deadlock may be detected between transactions **E** and **H**, which *directly* wait for each other. In the following, we present this first waiting relation.

- **Direct-waits-for-lock**
  A transaction **E** (lock requestor) directly waits for another transaction **H** (lock holder) if the mode of the lock requested by **E** is in conflict with the mode of the lock held by **H**. In Fig. 1, **E** cannot proceed until **H** does, and vice versa, i.e., both are waiting for each other.

  Considering the direct-waits-for-lock relations, direct-wait deadlocks can be found. However, to detect all possible deadlocks in nested transactions effectively, we have to represent more information about who is waiting for whom, i.e., more waiting relations. This is true no matter whether a deadlock occurs within a TL-transaction or among subtransactions of various TL-transactions. The next section approaches this topic.

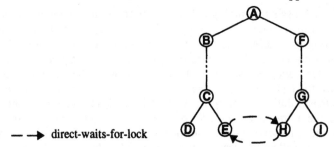

— —▶ direct-waits-for-lock

Fig. 1. Detection of a direct-wait deadlock.

3.2 Ancestor-Descendant Deadlocks

The scenario in Fig. 2 represents another kind of waiting situation. Transaction **I** directly waits for a lock held by **F**. Although progress has not stopped everywhere, because **F**, ..., **G** may proceed for some time, they cannot commit without aborting **I**, and therefore the best decision is to detect and resolve this ancestor-descendant deadlock immediately. A request of **I** causing a lock wait on its superior **F** can be detected by using the already introduced direct-waits-for-lock relation combined with another kind of waiting relation, which takes into account the hierarchical relationships of transactions – the *waits-for-commit relation*. This is explained in the following.

- **Waits-for-commit**
  Since a waiting lock requestor I cannot proceed with its work, all its superiors must wait as well for commit processing. In Fig. 2, G cannot commit until I does, G's parent cannot commit until G does, and so forth. In fact, all superiors of I cannot commit before I does. This kind of waiting relation is denoted *waits-for-commit*, and it can be represented by the parent-child relationships among the transactions in a hierarchy.

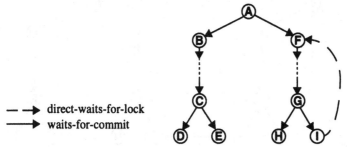

  — — ▶ direct-waits-for-lock
  ———▶ waits-for-commit

Fig. 2. Detection of an ancestor-descendant deadlock.

The combined use of direct-waits-for-lock and waits-for-commit relations turns out to be sufficient to detect existing cyclical waiting situations in nested transactions embodying both direct-wait as well as ancestor-descendant deadlocks. Hence, both relations are sufficient for detecting deadlocks in nested transactions [13]. However, to make this process more effective, Härder and Rothermel [9] have proposed the representation of an extra, refined waiting relation in order to detect opening-up deadlocks.

3.3 Opening-Up Deadlocks

Since a direct-waits-for-lock relation is only represented between the lock requestor and the lock holder (or, after commit of the lock holder, the current retainer), waiting situations between the lock requestor and all ancestors of the lock holder (retainer) are not explicitly established in the waits-for information thus far. In the context of nested transactions, however, these *indirect* waiting relationships should be taken into account to make early deadlock detection possible. If we examine only both kinds of waiting relations presented thus far (direct-waits-for-lock and waits-for-commit), the scenario of Fig. 3 represents a deadlock-free situation, since there is no cycle in the WFG involving only those relations. However, there is an emerging deadlock, because I indirectly waits for the oldest ancestor of M that is not an ancestor of I, in this case J. On the other hand, Q indirectly waits for the oldest ancestor of D that is not an ancestor of Q, i.e., A. If we evaluate this information (I → J, Q → A), we are able to immediately detect a cycle to be opening up. Hence, the representation of such indirect waiting situations as waiting relations in the WFG allows for the detection of *future* deadlocks. This waiting relation is introduced in the following.

- **Indirect-waits-for-lock**
  A lock requestor Q directly waits for a lock holder D if the mode of the lock requested by Q is in conflict with the mode of the lock held by D (this is the direct-waits-for-lock relation already presented). Further, let A be the highest ancestor of D that is not an ancestor of Q. Then, Q indirectly waits for A (see Fig. 3). This waiting situation is represented as an *indirect-waits-for-lock relation*.
  An optimistic attitude would not care about such an opening-up deadlock, since an abort of any transaction involved would eventually avoid the actual occurrence of the

deadlock before all progress ceases. However, transaction aborts are regarded as exceptions and should not be taken into account as a remedy to break opening-up deadlock cycles. In contrast, a pessimistic approach usually saves work [9]. However, the additional representation and management of indirect-waits-for-lock relations imposes some more overhead.

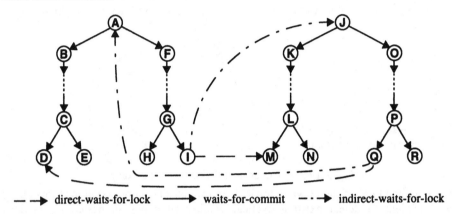

— —➤ direct-waits-for-lock   ——➤ waits-for-commit   —·—➤ indirect-waits-for-lock

Fig. 3. Detection of an opening-up deadlock.

This *indirect-waits-for-lock* relation is called *waits-for-retained-lock* by Härder and Rothermel [9]. We have renamed this relation here because when such a waiting situation occurs between subtransactions of different TL-transactions, as shown in Fig. 3, a subtransaction is not actually waiting for a *retained* lock (as the name suggests), but it in fact *indirectly* waits for a lock of the other TL-transaction hierarchy.

In addition, [9] proposes the representation of such indirect waiting relations for *all* ancestors of the lock holder up to the first non-common ancestor of the lock requestor. In the example of Fig. 3, not only the edges I → J and Q → A would be represented, but additionally I → L, ..., I → K as well as Q → C, ..., Q → B. We advocate that representing all these indirect-waits-for-lock relations is, as well as superfluous, very expensive for the deadlock manager. Therefore, for efficiency reasons, in our scheme we represent just one of them, namely the one involving the highest non-common ancestor between the two transactions, as shown in Fig. 3.

3.4 Overview of the Deadlock Detection Algorithm

Based on the previous discussions about the many waiting situations, we present in the following an overview of the algorithm for handling deadlocks. The algorithm is divided into four main bodies in order to capture all the inherent dynamism involved in the lifetime of transactions.

    A. *Whenever a transaction starts to wait for a lock:*

        A. i. Determine all transactions as well as the waiting relations (namely direct-waits-for-lock, waits-for-commit, and indirect-waits-for-lock) involved in this lock wait.

        A. ii. Insert all transactions as nodes in the WFG, if they are not already there.

        A. iii. Insert all waiting relations as directed edges between the corresponding nodes in the WFG.

A. iv. Initiate detection by means of navigating through all the nodes and edges in the WFG looking for all possible cycles.

A. v. If cycles are found, then choose, among the transactions involved in the cycles, victims for abortion (refer to Sect. 4).

B. *Whenever a TL-transaction commits:*

B. i. Check whether there is a node in the WFG for the committing TL-transaction.

B. ii. If there is such a node, then remove it and all its incoming edges from the WFG.

C. *Whenever a subtransaction commits:*

C. i. Check whether there is a node in the WFG for the committing sub-transaction.

C. ii. If there is such a node, then inherit all its incoming edges to the corresponding node of the committing subtransaction's parent and finally remove the node from the WFG.

D. *Whenever a transaction aborts:*[1]

D. i. Check whether there is a node in the WFG for the aborting transaction.

D. ii. If there is such a node, then remove it and all its incoming as well as outgoing edges from the WFG.

This could be a standard algorithm for deadlock detection in nested transactions using the waiting relations we have introduced so far. Surely, the most time-consuming aspect of this algorithm is the navigation process of looking for cycles in the WFG which involves traversing **all** its nodes and edges (step **A.iv.**). In the following, we present the detection arcs which substantially decrease such processing time.

3.5 The Detection Arcs

The main goal we have in mind here is to optimize the time-consuming process of looking for cycles in the WFG. The basic idea to achieve this goal is based on an extension of the indirect-waits-for-lock relations. We have seen previously that a transaction waiting for a lock indirectly waits for the oldest ancestor of the lock holder that is not itself an ancestor of the lock requestor. Using Fig. 4, transaction I directly waits for M and thus indirectly waits for J. However, if we analyze this waiting situation in more details, we can realize that not only I indirectly waits for J but also A, since A cannot commit before I does. Hence, the highest non-common ancestor of the lock requestor waits for the highest non-common ancestor of the lock holder. The representation of this waiting relation in the WFG – which we have called *detection arcs* – greatly alleviates the process of looking for cycles. In the following, we introduce detection arcs.

- **Detection arcs**
  A lock requestor I directly waits for a lock holder M if the mode of the lock requested by I is in conflict with the mode of the lock held by M (direct-waits-for-lock relation). Let A be the highest ancestor of I that is not an ancestor of M, and similarly, let J be the highest ancestor of M that is not an ancestor of I. Then, A indirectly waits for J through the direct wait between I and M. This waiting situation is represented as a *detection arc* in the WFG (Fig. 4).
  Essentially, a detection arc represents a higher level abstraction of the direct-waits-

---

1. We have not considered here partial rollbacks of transactions [11, 15]. However, a routine to cope with that feature can be thought of without serious difficulties.

for-lock and indirect-waits-for-lock relations between two transactions that have been caused by a lock wait. The most important advantage of the explicit detection arc representation is the process speed-up of looking for cycles in the WFG. We have previously seen the three kinds of deadlocks that can happen in nested transactions: direct-wait, ancestor-descendant, and opening-up deadlocks. With the help of the detection arcs, all direct-wait and opening-up deadlocks can be detected solely on their basis. Thus, in these cases the process of looking for cycles in the whole WFG can be reduced to looking for cycles only in a subset of the WFG, namely, the set of detection arcs. In Fig. 4, the cycle **A** → **F** → ... **G** → **I** → **J** → **O** → ... **P** → **Q** → **A** was reduced to the cycle **A** → **J** → **A** by means of detection arcs. Therefore, the detection of these kinds of deadlocks can be made much more efficient.

On the other hand, ancestor-descendant deadlocks cannot be detected with the help of the detection arcs. However, the detection of this kind of deadlock is in fact a very simple matter: whenever a lock wait happens, one must simply check whether the lock requestor is a descendant of the lock holder. Particularly in our implementation, this process was simplified even more, since we catch this information from the identifier of the requesting transaction which carries encoded information of all its ancestor transaction identifiers (refer to [18]). Therefore, whenever a transaction starts to wait for a lock, we check the inferior relationship between the requestor and the holder before the representation and derivation of the information for the WFG takes place. If they are in the same path of a transaction hierarchy, then there is a deadlock. If not, the algorithm for deadlock detection can proceed normally.

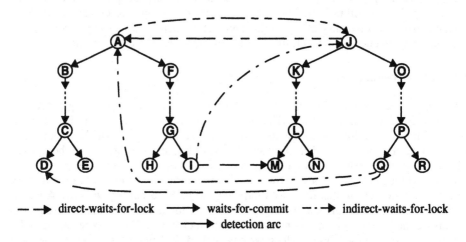

Fig. 4. Deadlock detection by means of detection arcs.

Furthermore, it is important to notice that finding a cycle involving the detection arcs only means, of course, that a deadlock has happened. All the transactions de facto involved in such a cyclical waiting situation are not determined. Hence, after having detected the deadlock occurrence, the usual routine for finding cycles in the whole WFG must be initiated. However, since the occurrence of a deadlock is generally considered to be a rare event [5], the time-consuming process of looking for cycles in the whole WFG is rarely started, namely, only when it is quite sure that a deadlock has occurred, and not every time a lock wait happens. Consequently, the overall performance of deadlock management is improved.

3.6 Deadlock Detection Algorithm Using Detection Arcs

In the following, we present an overview of the algorithm for handling deadlocks by means of detection arcs. In particular, only the first part (**A.**) of the previous algorithm needs to be adjusted, the other ones (**B.**, **C.**, and **D.**) remain unchanged (refer to Sect. 3.4). Furthermore, we have introduced in this algorithm a *counter* of the number of detection arcs between two nodes. Since the detection arcs represent a higher level abstraction of other waiting relations, there may appear several detection arcs between the very same nodes which in fact have the same meaning and purpose. The main idea behind such a counter is to restrict the number of detection arcs between two nodes. Having outlined the algorithm in the following, we discuss the main advantages of employing such counters.

A.   *Whenever a transaction starts to wait for a lock:*

A. i. Check the inferior relationship between the lock requestor and the lock holder. If they are in the same path of a transaction hierarchy, then choose the inferior transaction as a victim for abortion (refer to Sect. 4) and conclude the process.

A. ii. Determine all transactions as well as the waiting relations (namely direct-waits-for-lock, waits-for-commit, indirect-waits-for-lock, and detection arcs) involved in this lock wait.

A. iii. Insert all transactions as nodes in the WFG, if they are not already there.

A. iv. Insert the direct-waits-for-lock, indirect-waits-for-lock, and waits-for-commit (this one only if it is not already there) relations as directed edges between the corresponding nodes in the WFG.

A. v. Insert the detection arc as a directed edge between the corresponding nodes in the WFG. If there is already one such edge between both nodes, then only increment a corresponding counter.

A. vi. Initiate detection if and only if a new detection arc was inserted (i.e., if an existing counter was not incremented), by means of navigating only through the detection arcs of the WFG looking for possible cycles.

A. vii. If cycles are found, navigate through all the nodes and edges in the WFG looking for all possible cycles and then choose, among the transactions involved in the cycles, victims for abortion (refer to Sect. 4).

On the one hand, incrementing a counter whenever a detection arc is already available between the nodes (step **A.v.**) is necessary to cope with the deletion of the direct-waits-for-lock relations from the WFG. At that time, it can be efficiently decided by means of this counter whether the corresponding edge must be deleted as well, or whether there still are other direct-waits-for-lock relations below in the hierarchy subsumed under this edge.

On the other hand, another important aspect of this counter is that detection can be initialized only when a new detection arc is inserted in the WFG (step **A.vi.**). Of course, if the WFG is acyclic, after the insertion of an edge (detection arc) with the very same meaning between the very same nodes, it still remains acyclic. Therefore, this counter avoids the insertion of superfluous edges in the WFG. Furthermore, it allows for performance improvement, since the WFG becomes smaller and detection is initiated only when there is de facto the possibility of cycles being closed.

4 Deadlock Resolution

Since a deadlock does not go away by itself, after having been detected it must then be resolved. Deadlock resolution is typically done by means of the transaction (partial) rollback mechanism already available for fault tolerance: a deadlock victim must be found and rolled back. However, choosing the right victim for abortion is not a simple matter. In Fig. 5, suppose the last waiting situation signaled by the system is that transaction **F** waits for **B**. Until that point, the WFG was acyclic. However, after inserting the edge **F → B** (in this example, it does not matter which particular kind of waiting relation this edge represents), several cycles appear at once. Hence, finding the lowest-cost victim for abortion, the exact one which affects the minimal data granules of work lost and at the same time breaks all the cycles in the WFG, may be a time-consuming task.

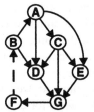

Fig. 5. Appearance of several cycles in a WFG at once.

Particularly in the case that the deadlock is of the kind ancestor-descendant, it is simple to find the victim: Since rollback of the ancestor transaction implies rollback of all its inferiors (committed and active), rollback of the descendant transaction is always cheaper than that of the corresponding ancestor, of course. In such a case, the descendant must be chosen as a victim and rolled back.

However, if the deadlock is either of the kind direct-wait or opening-up, then all transactions involved have to be considered to determine the lowest-cost victim for rollback and to break all the cycles appeared. There are several aspects that can influence the selection of the victim, as for example:
- the transaction level in the hierarchy and consequently the number of inferior transactions;
- the number of log records written thus far;
- the total execution time;
- objects changed so far;
- objects touched so far;
- processor time used so far; etc.

In contrast to Moss's nested transaction model [13], in other more flexible models – such as Camelot [20, 4], Clouds [2, 3], Eden [1, 14], LOCUS [12, 21], PRIMA [6, 8], KRISYS [17, 16], etc. – the transactions involved in the deadlock can occur everywhere in the transaction trees. Consequently, the derivation of the backout cost is much more complex; it must include the cost of aborting not only the victim transaction, but also of the corresponding transaction tree of committed and active subtransactions, and it must consider their work lost. Finally, when choosing the victim, the deadlock manager must be concerned about starvation, i.e., it must permit all transactions in the system to proceed eventually, in order to guarantee the progress of the system as a whole.

Particularly in the implementation of our multi-user knowledge base management system [16, 10], we have simplified the deadlock resolution process, since we believe that the costs for finding the ideal victim do not pay off compared to the remote possibility of eventually aborting the wrong transaction. Thus, when a deadlock of the kind ancestor-descendant happens, the deadlock manager requests the abortion of the descendant transaction, of course. Further, if the deadlock is either of the kind direct-wait or opening-up, then the deadlock manager considers just the transactions involved in the last waiting situation for aborting purposes. (Notice, therefore, that we do not need to start the process to look for cycles in the *whole* WFG after having detected the deadlock occurrence through the detection arcs, i.e., in our system the step **A.vii.** of the previous algorithm is saved.) On the basis of their transaction identifiers [18], the deadlock manager derives the information about the levels that those transactions are on and simply aborts the leaf-most one. Finally, if they are on the same level, the deadlock manager aborts the requesting transaction.

5 Performance Evaluation

5.1 The Conventional Strategy

The strategy we have chosen for comparison is exactly the one proposed by Härder and Rothermel [9] – here referred to as *conventional strategy*, to be compared with the *detection arcs strategy*. As previously presented, the waiting relations that are represented in the WFG by this strategy are: direct-waits-for-lock, waits-for-commit, and indirect-waits-for-lock (or *waits-for-retained-lock* according to their terminology).

5.2 The Algorithms and the Environment

The algorithms we have implemented, in C, may be gotten via *anonymous ftp* under *ftp.uni-kl.de* (131.246.94.94, /pub/informatik/software/rezende/Deadlock_NT). We have run the algorithms on a Sun Sparc Station 20^2, with 96 Mbytes of main memory, under Solaris 2.4^2, windows system Sun-X11R6^2. The time measurements have been made through the High-Resolution-Virtual-Timer of the Sun Workstation. We have performed the algorithms in hypothetical transaction hierarchies by varying depth as well as breadth and the number of direct-waits-for-lock relations, as will become clear in the next sections. Furthermore, we have repeated all functions ten thousand times in order to get good averages that are not so disturbed by occasional machine overloads. We have basically measured the detection process and the maintenance overhead of the WFG, both with respect to processing time.

5.3 Detection Process

In both strategies, the detection process (search for cycles in the WFG) is mainly influenced by the following factors:
(1) the level difference (*relative depth*) between the waiting transaction and the highest non-common ancestor of the awaited transaction;
(2) the *number of direct-waits-for-lock relations*; and
(3) the general *level of ramification* of the WFG, i.e., breadth as well as depth of the transaction hierarchies represented in the WFG.
    Of course, there are numerous possibilities of varying as well as combining these factors in order to analyze the performance of both strategies. Particularly in our investigation, we have considered four variations of these factors. We have kept the ramifi-

---

2. Registered trademark of Sun Microsystems, Inc.

cation level of the transaction hierarchies to the minimal value (i.e., only one path in each hierarchy) and varied then both the relative depth between waiting transaction and the highest non-common ancestor (Fig. 6) as well as the number of direct-waits-for-lock relations (Fig. 7). On the other hand, we have considered ramifications in the transaction hierarchies (two paths) and varied both factors as before, i.e., the relative depth (Fig. 8) and the number of direct-waits-for-lock relations (Fig. 9). As can be observed from the measurements, however, the behavior of both strategies relative to each other in non-ramified and ramified WFGs is very similar, just the time figures are somewhat different. In addition, it is important to notice here that the WFG in all its variations was prepared before the detection process was started, since we intended here to measure the processing time of the detection process when facing different situations. Therefore, the potential advantages of the counters of detection arcs discussed in Sect. 3.6 were not exploited in these measurements. In particular, we have considered that the left- and leaf-most transaction in the hierarchies has caused the last waiting situation; thus the detection process is started on it (shadowed circle in the forthcoming figures). In addition, the detection process has considered all necessary nodes and edges of the WFG – in fact, we have not closed any cycle in the WFG so that all nodes and edges must be transitiyely traversed. The maintenance overhead of the WFG is considered in the next section.

Fig. 6 illustrates the cost in time of the detection process of both strategies in non-ramified WFGs with varying relative depths between waiting transaction and the highest non-common ancestor. The processing time for the detection arcs strategy remains constant independent of the relative depth because the number of detection arcs in the WFG does not change when the depth is varied. On the other hand, the conventional strategy shows rising processing time as the depth is varied, since this strategy must traverse an increasing number of waiting relations in the WFG. In case of detection arcs, checking can be done directly on the representation, whereas the conventional strategy requests the iterative checking of all conceivable waiting relations.

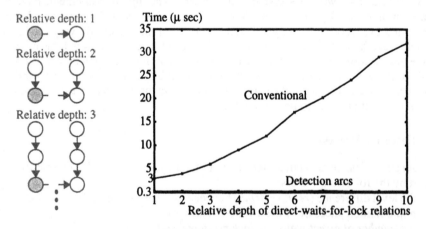

Fig. 6. Detection process in non-ramified WFGs – varying relative depths.

In Fig. 7, the performance of both strategies is shown when the number of direct-waits-for-lock relations is varied in non-ramified WFGs. As before, the conventional scheme similarly shows increasing time figures, since it must traverse an increasing number of waiting relations. In turn, the detection arcs strategy shows a slight increase in processing time because the number of detection arcs in the WFG has increased.

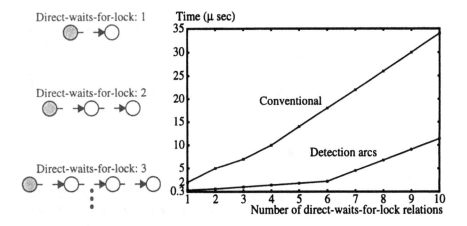

Fig. 7. Detection process in non-ramified WFGs – varying direct-waits-for-lock relations.

Considering now ramified WFGs, Fig. 8 illustrates the performance of both strategies when the relative depth is varied. In this case, the detection arcs strategy shows constant processing time because, as before, the number of detection arcs is not influenced by depth variations. On the other hand, the conventional strategy shows much worse processing times due to the high number of waiting relations caused by the ramifications in the WFG.

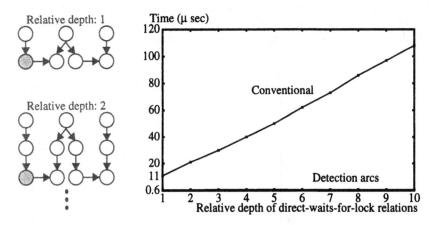

Fig. 8. Detection process in ramified WFGs – varying relative depths.

Finally, Fig. 9 illustrates the behavior of both strategies in ramified WFGs when the number of direct-waits-for-lock relations is varied. Similarly, the conventional strategy shows very high and constantly increasing processing times due to the ramifications in the WFG. On the other hand, the detection arcs strategy shows low but now rising processing times because again the number of detection arcs in the WFG has increased.

All in all, the detection arcs strategy achieves processing times for the detection of deadlocks drastically better than the conventional strategy. The general reason for that is what we have been affirming since the beginning of this paper: The number of edges of the WFG to be traversed by the detection process is substantially reduced through the representation and exploitation of the detection arcs.

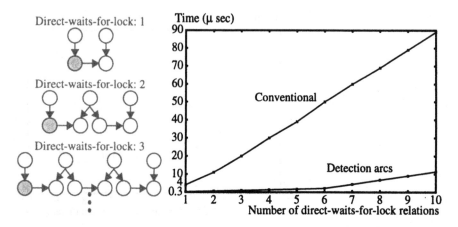

Fig. 9. Detection process in ramified WFGs – varying direct-waits-for-lock relations.

5.4 Maintenance Overhead of the Waits-For Graph

In order to analyze the maintenance overhead of the WFG in both strategies, we have considered insertion and deletion of nodes in the WFG and, as a consequence, the insertion and deletion of the corresponding waiting relations. Here, we have subsumed these operations under update operations in general. Fig. 10 illustrates the behavior of both strategies during the maintenance of the WFG. In particular, we have considered here a non-ramified WFG with varying relative depths; such variations, however, do not affect the behavior of both strategies relative to each other.

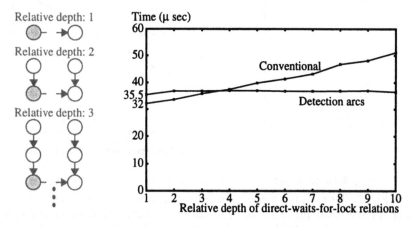

Fig. 10. Maintenance overhead for update operations.

The main difference in the performance of both strategies is due to the update of the varying number of waiting relations. In the detection arcs strategy, the maintenance overhead is almost constant independent of the depth of the transaction hierarchies. On the other hand, the conventional strategy shows a slightly-increasing overhead because the number of waiting relations (indirect-waits-for-lock) also increases when the trans-action hierarchies become deeper. Finally, the detection arcs strategy has a maintenance overhead greater than the conventional one in the beginning due to the higher costs to determine (twice) the highest non-common ancestor. However, this cost is paid off when the hierarchies are deeper because the conventional strategy must then cope with more waiting relations than the detection arcs strategy.

6 Conclusions

In order to correctly handle deadlocks in nested transactions, the concepts known for flat transactions must be extended with special waiting relations to reflect the properties of the nested structure of transactions. The usual direct-waits-for-lock relation reflects the idea that a lock requestor waits for a lock holder due to a conflict between requested and held lock modes. Such a waiting relation enables the detection of direct-wait deadlocks, where only lock requestor and holder are involved.

To detect deadlocks between ancestor and descendant, another kind of waiting relation, called waits-for-commit, must be represented in the WFG. This one reflects the hierarchical relationships between the transactions and represents the fact that an ancestor waits for the commitment of its inferiors. By such a means, a deadlock can be detected as soon as a descendant starts waiting for a lock held by any of its superiors.

If deadlocks are frequently anticipated, opening-up deadlocks should be detected as early as possible to save transaction work. For this purpose, we have additionally used the indirect-waits-for-lock relation. This one reflects the idea that the lock requestor waits for the highest ancestor of the lock holder which is not its ancestor. The representation of such a waiting relation allows for the detection of future deadlock cycles, thereby saving transaction work.

Furthermore, since the process of looking for cycles in the WFG considering all its nodes and edges may be extremely expensive, we have introduced a special kind of waiting relation which represents a high-level abstraction of the direct-waits-for-lock and indirect-waits-for-lock relations between two transactions, the detection arcs. With their help, the deadlock detection process can be made very efficient, because only a minimal subset of the WFG's edges needs to be navigated. Furthermore, such a detection process must be started only when a new detection arc is inserted in the graph, and not necessarily every time a lock wait happens.

We have also considered the principles of deadlock resolution in nested transactions. Essentially, deadlock resolution is based on transaction rollbacks. The transactions involved in the cyclical waiting situation have to be considered, and a victim for abortion must be chosen. The process of choosing such a victim is not trivial, because ideally the victim should be a transaction affecting the minimal data granules of lost work and at the same time breaking all the cyclical waiting situations. Particularly in our implementation, we have simplified this process by using some heuristics.

At last, we have realized many performance measurements, the most important of them we have shown here. With respect to all situations faced by the deadlock detection process, our detection arcs strategy has achieved processing times much better than the conventional one. In turn, the maintenance overhead of the WFG in both strategies has revealed no significant differences. Finally, with the algorithms we have made available via anonymous ftp, we hope to facilitate the work of the ones who might like to implement our ideas in their own systems.

References

1. Almes, G.T., Black, A.P., Lazowska, E.D., Noe, J.D.: The Eden System: A Technical Review. IEEE Trans. on Software Engineering SE-11 (1985) 43-58
2. Ahamad, M., Dasgupta, P., Blanc, R.J., Wilkes, C.T.: Fault Tolerant Computing in Object-Based Distributed Systems. Proc. IEEE Symp. on Reliability in Distributed Software and Database Systems (1987)
3. Dasgupta, P., Blanc, R.J., Appelbe, W.: The Clouds Distributed Operating System: Functional Description, Implementation Details and Related Work. Proc. 8th IEEE Int. Conf. on Distributed Computing Systems, San Jose, USA (1989)
4. Eppinger, J.L., Mummert, L.B., Spector, A.Z. (Eds.): Camelot and Avalon: A Distributed Transaction Facility. Morgan Kaufmann Publ., San Mateo, USA (1991)
5. Gray, J., Reuter, A.: Transaction Processing: Concepts and Techniques. Morgan Kaufmann Publ., San Mateo, USA (1993)
6. Härder, T., Meyer-Wegener, K., Mitschang, B., Sikeler, A.: PRIMA - A DBMS Prototype Supporting Engineering Applications. Proc. 13th Int. Conf. on Very Large Data Bases, Brighton, U.K. (1987) 433-442
7. Holt, R.C.: Some Deadlock Properties in Computer Systems. ACM Computing Surveys 4: 3 (1972) 179-196
8. Härder, T., Profit, M., Schöning, H.: Supporting Parallelism in Engineering Databases by Nested Transactions. SFB 124 Res. Report 34/92, Univ. of Kaiserslautern, Germany (1992)
9. Härder, T., Rothermel, K.: Concurrency Control Issues in Nested Transactions. VLDB Journal 2:1 (1993) 39-74
10. Mattos, N.M.: An Approach to Knowledge Base Management. LNAI 513, Springer-Verlag, Berlin, Germany (1991)
11. Mohan, C., Haderle, D., Lindsay, B.G., Pirahesh, H., Schwarz, P.: ARIES: A Transaction Recovery Method Supporting Fine-Granularity Locking and Partial Rollbacks Using Write-Ahead Logging. ACM Trans. on Database Systems 17:1 (1992) 94-162
12. Müller, E.T., Moore, J.D., Popek, G.A.: Nested Transaction Mechanism for LOCUS. Proc. 9th Symp. on Operating Systems Principles (1983) 71-89
13. Moss J.E.B.: Nested Transactions: An Approach to Reliable Distributed Computing. MIT Press, USA (1985)
14. Pu, C., Noe, J.D.: Nested Transactions for General Objects: The Eden Implementation. TR-85-12-03, Univ. of Washington, Washington D.C., USA (1985)
15. Rezende, F.F., Baier, T.: Employing Object-Based LSNs in a Recovery Strategy. Proc. 7th Int. Conf. on Database and Expert Systems Applications, Zurich, Switzerland (1996) 116-129
16. Rezende, F.F.: Transaction Services for Knowledge Base Management Systems - Modeling Aspects, Architectural Issues, and Realization Techniques. Doctor Thesis, Univ. of Kaiserslautern, Germany (1997)
17. Rezende, F.F., Härder, T.: Concurrency Control in Nested Transactions with Enhanced Lock Modes for KBMSs. Proc. 6th Int. Conf. on Database and Expert Systems Applications, London, U.K. (1995) 604-613
18. Rezende, F.F., Härder, T., Zielinski, J.: Implementing Identifiers for Nested Transactions. Proc. 16th Brazilian Computer Society Conference - 23rd Integrated Seminar on Software and Hardware (SBC/SEMISH'96), Recife, Brazil (1996) 119-130
19. Rukoz, M.: Hierarchical Deadlock Detection for Nested Transactions. Distributed Computing 4 (1991) 123-129
20. Spector, A.Z., Pausch, R.F., Bruell, G.: Camelot: A Flexible, Distributed Transaction Processing System. Proc. IEEE Spring Computer Conference, USA (1988)
21. Weinstein, M., Page, T., Livezey, B., Popek, G.: Transactions and Synchronization in a Distributed Operating System. Proc. 10th Symp. on Operating Systems Principles (1985) 115-126

Improved and Optimized Partitioning Techniques in Database Query Processing

Kjell Bratbergsengen and Kjetil Nørvåg

Department of Computer Science
Norwegian University of Science and Technology,
7034 Trondheim, Norway
{kjellb,noervaag}@idt.unit.no

Abstract. In this paper we present two improvements to the partitioning process: 1) A new dynamic buffer management strategy is employed to increase the average block size of I/O-transfers to temporary files, and 2) An optimal switching between three different variants of the partitioning methods that ensures minimal partitioning cost. The expected performance gain resulting from the new management strategy is about 30% for a reasonable resource configuration. The performance gain decreases with increasing available buffer space. The different partitioning strategies (partial partitioning or hybrid hashing, one pass partitioning, and multipass partitioning) are analyzed, and we present the optimal working range for these, as a function of operand volume and available memory.

Keywords: Relational algebra, partitioning methods, buffer management, query processing

1 Introduction

Relational algebra operations are time and resource consuming, especially when done on large operand volumes. In this paper, we present a new, dynamic, buffer management strategy for partitioning which can significantly reduce the execution time: *the circular track snow plow strategy*. Our approach is motivated from three observations:

1. When doing disk intensive operations, it is advantageous to process as large blocks as possible when doing disk accesses. Our strategy uses an optimal partitioning, which gives as large blocks as possible.
2. With the traditional fixed size block methods, only half the available memory is actually holding records. Our strategy, with variable size blocks, will with the same amount of available memory, double the average block size, and thus make much better use of available memory resources.
3. While it might be true that main memory on computers are large, and getting even larger, not all of this is available for one relational algebra operation. Often, several programs are running concurrently, several users are running queries concurrently, and queries can be quite complex, resulting in a large

tree of query operators. In this case, available memory for each operator can be rather small. As the comparison between the methods will show later in the paper, our method will be especially advantageous with small amounts of memory available, but it will always perform better than the traditional approach.

In the rest of the paper, we first present some related work in Sect. 2, and give an introduction to partitioning strategies in Sect. 3. The circular track snow plow strategy is introduced in Sect. 4. We present our cost model and assumptions in Sect. 5, and derive cost functions for the partitioning strategies. Finally, we compare these approaches in Sect. 6, and show a significant performance gain by using the snow plow strategy.

2 Related Work

Optimal splitting of source relations is discussed by Nakayama et. al. in [9]. Their conclusion is to partition the relation into as many partitions as possible. They say nothing about the block size, except that it is fixed. Their algorithms is beneficial to use when we have heavy data skew, but in other situations the small block size makes them expensive, as pointed out by Graefe [5]. Block size (clusters) has usually been determined from experiments, simulations, or just common sense, with Volcano [6] as an exception. Recently, the use of variable block size has also been recognized and studied by Davidson and Graefe [3], and Zeller and Gray [11], but these papers focuses on memory availability, rather than a thorough analysis by the use of cost functions.

3 Partitioning Strategies

With smaller operand volumes, nested loop methods are superior, requiring only one scan of the operands to create the resulting table. When the operand volume increases, nested loop methods are still employed in the final stage, but now after a hash partitioning stage, as described in [2, 1, 4].

Several partitioning strategies exists. They can be classified as *no splitting, partial, one pass, and multipass partitioning*. This first one, no splitting, is used when the smallest operand is less than or equal to available workspace. When this is the case, the whole operation can be done in main memory.

When the smallest operand is larger than available memory, one can split in one pass. All available workspace is used for splitting. We call this variant *one pass partitioning*. The number of partitions, p, is so large that each partition can be held in work space in the next stage.

When the smallest operand V is larger than the memory M, but less than some limit V_{ppu}, partial splitting (or hybrid hash) can be employed. Part of the memory is used for partitioning, the other part is used for performing the relational algebra operation. When the operand gets larger, more work space area is needed for splitting. The upper limit V_{ppu} is found when all available memory is best used for splitting the operand.

As the smallest operand gets very large, a large number of partitions is necessary when one pass partitioning is employed. The result is a small block size, because the block size $b = M/p$ (or, as we will see later, with our method, $b = 2M/p$). As this block size gets smaller, there is a limit where splitting is best done in several passes, *multipass partitioning*.

It is useful to classify the (smallest) operand size, relative to available workspace M, in four classes: small, medium, large, and huge operands. As is shown in Table 3, partitioning strategy is determined from operand class. How to decide the bounds for each class will be shown later in the paper. As pointed out in the introduction, it is important to keep in mind that not all of the main memory is available as workspace for the partitioning process.

Operand Class	Size of Smallest Operand	Strategy
Small	$V \leq M$	No partitioning
Medium	$M < V \leq V_{ppu}$	Partial partitioning
Large	$V_{ppu} < V \leq V_{opu}$	One pass partitioning
Huge	$V_{opu} < V$	Multipass partitioning

Table 1. Operand classes and corresponding partitioning strategies.

4 The Circular Track Snow Plow Strategy

With the traditional splitting strategy, as described in [2, 1, 7, 4, 10], we have a fixed size of memory for each group. When a new tuple arrive, it is moved to its block buffer. Whenever a block buffer is full, it is written to disk.

If we look closer at the fixed block size splitting, we see that only about half the available memory is actually holding records. If we do not divide the memory into fixed sized block buffers, but rather let work space be one common memory pool, we do not have to write records to disks until all memory is taken. Then we write the first group to disk. We now have a new period where all groups (part of partitions in memory) are growing at approximately the same speed. This holds if the hash partitioning formula gives an even distribution. Again when there is no room left, the next group is written to disk. After all groups have been written once to disk, we start over again with the first group. After a transient start up phase, we can see that the average size of the groups written to disk is approximately $b = 2M/p$. This method is analogous to the replacement selection sort which is used for initial sorting in sort-merge programs. Why the average block size is $2M/p$, is well described by Knuth in [8]. The situation can be compared to a snow plow on a circular track of length l. The plow is always plowing full depth snow. Just behind the plow, the depth is zero, and the average snow depth on the track is one half the full depth h. The total amount of snow on the track is $hl/2$. In our case, the full snow depth h corresponds to the block size b, and the track length l corresponds to the number of subfiles p. Then $bp/2 = M \Rightarrow b = 2M/p$. This is illustrated in Fig. 1, which shows the groups in memory during splitting. To the left we see the situation just before the first group (0) is written to disk. To the right we see a steady state situation just after group 3 has been written to disk. The next group to go is number 4, when the lower limit of available space is reached.

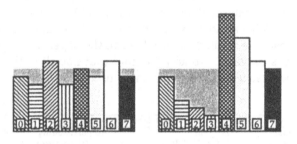

Fig. 1. Groups in memory during splitting.

4.1 Memory management

The memory is now used as a heap, storing records. The records are logically separated into p groups. This can be done using linked lists, pointer arrays, linked lists with pointers, etc. The group is determined using a hash formula on the operand key. Records are read and stored in memory until the amount of free memory reaches a lower limit. In the stationary situation, the amount of memory used is the same as the amount released. The addresses of the free space slots could be stored on a small stack. Memory management is especially simple if all records have the same size, however, if there are variable length records, more elaborate schemes should be used. Memory management at this level is important, because it could take a lions share of CPU time.

4.2 Writing Blocks to Disk

To take full advantage of this method, each group should be written to the disk as one block. Because of the stochastic nature of the group size, groups do not in general have the same size. Also, in the initialization phase, the average group size is rapidly growing from M/p to $2M/p$.

Despite the groups in memory are of different sizes, each group could be stored as a chain of fixed sized blocks on the disk. We should set aside two buffers to allow for double buffering. Each buffer should be $2M/p$ bytes. When a group is ready for output, its records are moved to the free output buffer. In the startup transient phase, we would not be able to fill the buffer before we have to write it, but in the stationary phase most of the time it will be nearly full. Sometimes we have to leave some records of the group behind, they will have to go to the next block for that group. To better fill the output buffer, we could change the *round robin* sequence strategy for writing groups to disk, to a *largest group first strategy* (LGF). This strategy might even lead to a larger average block size than $2M/p$.

It would be even better if we could get user level functionality enabling us directly to write to, and read from, the SCSI port. This requires some redesign of the ASPI interface. The current ASPI interface provides only a traditional block transfer I/O command. The command specifies a block address, buffer address and block length. No constructive interaction is possible until the command has finished, i.e. transferred a complete block. We would need new functionality, like moving single words or smaller blocks between SCSI port and user memory. This is effectively a *gather write* function available at the user level. This could save a lot of unnecessary copying.

4.3 Disk Layout

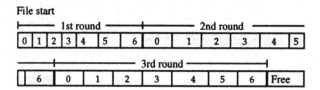

Fig. 2. The disk image after all groups have been emptied three times.

If we write the disk with fixed sized blocks, there is no problem finding all blocks of one group, they are chained together. The following is about disk layout when the disk is written with variable sized blocks (groups). When the groups are written to disk, we will get a pattern similar to that shown in Fig. 2, if neighboring groups are written contiguously onto disk. A *Round* in the figure is *one round around the circular track*, processing each group once. The numbers are group numbers. Writing groups contiguously gives a bonus when we flush all groups at end of input. This can be done in one operation. It is also necessary if we want to create *supergroups*, by joining neighboring groups into one supergroup. This is useful when the operand(s) has been over-partitioned (the operand has been partitioned into a larger number of partitions than necessary). This can happen if we are uncertain about the number of subfiles we need, and choose to overpartition to err on the right side. The overpartitioning causes more disk accesses than necessary during the splitting phase. The extra cost of overpartitioning should be removed from the reading phase, and we can

Round	Address	g0	g1	g2	g3	g4	g5	g6
0	0	10	12	14	15	17	18	21
1	107	19	23	22	20	21	22	22
2	256	21	21	18	20	21	20	21
3	398	22	19	23	17	15	12	9
4	515	7	3	1	0	0	0	0
Size	526	79	78	78	72	74	72	73

Table 2. Index table, where the last row holds accumulated values (the size) for each group in number of address units.

do so by joining neighboring groups into supergroups. This is easy as long as all groups are written contiguously onto the same disk.

Because of the variable block size, we need an index to efficiently retrieve blocks when we read back one or more groups. The index is a table with one column for each group (subfile), and one row for each round in the Round Robin output process. The corresponding table element would then contain the size of each block. The size of the index table depends on the number of groups and the number of rounds. To speed up address calculations, it would be useful to add one column to the index table, holding the address of the first block in each round. It is shown in Table 4.3 how an index table might look like.

The size of each block could be in bytes, sectors or some other unit. The total size of each subfile after partitioning is found by adding the numbers in each column. This information will tell how many subfiles can be read together, or how much space is needed to hold the largest subfile during the final algebra operation.

Even for large data volumes, the index table should be stored in memory without eating up to much space: Suppose that for every round, approximately $2M$ data is written to disk. The size of the index table, in number of variable sized blocks is $s = \frac{Vp}{2M}$. If $V = 1$ GB, $p = 100$ and $M = 50$ MB, the size s is 1000 integers.

4.4 Estimation of the Free Space Limit

The free space limit should be as small as possible, however there are some constraints. If we have only one SCSI bus, we have no real I/O overlapping. An initiated I/O operation must be completed until another operation could be started. If we started a read operation and could not complete it because of lack of input buffer space, we would have a deadlock. Then we would not be able to free space by writing a group to disk. Before we start a read, we should make sure that we have enough free space to accommodate all data read.

4.5 The Minimum Block Size

Writing a group should be skipped if it is below a minimum size. This will happen only when the hashing formula works poorly, producing uneven sized groups, or we try to stress the system, having uncoordinated parameters. The minimum block size should be in the vicinity of 4 KB, and this should be far below the normal group size when M has some reasonable value (above 100 KB, at least). If we use the LGF strategy there will be no minimum block size problem.

4.6 Multiuser Environments

It is also worth noting that the size of M can change dynamically, this only affects the size of the groups. Partitioning strategy, however, is done at operation startup time. Thus, if available memory decreases, an extra pass might be needed.

5 Cost Functions

Our cost model is based on I/O transfer only. This is the most significant cost factor, and in reasonable implementations, the CPU processing should go in parallel with I/O transfer making the CPU cost "invisible". Our disk model is traditional. Disk transfers are done blockwise. One block is the amount of data transferred in one I/O command. The main cost comes from two contributors: *the start up cost* and *transfer cost*. Start up cost comes from command software and hardware overhead, disk positioning time, and disk rotational delay.

In our model, the average start up cost is fixed, and is set equivalent to t_r, the time it takes to do one disk revolution. The transfer cost is directly proportional to the block size, and is equivalent to reading disk tracks contiguously, e.g., transfer cost is equal to $\frac{b}{V_s} t_r$, where V_s is the amount of data on one track and b is the block size to be transferred. For very large blocks, it is likely that several tracks and also tracks in different cylinders are read contiguously. This implies positioning, but we assume that the times used for this is insignificant compared to transfer time. The time it takes to transfer one block is $t_b = t_r(1 + \frac{b}{V_s})$. The time to transfer a data volume V using block size b is:

$$T_T = \frac{V t_r}{b} + \frac{V t_r}{V_s} = V t_r \left(\frac{1}{b} + \frac{1}{V_s} \right) \qquad (1)$$

Our emphasis is to find optimal parameters and the best working range for each method. To be able to handle the different equations mathematically we regard them as continuous functions rather than discontinuous functions resulting from applying ceiling and floor functions. This approximation gives a better overall view, but could cause small errors compared to the exact mathematical description.

To get smooth input and output streams, double buffering can be employed. However, to simplify the computations, the space for input buffers and extra output buffers is not counted within the memory M in our cost functions. Thus, the memory M, can be thought of as the available memory *after reservation of memory for the extra input and output buffers.*

The splitting is based on a hash formula applied to the operation key. The subtables will vary in size due to statistical variations and the "goodness" of the selected hash formula, in a real system it would be beneficial to let the average subtable be slightly smaller than the workspace. With good approximation we can ignore this and we are also ignoring space needed for structural data.

5.1 One Pass Partitioning

We will start with a simple partitioning strategy. If the input table is larger than available work space, we will split the table in subtables, such that each subtable fits into work space M. The subtables are are written to temporary files. The necessary split factor is: $p = \lceil \frac{V}{M} \rceil$, and the time used is:

$$T_{1p} = 2T_T = 2Vt_r \left(\frac{1}{b} + \frac{1}{V_s} \right) = 2Vt_r \left(\frac{V}{M^2} + \frac{1}{V_s} \right)$$

The actual block size with fixed block size, assuming we are free to select the block size, is $b = \lfloor \frac{M}{p} \rfloor \approx \frac{M^2}{V}$, which gives:

$$T_{1p}^F = 2Vt_r \left(\frac{V}{M^2} + \frac{1}{V_s} \right)$$

and with variable block size, we get on the average $b = \frac{2M}{p} \approx \frac{2M^2}{V}$, which gives:

$$T_{1p}^V = 2Vt_r \left(\frac{V}{2M^2} + \frac{1}{V_s} \right)$$

For operand volumes slightly larger than M, we see that it would probably be better to let some of the work space be used for holding records participating in the final algebra stage, and use only a portion of the work space for split buffer. This leads us to the partial partitioning or hybrid hash algorithm. At the other end, we see that when operand volumes are very large, the split factor increases and the block size goes down. Small I/O blocks are severely slowing down the I/O process. It may be better to split the data repeatedly, using larger blocks, rather than using smaller blocks and reaching the correct subfile size in one pass. This leads us to the multipass splitting method.

5.2 Partial Partition

Partial partitioning is especially advantageous for operand volumes larger than M, but so small that we do not need all available memory for efficient splitting. A part of the memory is used for holding a number of complete groups, to avoid the unnecessary I/O caused by the splitting. If the operand volume V is known in advance, we can compute the optimum memory size x, not used for splitting. x is thus also the amount of data which is not split. We ignore floor and ceiling functions to keep the equations mathematically tractable.

Fixed Block Size. The number of subfiles is $N = (V - x)/M$. The complete split is done in one pass, hence $N = p$, the split factor. The average block size using fixed block size splitting is:

$$b = \frac{(M - x)}{p} = \frac{M(M - x)}{V - x}$$

which gives the split time by substitution of b into Eq. 1 is:

$$T_{pp}^F = 2(V - x)t_r\left(\frac{1}{b} + \frac{1}{V_s}\right) = 2(V - x)t_r\left(\frac{V - x}{M(M - x)} + \frac{1}{V_s}\right)$$

The time will vary with x, a large x reduces transferred volume, however, the average block size is decreased, and the time spent may increase. To find a minimal value for T_{pp}, we have to find the value of x that will give the minimum value of T_{pp}. This can be done by solving:

$$\frac{dT_{pp}^F(x)}{dx} = 2t_r\left(\frac{-2(V - x)M(M - x) + M(V - x)^2}{M^2(M - x)^2} - \frac{1}{V_s}\right) = 0$$

To solve this equation we substitute $\lambda = M/V_s$ and

$$z = \frac{V - x}{M - x} \tag{2}$$

Then we obtain the following equation in z giving:

$$z^2 - 2z - \lambda = 0 \Rightarrow z = 1 \pm \sqrt{1 + \lambda}$$

Back substitution of z into Eq. 2 gives:

$$x = \frac{zM - V}{z - 1}$$

x should never be negative, which implies: $z > 0$ and $zM - V \geq 0$. This sets a restriction on V, which must be less than zM. It does not make sense to use partial partitioning when operand volumes are greater than zM. When $V \leq M$, splitting is not at all employed. This limits the working range of partial partitioning to: $M < V \leq zM$.

Variable Block Size. Derivation in the case of variable block size is done the same way as for fixed block size. The only difference is that we are doubling the effective block size, which gives:

$$T_{pp}^V = 2(V - x)t_r\left(\frac{1}{b} + \frac{1}{V_s}\right) = 2(V - x)t_r\left(\frac{V - x}{2M(M - x)} + \frac{1}{V_s}\right)$$

5.3 Multipass Partitioning

Data are read from an input file and hashed into a number of subfiles. The actual block size with fixed size blocks is: $b = \lfloor \frac{M}{p} \rfloor \approx \frac{M}{p}$. The necessary number of subfiles at the end is $N = \lceil \frac{V}{M} \rceil \approx \frac{V}{M}$. Depending on the operand volume, it may be beneficial to partition the operand in several passes. This is equivalent to the merging used in sort-merge processing, and the approximate number of operand passes is $w = \log_p N$. When we substitute for N, we get $w = \log_p \frac{V}{M}$. The total amount of data read and written to disk to complete a partitioning and the final relational algebra step is $V_T = 2Vw$, which gives a total partitioning time of:

$$T_{mp} = V_T T_T = 2V t_r \log_p \frac{V}{M} \left(\frac{1}{b} + \frac{1}{V_s} \right)$$

Substituting for $\log_p \frac{V}{M} = \frac{\ln V/M}{\ln p}$:

$$T_{mp} = 2V \frac{\ln V/M}{\ln p} t_r \left(\frac{p}{M} + \frac{1}{V_s} \right) \tag{3}$$

An optimum block size exist because when we split into many subfiles in one pass, each subfile need an output buffer, hence they get smaller. We can minimize Eq. 3 by noting that the variable part of this expression is:

$$f(p) = \frac{1}{\ln p} \left(\frac{1}{b} + \frac{1}{V_s} \right)$$

To find a minimum value for $f(p)$, we derive $f(p)$ with respect to p, and the optimum value for p is when $f'(p) = 0$:

$$p(\ln p - 1) - \frac{M}{V_s} = 0$$

It is easily seen that p is a function of the quotient $\lambda = \frac{M}{V_s}$:

$$p(lnp - 1) - \lambda = 0$$

This equation can be solved numerically, to find the value for p. Thus, the function for multipass partitioning with fixed block size is given by:

$$T_{mp}^F = 2V t_r \log_p \frac{V}{M} \left(\frac{p}{M} + \frac{1}{V_s} \right)$$

With the same method, we can find an optimum value for p in the case of variable block size (where $b = \frac{2M}{p}$):

$$T_{mp}^V = 2V t_r \log_p \frac{V}{M} \left(\frac{p}{2M} + \frac{1}{V_s} \right)$$

As an example, Table 5.3 shows optimal split factors, block size, and number of passes for different sizes of memory, with operand volume held constant on $V = 1000$ MB and $V_s = 50$ KB.

$\lambda = M/V_s$: (M in MB:)	1 (0.05)	2 (0.1)	5 (0.25)	10 (0.5)	20 (1.0)	50 (2.5)	100 (5)	200 (10)	500 (25)	1000 (50)
Fixed block size:										
Optimal p	3	4	6	8	12	23	37	63	129	226
b	17	25	42	62	83	109	135	159	194	226
w	9.01	6.64	4.63	3.66	2.78	1.91	1.47	1.11	1.00	1.00
Var. block size:										
Optimal p	4	5	8	12	20	37	63	108	226	400
b	25	40	62	83	100	135	159	185	221	250
w	7.14	5.72	3.99	2.31	1.66	1.28	1.00	1.00	1.00	1.00

Table 3. Optimal split factors, block size and number of passes for different sizes of memory.

Strategy:	Partial	One Pass	Multipass
Range:	$M < V \le zM$ (medium operands)	$zM < V \le p_{mp}M$ (large operands)	$V > p_{mp}M$ (huge operands)
Fixed Size, T^F: $z = 1 + \sqrt{1+\lambda}$ $p(\ln p - 1) - \lambda = 0$	$2(V-x)t_r\left(\frac{V-x}{M(M-x)} + \frac{1}{V_s}\right)$	$2Vt_r\left(\frac{V}{M^2} + \frac{1}{V_s}\right)$	$2Vt_r \log_p \frac{V}{M}\left(\frac{P}{M} + \frac{1}{V_s}\right)$
Variable size T^V: $z = 1 + \sqrt{1+2\lambda}$ $p(\ln p - 1) - 2\lambda = 0$	$2(V-x)t_r\left(\frac{V-x}{2M(M-x)} + \frac{1}{V_s}\right)$	$2Vt_r\left(\frac{V}{2M^2} + \frac{1}{V_s}\right)$	$2Vt_r \log_p \frac{V}{M}\left(\frac{P}{2M} + \frac{1}{V_s}\right)$
Supporting values: $\lambda = M/V_s$	$x = \frac{zM-V}{z-1}$		$w = max\left(1.0, \frac{\ln V/M}{\ln p}\right)$

Table 4. Cost functions for splitting.

5.4 Summary and Application of the Cost Functions

The cost functions and their working areas are summarized in Table 5.4. To demonstrate the relationship between the three variants, we have computed the partitioning times for different operand volumes. By using $V_s = 50$ KB, $t_r = 11$ ms, and $M = 1$ MB, we get the partitioning times as shown in Table 5.4.

From the table, we can see that for fixed size blocks, partial partitioning is best for volumes from 2 to 5 MB. Multipass is better when operands are larger than 12 MB. For variable blocks, partial partitioning is best for the volumes from 2 to 7 MB. Then one pass takes over, multipass partitioning is better when operands are larger than 20 MB. The different working areas for the variants of partitioning is illustrated in Fig. 3.

V (in MB)	Fixed sized blocks $\lambda = 20, z = 5.6, p_{mp} = 12$			Variable sized blocks $\lambda = 20, z = 7.4, p_{mp} = 20$		
	T_{pp}	T_{1p}	T_{mp}	T_{pp}	T_{1p}	T_{mp}
2	0.69	0.98	1.39	0.61	0.93	1.33
3	1.39	1.53	2.19	1.22	1.43	2.00
4	2.08	2.13	2.92	1.83	1.96	2.37
5	2.77	2.78	3.65	2.44	2.50	3.33
6	-	3.47	4.38	3.04	3.07	4.00
7	-	4.20	5.11	3.65	3.66	3.67
8	-	4.98	5.84	-	4.27	5.34
16	-	12.8	12.7	-	9.96	10.7
32	-	37.0	31.7	-	25.6	24.7
64	-	119.5	76.1	-	74.0	59.2
128	-	421.0	177.6	-	238.9	138.2
256	-	1570.0	405.9	-	842.0	315.9

Table 5. Partitioning times for different operand volumes and different basic partitioning methods.

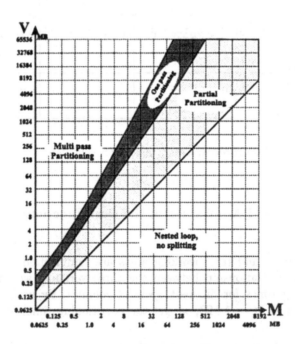

Fig. 3. Working areas for different algebra methods, with numbers from variable block size.

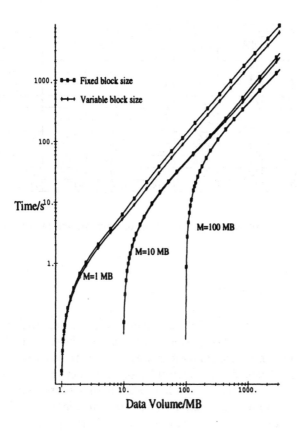

Fig. 4. Execution time with snow plow splitting.

6 Comparison

To compare the effect of increased average block size, we compare the traditional and new methods for three representative cases: $M = 1$ MB, $M = 10$ MB, and $M = 100$ MB. In Fig. 4 we have plotted the functions for variable and fixed block size. We have for each value of V used the partitioning strategy (no/partial/one pass/multipass) that gives the best time. It is important to keep in mind that this is a log-log-plot, and therefore the difference in execution time between fixed and variable block size is not large in the figure. The improvement can be better illustrated by looking at the performance gain, which is computed in Table 6 and illustrated in Fig. 5. In the table, blank fields denotes no splitting.

As expected, the improvements are most noticeable for smaller work space areas. For larger work spaces, the number of blocks is relatively small, and the block access time is negligible compared to the transfer time.

V (in MB)	$M = 1$ MB, $\lambda = 20$			$M = 10$ MB, $\lambda = 200$			$M = 100$ MB, $\lambda = 2000$		
	fixed	var	imp %	fixed	var	imp %	fixed	var	imp %
1									
2	0.7	0.6	14						
4	2.1	1.8	14						
8	5.0	4.3	17						
16	12.7	10.0	27	3.1	2.9	4.2			
32	31.7	24.7	29	11.3	10.8	4.2			
64	76.1	59.2	29	27.6	26.5	4.2			
128	177.6	138.2	29	60.4	58.0	4.2	13.0	12.8	1.3
256	405.9	315.9	29	128.3	121.1	6.0	72.5	71.6	1.3
512	913.2	710.8	29	285.8	256.7	11.3	191.5	189.2	1.3
1024	2029	1580	29	668.6	571.6	17.0	429.4	423.6	1.3
2048	4464	3475	29	1538	1314	17.0	905.4	893.2	1.3

Table 6. Performance improvement as a function of operand volume and workspace size.

7 Conclusions and Future Work

We have described a novel method for partitioning, the circular track snow plow buffer management strategy. This strategy makes more efficient use of memory compared to traditional methods, and effectively doubles the average block size. Doubling the effective block size can give substantial reductions in I/O transfer time, and by the use of cost models we have shown that performance gains of 10-20% can be expected for reasonable resource configurations.

In this paper we have made the assumption that the operand volume is known. This is not always true, and we are now investigating a dynamic or adaptive strategy, based on the snow plow principle, which is applicable when the operand volume is unknown. We are also working with the new buffer management strategy employed in other areas as file loading and transaction log.

In the development og this methods, we have also discovered how a more efficient set of routines for communication with the SCSI buss system could be used to avoid the unnecessary transfer of data to an internal block buffer. Direct transfer to the user program area can save the internal bus from considerable traffic. This is clearly interesting, and should be studied further.

References

1. K. Bratbergsengen. Hashing Methods and Relational Algebra Operations. In *Proceedings of the 10th International Conference on VLDB*, 1984.
2. K. Bratbergsengen, R. Larsen, O. Risnes, and T. Aandalen. A Neighbor Connected Processor Network for Performing Relational Algebra Operations. In *Fifth Workshop on Computer Architecture for Non-Numeric Processing, March 11-14, 1980 (SIGIR Vol. XV No. 2, SIGMOD Vol.X No. 4)*, 1980.
3. D. L. Davidson and G. Graefe. Memory-Contention Responsive Hash Joins. In *Proceedings of the 20th International Conference on VLDB*, 1994.

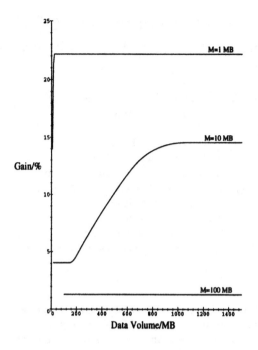

Fig. 5. Performance gain by using the snow plow strategy.

4. D. DeWitt, R. Katz, F. Olken, L. Shapiro, M. Stonebraker, and D. Wood. Implementation Techniques for Main Memory Database Systems. In *Proc. ACM SIGMOD Conf.*, 1984.
5. G. Graefe. Query Evaluation Techniques for Large Databases. *ACM Computing Surveys*, 25(2), 1993.
6. G. Graefe. Volcano — An Extensible and Parallel Query Evaluation System. *IEEE Transactions on Knowledge and Data Engineering*, 6(1), 1994.
7. M. Kitsuregawa, H. Tanaka, and T. Motooka. Application of Hash to Data Base Machine and its Architecture. *New Generation Computing*, 1(1), 1983.
8. D. Knuth. *The Art of Computer Programming. Sorting and Searching.* Addison-Wesley Publishing Company Inc., 1973.
9. M. Nakayama, M. Kitsuregawa, and M. Takagi. Hash-Partitioned Join Method Using Dynamic Destaging Strategy. In *Proceedings of the 14th International Conference on VLDB*, 1988.
10. L. D. Shapiro. Join Processing in Database Systems with Large Main Memories. *ACM Transactions on Database Systems*, 11(3), 1986.
11. H. Zeller and J. Gray. An Adaptive Hash Join Algorithm for Multiuser Environments. In *Proceedings of the 16th International Conference on VLDB*, 1990.

Query Evaluation in CROQUE*
– Calculus and Algebra Coincide –

Torsten Grust[1], Joachim Kröger[2], Dieter Gluche[1], Andreas Heuer[2], and
Marc H. Scholl[1]

[1] University of Konstanz
Database Research Group
P.O. Box D188, D-78457 Konstanz, Germany
e-mail: ⟨*firstname*⟩.⟨*lastname*⟩@uni-konstanz.de
[2] University of Rostock
Database Research Group
D-18051 Rostock, Germany
e-mail: {jo,heuer}@informatik.uni-rostock.de

Abstract. With the substantial change of declarative query languages
from plain SQL to the so-called "object SQLs", in particular OQL, there
has surprisingly been not much change in the way problems of query representation and optimization for such languages are tackled. We identify
some of the difficulties pure algebraic approaches experience when facing object models and the operations defined for them. Calculus-style
formalisms suite this challenge better, but are said not to be efficiently
implementable in the database context.

This paper proposes a hybrid query representation and optimization approach, combining the strengths of a many-sorted query algebra and
the monoid comprehension calculus. We show that efficient execution
plans beyond nested-loop processing can be derived – not only for σ-
π-$\bowtie$ queries – in such a framework. The translation process accounts
for queries manipulating bulk-typed values by employing various join
methods of the database engine, as well as queries that use aggregation,
construction of arbitrary values, and arithmetics.

1 Introduction

The choice of the intermediate representation for a declarative query language
such as OQL is guided by the vital characteristics that we demand from such a
representation, namely

(a) the ability to capture the concepts (operations and types) of the query language *completely*, and

---

* CROQUE (Cost- and Rule-based Optimization of object-oriented **Queries**) is a
research project funded by the German Research Association (DFG) under contracts
He 1768/5-2 and Scho 554/1-2.

(b) the suitability to serve as a starting point for a mapping from this representation to the primitives of the underlying persistent storage manager (for efficient execution).

Traditional call interfaces to storage managers and query engines have been designed to be driven by algebraic query plans. Given a tree or DAG representing the (optimized) query expressed in terms of the system's object algebra, an interpreter or intermediate compiler generates calls to the storage manager to perform the algebraic manipulations. In fact, some of these calls implement certain algebra operators within the storage subsystem itself. Among them are selections, $\sigma[p]$, some projections, π, several join types, like $\bowtie_p$ (join), $\ltimes_p$ (semijoin), $\overline{\ltimes}_p$ (antijoin, the complement to $\ltimes$), and $\bowtie_p$ (two-sided outerjoin) as long as predicate p fulfills simplicity restrictions. All other operations are carried out during a postprocessing phase that mainly takes place in memory.

Algebraic approaches to query representation fit into this scenario. The initial algebraic expression is rewritten so that large subtrees of the query tree can be processed under the responsibility of the storage subsystem. Apparently, algebras fulfill requirement (b) well. However, with the substantial change of declarative query languages from plain SQL to so-called "object SQLs", in particular OQL, there has surprisingly been almost no change in the way the problems of query representation and optimization are tackled. In some sense, query processors did not reflect the shift in paradigm the query languages themselves went through.

Algebras that have been derived from the well-known nested relational algebras (NRAs) still dominate the research work in this evolving field by far. Most of these approaches did not add expressiveness to NRA, though, which made them cover the classic SQL subset of OQL only. Notable exceptions are the efforts of [12] and [13], and their query algebras AQUA and PFL, respectively.

The AQUA data model and algebra has been designed to serve as a "standard" intermediate representation for object query languages. AQUA's operators may operate on scalars as well as values of various bulk types. AQUA gains this generality by defining operators as higher-order functions that themselve take functions as parameters. Among other uses, these function parameters represent value constructors (e.g. set union or list concatenation), thus turning a set-manipulating operator into a list manipulator by appropriate parameterization.

Poulovassilis and Small's functional query language PFL realizes the general application of functions and iteration abstractions (like fold) which are needed to implement OQL. The semantically clean foundation of PFL allowed for the derivation of a large body of equivalences, the basis for the development of a PFL query optimizer.

The issue of efficiently mapping such languages to database query engine programs, however, are not dicussed. It is one of the core work items of our CROQUE project to bridge this gap for a language similar to PFL, the *monoid calculus* [8]. The calculus is expressive enough to represent OQL completely. Translating OQL into the monoid calculus results in uniform program schemes (*monoid comprehensions*) which help to keep the expected size of an optimizer rewrite rule base as well as its search space in tractable bounds.

In [5], Daniel Chan proposed collection comprehensions (over sets, bags, and lists) as an intermediate representation for object SQLs. We map quantification and aggregation to comprehensions too, making the intermediate query forms even more uniform. Further processing phases (mappings A_0 and A_1 to be introduced in Sect. 3) benefit from this simplicity. Chan's execution engine is non-standard in the sense that it does not support joins, but *map* and *reduce* (*fold*). Instead, our query compilation process assumes a richer algebraic query engine as sketched above (with extensions) as its translation target.

We proceed as follows. In Section 2, some light is shed on the consequences of understanding OQL as "a better SQL" only. Section 3 introduces CROQUE's internal hybrid representation of OQL which, we believe, overcomes the major deficiencies of the pure algebraic query processing strategies. The query compilation process assumes an algebraic query engine as sketched above (with extensions) as its translation target. Section 4 summarizes.

2 Algebraic Representations for OQL

Having the instruments of NRA at hand, there is a tendency to view OQL queries as "advanced" SQL queries, with an explicit emphasis on the efficient translation of *nested subqueries* [11,6,15].

2.1 Nested selects

The following `select-from-where` clause is understood as the basic building block of complex queries (let $\bar{e}$ denote $e_1, \ldots, e_n$):

$$
\begin{aligned}
&\texttt{select struct}(a_1\!:\!e_{k_1}, \ldots, a_k\!:\!e_{k_k}) \\
&\quad\texttt{from } E_1 \texttt{ as } e_1, \ldots, E_n \texttt{ as } e_n \\
&\quad\texttt{where } p(\bar{e})
\end{aligned}
$$

The obvious algebraic translation would be

$$
\pi_{e_{k_1}, \ldots, e_{k_k}} (\sigma[\lambda\bar{e}.p(\bar{e})](E_1 \times \ldots \times E_n))
$$

(query optimizers then convert the Cartesian products into real joins if possible).

Note that the OQL `select-from-where` block delivers a *bag* (multiset) as its result type, which already demands a non-standard interpretation of the former set-based algebraic operators, especially π and $\times$ in this case. Now, nested subqueries may occur in the `where`-clause (which has been allowed since the early days of SQL and has been extensively studied, e.g. in [11] and a whole series of follow-up papers) and the `from`-clause. Nested subqueries in the `select`-clause have been investigated more recently. Consider

$$\texttt{select struct}(a_1:e_1, a_2:\texttt{select } f(e_1,e_2)$$
$$\texttt{from } E_2 \texttt{ as } e_2$$
$$\texttt{where } p'(e_1,e_2))$$
$$\texttt{from } E_1 \texttt{ as } e_1$$
$$\texttt{where } p(e_1)$$

The above form immediately leads to a nested projection if we apply the above algebraic translation scheme. Execution of such plans often results in inefficient nested loop processing. Consequently, recent work proposed non-standard join operators such as *binary grouping* (Γ, [6]), *hierarchical joins* [14], or the *nestjoin* (Δ, [15]), which we will look upon more closely in the following. Actually, the above query is implemented by a single nestjoin which performs a join over predicate p' and a grouping with regard to function f simultaneously:

$$(\sigma[\lambda e_1.p(e_1)](E_1))\underset{\lambda e_1.\lambda e_2.f(e_1,e_2);\lambda e_1.\lambda e_2.p'(e_1,e_2)\to a_2}{\Delta} E_2$$

The nestjoin allows for unnesting the subquery; operand E_2 appears at the top-level, giving us several alternatives of implementing this query efficiently.

In $R \Delta_{f,p\to M} S$, for each $r \in R$, predicate p tests for each $s \in S$ if s is member of the group (named M in the result) belonging to r, and, if so, adds the result of $f(r,s)$ to the group. As a simple example from the relational domain, consider

R			S		R		$\underset{\lambda r.\lambda s.(r.A+s.B),\lambda r.\lambda s.(r.\#=s.\#)\to M}{\Delta}$		S
#	A		#	B	#	A	M		
a	1		a	10	a	1	$\{11, 21\}$		
b	2		a	20	b	2	$\{\}$		
c	3		c	30	c	3	$\{33\}$		

In contrast to the equivalent *join-group-map* sequence there is no need to introduce *null* values: empty groups are represented as empty collections which are part of the data model.

2.2 Non-linear Translations

We already end up with significantly more complex translations if we take the freedom to construct arbitrary values in the **select**-clause from the variables we declared in the **from**-clause, like OQL allows us to:

$$\texttt{select struct}(x:e.x, y:e.y, M:\texttt{set}(e.x, e.y))$$
$$\texttt{from } E \texttt{ as } e$$

First, note that this query deals with bags and sets simultaneously, which is quite typical for OQL queries but in no way common for proposed algebraic approaches. Let us ignore this fact for the sake of this example.

We cannot translate this query by a standard projection (note that we use the same values, e.g. $e.x$ and $e.y$, more than once to build the complex result) or nesting (set M includes values of different columns of E). Rather, a translation would be

$$E \underset{id;\lambda e_1.\lambda e_2.(e_1.x=e_2\vee e_1.y=e_2)\to M}{\overset{\Delta}{}}(\pi_x(E)\cup\pi_y(E))$$

(where $id = \lambda x.x$ denotes the identity mapping). This translation is *non-linear* in the sense that expression E has to be copied and further processed every time we reference a variable that ranges over it (here e) to construct our complex value. This is an inherent problem of all algebraic approaches, being variable-less formalisms by nature. The translation is likely to be inefficient. A formalism that incorporates variables, like an appropriate calculus, would allow for a direct translation. Consider

$$bag\{\langle x = e.x, y = e.y, M = set\{e.x, e.y\}\rangle \mid e \leftarrow E\}$$

which denotes a *bag comprehension*, an expression of the *monoid calculus* we introduce shortly. Variable e gets sequentially bound to the elements of E and can be used in the head of the comprehension to construct values which are then collected to make up the resulting bag. More importantly, the representation is linear.

If we abstract from the problem of value construction to the general application of functions under the variable bindings generated by the from- and where-clauses, we obtain a more general view of the basic **select**-block in OQL:

$$
\begin{aligned}
&\textbf{select } f(\bar{e}) \\
&\quad \textbf{from } E_1 \textbf{ as } e_1, \ldots, E_n \textbf{ as } e_n \\
&\textbf{where } p(\bar{e})
\end{aligned}
$$

Algebras have been enriched by a very powerful operator, namely **map**$[f]$, to account for this generalization. $\text{map}[f](E)$ applies function f to every element of E, making

$$\text{map}[f](\sigma[\lambda\bar{e}.p(\bar{e})](E_1 \times \ldots \times E_n))$$

a translation of the above **select**. Note that f may be quite complex, in particular an expression of the enhanced NRA itself.

2.3 Queries with Aggregates

If we consider more than just **select-from-where** (i.e. π-σ-$\bowtie$ respective map-σ-$\bowtie$) queries, we again have to enrich algebras. As an example, consider query Q_1:

$$
\begin{aligned}
Q_1 = \text{sum}(&\textbf{select } x \\
&\textbf{from flatten}(E) \textbf{ as } x \\
&\textbf{where } x > 0)
\end{aligned}
$$

The **sum** aggregate – or operator **+** in general – has no algebraic counterpart yet. We could resort to treating such operators as "black boxes" that are just moved around during the query rewriting process. An optimizer that knows about +'s properties (like being commutative, associative, and having identity 0), however, has the choice of *folding* the aggregation into the program evaluating the **select-from-where** block, thus reducing the need for extra summation loops. This applies to aggregations in general, covering OQL's **count**, **max/min**, **avg**, **exists**, and **forall** (where the latter two aggregate boolean values).

The incorporation of general aggregations has been realized by means of **fold** operators of various sorts [1,2,17,7,13]. $\text{fold}[\oplus; f](E)$ applies function f to every element of E and accumulates the function results via the binary operator $\oplus$. $\text{sum}(E)$ is thus implemented by $\text{fold}[+; \text{id}](E)$. The uses of fold are manifold. We will use folding of boolean values to implement quantification as well. Consider $\text{fold}[\lor; \lambda e.e > 10](E)$ which implements the predicate $\exists e \in E : e > 10$.

The use of aggregation, operations on scalars like arithmetics, and multiple collection types in one query are not captured by the algebras proposed in the vast majority of work on query algebras for object SQLs. Being strict, we would have to say that these algebras miss requirement (a) and therefore fail to be complete representations of OQL-like languages at all. To summarize, let us list the features we identified as crucial for an adequate OQL representation that fulfills both requirements:

(1) We clearly need **specialized join operators** (such as Δ) which can cope with certain nesting cases.
(2) We need a means to express general **function application** (map), the **construction of arbitrary values** in particular.
(3) There have to be ways to reason about **aggregation** and quantification (which we can look at as aggregation over boolean values), i.e. fold.
(4) The **treatment of the diverse collection types** (sets, bags, lists) should be uniform to avoid special operators like *list-set-join* or *bag-projection*. Incorporation of new collection types should be possible seamlessly.

2.4 The Monoid Comprehension Calculus

CROQUE's approach incorporates the monoid comprehension calculus into its query representation to achieve these fundamental goals. The monoid calculus actually does fulfill the features (2)–(4), thus meeting requirement (a) from Sect. 1. However, calculi are said to be not efficiently implementable in the database context, since the calculus expressions inherently describe nested loop processing strategies. Section 3 will present a *hybrid approach*, comprising an algebra and the monoid calculus, which shows that query execution plans beyond nested loop processing are in fact derivable in this framework. This will finally provide us with a framework that meets both characteristics we identified in the Introduction.

We will introduce the ideas of the **monoid comprehension calculus** only briefly here, [16,18,3,8] give comprehensive surveys. The calculus can be looked at as a generalization of the well-known relational calculus. It is more general in the sense that we gain the ability to manipulate not only sets, but any type that possesses the properties of a monoid. A monoid $\mathcal{M}$ is an abstract algebraic structure equipped with an associative binary operation $merge[\mathcal{M}]$, having the distinguished element $zero[\mathcal{M}]$ as its identity. Monoids that represent collections additionally specify the function $unit[\mathcal{M}]$ that constructs a singleton value of that collection type. Within the monoid framework, we now represent the bulk types *set*, *bag*, and *list* as triples $(zero[\mathcal{M}], unit[\mathcal{M}], merge[\mathcal{M}])$, resulting in $(\{\}, \{e\}, \cup)$, $(\{\!\!\{\ \}\!\!\}, \{\!\!\{ e \}\!\!\}, \uplus)$, and $([], [e], +\!\!+)$ respectively. The properties of $merge[\mathcal{M}]$ (being idempotent, commutative, or both), in fact, make the three collection types different. Our primary focus is the manipulation of bulk data, but the diverse types of aggregation and arithmetic operations we encounter during the translation of OQL fit into this framework as well. Examples of such non-collection monoids are $sum = (0, \mathrm{id}, +)$, $some = (false, \mathrm{id}, \vee)$, and $all = (true, \mathrm{id}, \wedge)$. While sum serves the obvious purpose, $some$ and all implement existential and universal quantification. Similar monoid instances are *max*, *min*, and *prod*.

Queries are represented as a subclass of special monoid mappings, **monoid homomorphisms**, which we write down as monoid comprehensions, the corresponding generalization of set comprehensions or ZF-expressions. The homomorphisms provide us with a semantically clean way to reason about queries that involve multiple collection and scalar types since the range and destination monoids of these mappings may not be the same [8,10].

In the **monoid comprehension** $\mathcal{M}\{f \mid q_1, \ldots, q_n\}$ the **qualifiers** q_i are either **generators** of the form $e \leftarrow E$ or **predicates** p. A generator q_i sequentially binds variable e to the elements of its range E; e is bound in $q_{i+1}, \ldots, q_n$ and f. The binding of e is propagated until a predicate evaluates to *false* under this binding. Function f, the **head**, is evaluated under all bindings that pass, and the function results are then accumulated via $merge[\mathcal{M}]$ to make up the final result. Comprehensions nest to arbitrary depth. Abstracting monoid element operations this way gives us the ability to reason about equivalences and rewriting rules independent of particular collection types. E.g.

$$\mathcal{M}\{f \mid \overline{q_1}, e \leftarrow zero[\mathcal{N}], \overline{q_2}\} \equiv zero[\mathcal{M}]$$

(where the $\overline{q_i}$ denote sequences of qualifiers) holds for any instantiation of monoids $\mathcal{M}$ and $\mathcal{N}$, making the expected size of an optimizer rewrite rule base more manageable.

Examples of comprehensions are the following mapping from lists to bags

$$bag\{e \mid e \leftarrow [1, 2, 3, 1], e \neq 2\} = \{\!\!\{ 1, 1, 3 \}\!\!\}$$

or

$$set\{\langle e_1, e_2 \rangle \mid e_1 \leftarrow E_1, e_2 \leftarrow E_2, some\{e_1 = c \mid c \leftarrow e_2.M\}\}$$

which computes the join of E_1 and E_2 with regard to predicate $e_1 \in e_2.M$.

Note that for E of type $\mathcal{N}$ and $\oplus$ denoting $merge[\mathcal{M}]$ of some monoid $\mathcal{M}$, the comprehension $\mathcal{M}\{e_1 \mid e \leftarrow E, e_1 \leftarrow f(e)\}$ is equivalent to $fold[\oplus; f](E)$, i.e. the operation we identified as crucial for our query evaluation purposes:

$$
\begin{aligned}
\text{fold}[\oplus; f](zero[\mathcal{N}]) &= zero[\mathcal{M}] \\
\text{fold}[\oplus; f](unit[\mathcal{N}](e)) &= f(e) \\
\text{fold}[\oplus; f](merge[\mathcal{N}](e_1, e_2)) &= f(e_1) \oplus \text{fold}[\oplus; f](e_2)
\end{aligned}
$$

These three equations reflect the way of how values are constructed by the calculus, namely by the application of $zero[\mathcal{M}]$, $unit[\mathcal{M}]$, and $merge[\mathcal{M}]$ exclusively.

In fact, one can show that fold's expressiveness is sufficient to capture OQL. In [10] we actually gave a complete mapping of OQL to the monoid comprehension calculus. Summing things up, what we gain with the monoid calculus is (1) the necessary expressive power to capture OQL-like languages, (2) a uniform and extensible way of manipulating values of diverse collection types, (3) a uniform treatment of arithmetics, quantification, and aggregation, and (4) a formalism that can handle variables and bindings like the source query language can.

Mapping the source language, OQL, to the monoid calculus as the target formalism is actually a straightforward process. The OQL from-clause translates into a sequence of generators, predicates in the where-clause introduce filters, while the select-clause corresponds to a comprehension's head, i.e. function application. Let $\mathbb{T}$ be the mapping from OQL to the monoid calculus. The core of $\mathbb{T}$ would then read

$$
\mathbb{T}\left(\begin{matrix}\text{select } f(\bar{e}) \\ \text{from } E_1 \text{ as } e_1, \ldots, E_n \text{ as } e_n \\ \text{where } p(\bar{e})\end{matrix}\right) = bag\{\mathbb{T}(f(\bar{e})) \mid e_1 \leftarrow \mathbb{T}(E_1), \\ \ldots, \\ e_n \leftarrow \mathbb{T}(E_n), \mathbb{T}(p(\bar{e}))\}
$$

This meets the OQL semantics, including the case of one or more E_i being empty collections: the overall result will be empty. [10] extends $\mathbb{T}$ to capture the complete specification of OQL 1.2 [4]. The problems we experienced with the construction of complex values, especially non-linear translations caused by the use of variables, do not affect the calculus, as we have mentioned before. Consider

$$
\begin{aligned}
Q_2 = \ &\text{select distinct } e \\
&\text{from } E \text{ as } e \\
&\text{where exists } x \text{ in } M: N \text{ <= set}(e, x)
\end{aligned}
$$

(where <= denotes the set inclusion predicate) and its image under $\mathbb{T}$

$$
\mathbb{T}(Q_2) = set\{e \mid e \leftarrow E, some\{N \subseteq set\{e, x\} \mid x \leftarrow M\}\}
$$

However, how are we supposed to find an efficient algebraic execution plan for a nested comprehension like this?

3 A Hybrid Translation and Optimization Schema for OQL

We just observed that monoid comprehensions basically correspond to nested folds when translated into an extended nested algebra. While this is true, this observation may lead to the impression that one is stuck with nested loops when it comes to finding execution plans for comprehensions: fold$[\oplus; f]$ accesses each element of the argument collection (possibly even in order, if applied to a list), applies function f and then merges the result via $\oplus$. There is no obvious strategy for the efficient evaluation of monoid calculus expressions like the strategy for NRA we sketched in the Introduction. We miss a mapping of nested comprehensions to the primitives of query engines which are tailored to evaluate terms of a particular algebra.

On the other hand there are classes of OQL queries that clearly are of algebraic nature, e.g., compute joins, perform selections, simple projections, grouping, and nesting, and we are better off to translate these queries into algebraic plans directly. The large body of knowledge of optimization methods in this field should clearly be reused if possible.

The apparent potential of the monoid calculus and the latter observation motivated the *hybrid approach* to OQL representation and optimization that we pursue in the CROQUE project:

- Translate the source OQL query into a mix of monoid calculus and algebra, which we will introduce below. If we are able to detect subqueries that can be computed by algebraic terms at this point, we choose an algebraic representation for these subqueries. To ensure a clean semantics for such mixed representations we will define the algebra operators by means of monoid calculus terms. In addition, these definitions will provide a definite semantics for the operators when applied to the different collection types. We obtain a many-sorted query algebra this way.
- Perform rewriting on this representation. The whole body of rule-based algebraic rewriting techniques applies. We additionally may apply calculus rewrite rules which above all allow for simple unnesting of complex subqueries. Comprehension normalization (which basically is accomplished by applying the rewriting rules of Fig. 3) actually implements numerous unnesting techniques found in the literature. Calculus expressions may be translated into algebra and vice versa. The rewriting process follows the heuristic of translating calculus into equivalent algebraic terms.
- As a final step, convert remaining calculus terms into folds. We will show shortly how this can be done. It is a requirement for the underlying query execution engine to provide facilities for the evaluation of fold.

In the remainder, we will present the strategy sketched above. Let us continue by introducing the query algebra to the depth needed.

3.1 A Monoid-Aware Algebra

The following introduces some operators of the algebra by putting the operators' definitions down to the equivalent monoid comprehensions as mentioned above. We gain several advantages with this approach: (1) a semantically clean interaction of the algebra with the calculus is guaranteed. Calculus terms may play the role of selection or join predicates, may represent functions (e.g., as they are needed as parameters for map and fold), or may be arguments to algebra operators in general. (2) The generic definitions hold for any monoid instantiation, as long as well-definedness conditions are obeyed. The algebra will operate on multiple collection types, not only sets. (3) We uncover the control structure of the operators. Unfolding and loop fusion becomes possible.

Due to space restrictions, we merely present the basic ideas here, but the design of the operators follows a common principle; [9] contains a comprehensive list of all operators.

In the following, read symbol :: as *has type*. Let *int*, *bool*, and *string* be atomic types. $\langle a_1 :: \alpha_1, \ldots, a_n :: \alpha_n \rangle$ is a record with field tags a_i and respective field types α_i; $\otimes$ concatenates records. With $\mathcal{M}$ being a collection monoid (*set, bag, list*), and α being some type, $\alpha\mathcal{M}$ is the type denoting a $\mathcal{M}$-collection of α-members, e.g. *int list*.

The core of the algebra is fold$[\oplus; f](E)$, which applies f to the elements of E. It then uses $\oplus$, the *merge* operation of some monoid $\mathcal{M}$, to collect the result. In particular, if we have $E :: \alpha\mathcal{M}, f :: \alpha \to \beta\mathcal{M}, \oplus :: \beta\mathcal{M} \times \beta\mathcal{M} \to \beta\mathcal{M}$, we define

$$\text{fold}[\oplus; \lambda e.f(e)](E) = \mathcal{M}\{e' \mid e \leftarrow E, e' \leftarrow f(e)\}$$

The result's type is $\beta\mathcal{M}$.

The semijoin $E_1 \ltimes_p E_2$ is a join variant that delivers only those left operand objects that have at least one join partner with respect to the predicate p. Implementation can be efficient in terms of space (buffers or files that hold the intermediate result only carry E_1 objects) and time (as soon as any join partner is found for an E_1 object, it belongs to the result; no other E_2 object has to be touched). Let $E_1 :: \alpha\mathcal{M}, E_2 :: \beta\mathcal{N}, p :: \alpha \times \beta \to \text{bool}$, then we define

$$E_1 \underset{\lambda e_1.\lambda e_2.p(e_1,e_2)}{\ltimes} E_2 = \mathcal{M}\{e_1 \mid e_1 \leftarrow E_1, some\{p(e_1,e_2) \mid e_2 \leftarrow E_2\}\}$$

The aforementioned nestjoin, $E_1 \Delta_{f; p \to A} E_2$ is a non-standard join between E_1 and E_2 in the sense that for each E_1 object we create a group A of E_2 objects that match the join predicate p. On creation of this group we apply f. Types are as follows: $E_1 :: \alpha\mathcal{M}, E_2 :: \beta\mathcal{N}, f :: \alpha \times \beta \to \gamma, p :: \alpha \times \beta \to \text{bool}$. We then have

$$E_1 \underset{\substack{\lambda e_1.\lambda e_2.f(e_1,e_2);\\ \lambda e_1.\lambda e_2.p(e_1,e_2) \to A}}{\Delta} E_2 = \mathcal{M}\{e_1 \otimes \langle A = \mathcal{N}\{f(e_1,e_2) \mid e_2 \leftarrow E_2, \\ p(e_1,e_2)\}\rangle \mid e_1 \leftarrow E_1\}$$

The result is of type $\alpha \times \langle A :: \gamma\mathcal{N}\rangle\mathcal{M}$. Δ is valuable when translating queries with nesting in the **select** clause, as well as for the evaluation of complex predicates between **select** blocks. Efficient techniques for the evaluation of grouping, e.g. sorting or indices, apply to the implementation of Δ, too.

3.2 Execution Strategies for Monoid Comprehensions

Achieving good execution plans for the monoid calculus is not as obvious as for algebras. Provided we believe the calculus to be a valuable approach to object SQL query processing, we face the problem of how to find good QEPs for potentially deeply nested comprehension expressions. In what follows we will present a mapping, A, from the calculus to a hybrid representation employing the monoid-aware nested algebra, which we assume to be the target language of the query execution engine.

Successive applications of A will replace monoid calculus terms by algebraic equivalents. The intermediate results of A are subject to algebraic and calculus-based rewriting, to the results of which A is applied again. Since any calculus term at least has its canonical fold representation we are guaranteed to have a way out of this process. The rewriting finally yields a term of the target algebra we introduced, i.e. a program for our query engine. The degrees of freedom in this process define the dimensions of the search space along which we look for the optimal representation of our query: calculus $\rightarrow$ calculus, calculus $\leftrightarrow$ algebra, and the classical algebra $\rightarrow$ algebra.

After introducing the ideas of A we will present the derivation of execution plans in this framework by example, including the problematic queries Q_1 and Q_2 from Sect. 2. Let us start with a first basic version A_0 of the mapping and improve A as we go.

A_0 – Comprehensions Implemented by fold.

The initial mapping A_0 puts the comprehensions down to their nature of being monoid homomorphisms, which, in turn, are implemented by the algebra's fold operator (see Fig. 1). A_0 is defined via structural recursion over the list of qualifiers. Constants (Rule 1) and database variables (2), e.g. globally named collections, provide the base cases for the recursion. Rules (3)–(5) reduce the qualifier list from its head on. Rule (4) introduces a fold over a generator's range. Predicates are handled via a conditional (5) that replaces non-qualifying elements by $\mathcal{M}$'s identity $zero[\mathcal{M}]$, which does not contribute to the result.

$$A_0(c) \rightarrow c \tag{1}$$
$$A_0(v) \rightarrow v \tag{2}$$
$$A_0(\mathcal{M}\{f \mid \}) \rightarrow unit[\mathcal{M}](A_0(f)) \tag{3}$$
$$A_0(\mathcal{M}\{f \mid e \leftarrow E, \bar{q}\}) \rightarrow fold[merge[\mathcal{M}]; \lambda e.A_0(\mathcal{M}\{f \mid \bar{q}\})](A_0(E)) \tag{4}$$
$$A_0(\mathcal{M}\{f \mid p, \bar{q}\}) \rightarrow \text{if } A_0(p) \text{ then } A_0(\mathcal{M}\{f \mid \bar{q}\}) \text{ else } zero[\mathcal{M}] \tag{5}$$

Fig. 1. Mapping A_0. Implement comprehensions by nested folds.

Note that it would be sufficient for A_0's target query engine to implement fold, the respective monoid operations, and a conditional to execute the resulting plans. While this at least provides a complete mapping from comprehensions to the algebra, we always end up with nested applications of fold because of (4), i.e. nested-loop processing. Consider the result of A_0's application to $T(Q_2)$ in which the inner fold implementing the existential quantification is executed for each $e \in E$:

$(A_0 \circ T)(Q_2)$

$$\underset{(4)}{=} A_0(set\{e \mid e \leftarrow E, some\{N \subseteq set\{e, x\} \mid x \leftarrow M\}\})$$

$$\underset{(4)}{=} fold[\cup; \lambda e.A_0(set\{e \mid some\{N \subseteq set\{e, x\} \mid x \leftarrow M\}\})](A_0(E))$$

$$\underset{(5)}{=} fold[\cup; \lambda e.\text{if } A_0(some\{N \subseteq set\{e, x\} \mid x \leftarrow M\}) \text{ then } A_0(set\{e \mid \}) \\ \text{else } \{\}](E)$$

$$\underset{(4)}{=} fold[\cup; \lambda e.\text{if } fold[\vee; \lambda x.A_0(some\{N \subseteq set\{e, x\} \mid \})](M) \text{ then } \{A_0(e)\} \\ \text{else } \{\}](E)$$

$$\underset{(3)}{=} fold[\cup; \lambda e.\text{if } fold[\vee; \lambda x.N \subseteq \{e, x\}](M) \text{ then } \{e\} \text{ else } \{\}](E)$$

A_0 fails to employ the more efficient algorithms of the query engine.

However, since the query engine's operators have been put down to monoid calculus terms, we have the possibility to incorporate join strategies into the mapping.

A_1 – **Reduction by Pattern Matching.** The extended version A_1 understands the algebra operator definitions as *patterns* to be detected in the comprehension expressions. On a successful match, A_1 replaces the match by its equivalent algebraic term. We derive an initial A_1 by adopting the rules of A_0 and adding the cases of Fig. 2 which improve the processing of predicates and quantifiers. More than one rule may match at a time and any rule may then be selected arbitrarily. However, we listed the rules in the order an optimizer heuristic should try to match, e.g. we prefer to implement universal quantification by $\overline{\ltimes}$ (7) before resorting to a σ with a nested fold as its predicate (10). Note that (10) covers (5); we can therefore drop (5) and the if-then-else conditional completely. Since the $\overline{\ltimes}$ is feasible only if no dependencies (besides the join predicate) between the join partners exist, we check this condition by examining the set of free variables $F(\cdot)$. Some rules introduce new generator variables and we adapt the comprehension head accordingly, mainly by renaming variables, thus turning f into f' in (8) and (10). Finally, the comprehension pattern of (11) serves as a catch-all case and implements the application of f via map as discussed in Sect. 2.2.

If we turn back to query Q_2 again, we now rewrite as follows:

$A_1(set\{e \mid e \leftarrow E, some\{N \subseteq set\{e, x\} \mid x \leftarrow M\}\})$

$$\underset{(6)}{=} A_1(set\{e' \mid e' \leftarrow E \underset{\lambda e.\lambda x.A_1(N \subseteq set\{e, x\})}{\ltimes} M\})$$

$$\underset{(4)}{=} fold[\cup; \lambda e'.A_1(set\{e' \mid \})](E \underset{\lambda e.\lambda x.N \subseteq \{e, x\}}{\ltimes} M)$$

$$\underset{(3)}{=} fold[\cup; \lambda e'.\{e'\}](E \underset{\lambda e.\lambda x.N \subseteq \{e, x\}}{\ltimes} M)$$

in which we can drop the outer fold if $E :: \alpha$ set (the fold merely implements a type coercion from the semijoin's output type to α set).

$$A_1\left(\mathcal{M}\{f \mid \overline{q}, e \leftarrow E, \atop some\{p \mid \overline{q_1}\}\}\right) \rightarrow A_1\left(\mathcal{M}\{f \mid \overline{q}, e \leftarrow A_1(E) \underset{A_1(p)}{\ltimes} A_1(\overline{q_1})\}\right)$$

$$\text{if } e \notin F(\overline{q_1}) \tag{6}$$

$$A_1\left(\mathcal{M}\{f \mid \overline{q}, e \leftarrow E, \atop all\{p \mid \overline{q_1}\}\}\right) \rightarrow A_1\left(\mathcal{M}\{f \mid \overline{q}, e \leftarrow A_1(E) \underset{\neg A_1(p)}{\overline{\ltimes}} A_1(\overline{q_1})\}\right)$$

$$\text{if } e \notin F(\overline{q_1}) \tag{7}$$

$$A_1\left(\mathcal{M}\{f \mid \overline{q}, e_1 \leftarrow E_1, \atop e_2 \leftarrow E_2\}\right) \rightarrow A_1\left(\mathcal{M}\{f' \mid \overline{q}, e \leftarrow A_1(E_1) \times A_1(E_2)\}\right)$$

$$\text{if } e_1 \notin F(E_2) \tag{8}$$

$$A_1\left(\mathcal{M}\{f \mid \overline{q}, p_1, p_2\}\right) \rightarrow A_1\left(\mathcal{M}\{f \mid \overline{q}, p_1 \wedge p_2\}\right) \tag{9}$$

$$A_1\left(\mathcal{M}\{f \mid \overline{q}, p\}\right) \rightarrow A_1\left(\mathcal{M}\{f' \mid e \leftarrow \sigma[A_1(p)](A_1(\overline{q}))\}\right) \tag{10}$$

$$A_1\left(\mathcal{M}\{f \mid \overline{q}\}\right) \rightarrow \text{map}[A_1(f)](A_1(\overline{q})) \tag{11}$$

Fig. 2. Mapping A_1. Operator pattern matching.

Figure 2 only shows a subset of the rewriting rules, since each algebra operator introduces at least one rule according to its definition. See [9] for the complete A_1 rewrite rule base. An actual optimizer based on our approach will, however, certainly feature a larger set of rules.

Up to now, we have improved the calculus $\mapsto$ algebra mapping. By adding the rules of Fig. 3 we extend the translation scheme once more and introduce the calculus $\mapsto$ calculus (i.e. comprehension level) rewriting dimension. While (12) and (13) allow for selection pushdown and join reordering, respectively, (14) unnests a comprehension (over monoid $\mathcal{N}$). The binding $e \equiv f'$ makes e a synonym for f' in the comprehension's head. This last rule, together with (18) and (15), serves to remove dependencies between potential join partners, thus increasing the chance of introducing efficient joins and abandoning nested loop processing.

By translating algebra operators, aggregations, quantifiers, and predicates into their comprehension equivalents, we uncover their control structure. E.g., we may view $N \subseteq M$ as some atomic set predicate for which we expect a corresponding query engine procedure, but as well may carry out the subset test explicitly: $all\{some\{y = z \mid z \leftarrow M\} \mid y \leftarrow N\}$. This opens possibilities for join pattern detection or loop fusion. The latter is not feasible if we view the operators only as black box functions that fulfill certain abstract algebraic properties. The translation of Q_2 backs up this claim. Uncovering $\subseteq$ makes an antijoin applicable and we are actually able to deduce a pure algebraic plan:

$$A_1(\mathcal{M}\{f \mid \overline{q}, e \leftarrow E, p\}) \rightarrow A_1(\mathcal{M}\{f \mid \overline{q}, p, e \leftarrow E\})$$
$$\text{if } e \notin F(p) \tag{12}$$

$$A_1(\mathcal{M}\{f \mid \overline{q}, e_1 \leftarrow E_1, e_2 \leftarrow E_2\}) \rightarrow A_1(\mathcal{M}\{f \mid \overline{q}, e_2 \leftarrow E_2,$$
$$e_1 \leftarrow E_1\})$$
$$\text{if } e_1 \notin F(E_2) \tag{13}$$

$$A_1(\mathcal{M}\{f \mid \overline{q}, e \leftarrow \mathcal{N}\{f' \mid \overline{q_1}\}\}) \rightarrow A_1(\mathcal{M}\{f \mid \overline{q}, \overline{q_1}, e \equiv f'\})$$
$$\text{if } \mathcal{N} \preceq \mathcal{M} \tag{14}$$

$$A_1(\mathcal{M}\{f \mid \overline{q}, some\{p \mid \overline{q_1}\}, \overline{q_2}\}) \rightarrow A_1(\mathcal{M}\{f \mid \overline{q}, \overline{q_1}, p, \overline{q_2}\})$$
$$\text{if } merge[\mathcal{M}] \text{ is idempotent} \tag{15}$$

$$A_1(\mathcal{M}\{f \mid \overline{q}, e \leftarrow zero[\mathcal{N}], \overline{q_1}\}) \rightarrow zero[\mathcal{M}] \tag{16}$$

$$A_1(\mathcal{M}\{f \mid \overline{q}, e \leftarrow unit[\mathcal{N}](e'), \overline{q_1}\}) \rightarrow A_1(\mathcal{M}\{f \mid \overline{q}, e \equiv e', \overline{q_1}\}) \tag{17}$$

$$A_1(\mathcal{M}\{f \mid \overline{q}, e \leftarrow merge[\mathcal{N}](E_1, E_2), \overline{q_1}\}) \rightarrow merge[\mathcal{M}]$$
$$(A_1(\mathcal{M}\{f \mid \overline{q}, e \leftarrow E_1, \overline{q_1}\}),$$
$$A_1(\mathcal{M}\{f \mid \overline{q}, e \leftarrow E_2, \overline{q_1}\}))$$
$$\text{if } \mathcal{M} \text{ is commutative} \tag{18}$$

Fig. 3. A_1 extended. Comprehension level rewriting.

$$A_1(set\{e \mid e \leftarrow E, some\{all\{some\{y = z \mid z \leftarrow \{e, x\}\} \mid y \leftarrow N\} \mid x \leftarrow M\}\})$$
$$\underset{(15)}{=} A_1(set\{e \mid e \leftarrow E, x \leftarrow M, all\{some\{y = z \mid z \leftarrow \{e, x\}\} \mid y \leftarrow N\}\})$$
$$\underset{(18)}{=} A_1(set\{e \mid e \leftarrow E, x \leftarrow M, all\{y = e \vee y = x \mid y \leftarrow N\}\})$$
$$\underset{(8)}{=} A_1(set\{e \mid e' \leftarrow E \times M, e \equiv e'_E, x \equiv e'_M, all\{y = e \vee y = x \mid y \leftarrow N\}\})$$
$$\underset{(7)}{=} A_1(set\{e''_E \mid e'' \leftarrow (E \times M) \underset{\lambda e'.\lambda y.y \neq e'_E \wedge y \neq e'_M}{\overline{\ltimes}} N\})$$
$$\underset{(11)}{=} \pi_E((E \times M) \underset{\lambda e'.\lambda y.y \neq e'_E \wedge y \neq e'_M}{\overline{\ltimes}} N)$$

In the above, a subscripted variable e_M denotes e's value projected onto the fields $l_1, \ldots, l_n$ if $M :: \langle l_1 :: \tau_1, \ldots, l_n :: \tau_n \rangle C$ for any collection constructor C (record projection).

To conclude the example rewritings, let us turn back to query Q_1 and track the rewriting steps that an optimizer equipped with the complete rule base could undertake. Recall, that Q_1 flattened E, a bag of collections, and then added all elements being greater than zero to obtain the final result:

$$(A_1 \circ T) \begin{pmatrix} \texttt{sum(select } x \\ \qquad \texttt{from flatten}(E) \texttt{ as } x \\ \qquad \texttt{where } x > 0) \end{pmatrix}$$

$$\underset{(T)}{=} A_1\left(sum\{e \mid e \leftarrow bag\{A_1(x) \mid x \leftarrow A_1(\texttt{flatten}(E), A_1(x > 0)\}\}\right)$$

$$\underset{(\texttt{flatten})}{=} A_1\left(sum\{e \mid e \leftarrow bag\{x \mid x \leftarrow bag\{z \mid z' \leftarrow E, z \leftarrow z'\}, x > 0\}\}\right)$$

$$\underset{(10)}{=} A_1\left(sum\{e \mid e \leftarrow \sigma[\lambda x.x > 0](bag\{z \mid z' \leftarrow E, z \leftarrow z'\})\}\right)$$

$$\underset{(A_0)}{=} A_1\left(sum\{e \mid e \leftarrow \sigma[\lambda x.x > 0](\text{fold}[\uplus; \text{id}](E))\}\right)$$

$$\underset{(A_0)}{=} \text{fold}[+; \text{id}](\sigma[\lambda x.x > 0](\text{fold}[\uplus; \text{id}](E)))$$

In principle, the resulting program performs three loops to accomplish its task. Loop fusion techniques, however, allow us to transform the query into a program that only needs two loops. Instead of flattening, each collection in E is summed up, mapping elements less than or equal to zero to $+$'s identity 0, giving a bag of intermediate sums. A second outer loop then sums up: $\text{fold}[+; \lambda e.\text{fold}[+; \lambda x.\text{if } x > 0 \text{ then } x \text{ else } 0](e)](E)$. This superior alternative may directly be derived by A_0, i.e. actually is element of our optimizer's solution space.

Since $+$ is a first-class operator in the monoid framework and its algebraic properties are well known (esp. having identity 0), we can apply loop fusion here. Lifting any type onto the monoid level makes the operations of these types transparent and therefore subject to further analysis and optimization. This is a consequence of the basic requirement (a) we stated at the very beginning: A *complete* representation of the query languages' types and operations in which no "black boxes" remain has to be aspired.

A basic rewriting strategy for an optimizer based on the A_1 rules would try to unnest nested comprehensions (i.e. subqueries) using (14), (15), and (18). The goal is to remove variable dependencies that prevent the introduction of joins. [19,8] discuss a normal form for monoid comprehensions that realizes a minimal number of such dependencies. We move along the calculus $\mapsto$ calculus dimension this way. Then, moves in the calculus $\mapsto$ algebra dimension are carried out in order to introduce joins and the other algebra operators. Rules (6)–(11) implement such moves. This is based on the assumption that the query engine knows about efficient implementations for these operators. All these rewriting steps may be interleaved by algebraic as well as comprehension level rewriting. To obtain a program for the query execution engine, all remaining calculus terms are converted into folds as a final step.

4 Conclusions and Further Work

Facing todays "object SQLs", in particular OQL, this paper proposed to let the monoid play the role sets played in the relational setting. The monoid calculus has been shown to provide the expressiveness that is needed to completely capture OQL. In order to obtain efficient execution plans for algebra-tailored query engines beyond nested-loop processing, we introduced a monoid-aware fold algebra. $A_1 \circ T$ implemented a rewrite-based mapping from the source query language OQL to this target algebra, employing non-standard joins. This hybrid approach, combining algebra and calculus, takes advantage of the strengths of both formalisms during the derivation of query engine programs.

Some issues are still open. Most importantly, a rewriting strategy based on A_1 and its successors has to be developed. Moves in the three rewriting dimensions have to be coordinated. Should the algebra be extended to cope with further particular nesting cases, in the spirit of Δ? Which influence does fold have on the construction of a suitable query engine? Additionally, incorporating the calculus into the evaluation framework opens new possibilities to exploit further program transformation techniques, like loop fusion, thus widening the view of database query optimization. Advanced query optimization techniques, like bypass processing for disjunctive queries, have to be adapted to fit the hybrid approach. [10] already took a step in this direction. Our CROQUE project is underway implementing the setup we discussed in this paper. Although based on a subset of rules of A_1 and a limited set of algebra operators only, first tests showed promising translation results for a broad range of OQL queries.

References

1. Francois Bancilhon, Ted Briggs, Setrag Khoshafian, and Patrick Valduriez. FAD, a Powerful and Simple Database Language. In Peter M. Stocker, William Kent, and Peter Hammersley, editors, *Proceedings of the 13th Int'l Conference on Very Large Databases (VLDB)*, pages 97–105. Morgan Kaufmann Publishers, September 1987.
2. Catriel Beeri and Yoram Kornatzky. Algebraic Optimization of Object-Oriented Languages. In Paris C. Kanellakis and Serge Abiteboul, editors, *Proceedings of the 3rd Int'l Conference on Database Theory (ICDT)*, volume 470 of *LNCS*, pages 72–88. Springer Verlag, December 1990.
3. Peter Buneman, Leonid Libkin, Dan Suciu, Val Tannen, and Limsoon Wong. Comprehension Syntax. In *SIGMOD Record*, volume 23, pages 87–96, March 1994.
4. Rick G. Cattell, editor. *The Object Database Standard: ODMG-93*, chapter 4, Object Query Language (Release 1.2), pages 65–96. Morgan Kaufmann Publishers, 1995. Updates to Release 1.1.
5. Daniel Chan. *Object-oriented Language Design and Processing*. PhD thesis, Computer Science Department, University of Glasgow, 1994.
6. Sophie Cluet and Guido Moerkotte. Nested Queries in Object Bases. In *Proceedings of the 4th Int'l Workshop on Database Programming Languages (DBPL)*, September 1993.
7. Leonidas Fegaras. Efficient Optimization of Iterative Queries. In *Proceedings of the 4th Int'l Workshop on Database Programming Languages (DBPL)*, pages 200–225, September 1993.
8. Leonidas Fegaras and David Maier. Towards an Effective Calculus for Object Query Languages. In *Proceedings of the 1995 ACM SIGMOD Int'l Conference on Management of Data*, May 1995.

9. Torsten Grust, Joachim Kröger, Dieter Gluche, Andreas Heuer, and Marc H. Scholl. Query Evaluation in CROQUE: Calculus and Algebra Coincide. Technical Report in preparation, Department of Mathematics and Computer Science, Database Research Group, University of Konstanz, April 1997.

10. Torsten Grust and Marc H. Scholl. Translating OQL into Monoid Comprehensions — Stuck with Nested Loops? Technical Report 3a/1996, Department of Mathematics and Computer Science, Database Research Group, University of Konstanz, September 1996.

11. Won Kim. On Optimizing an SQL-like Nested Query. *ACM Transactions on Database Systems*, 7(3):443–469, September 1982.

12. Theodore W. Leung, Gail Mitchell, Bharathi Subramanian, Stanley B. Zdonik, and other. The AQUA Data Model and Algebra. In *Proceedings of the 4th Int'l Workshop on Database Programming Languages (DBPL)*, September 1993.

13. Alexandra Poulovassilis and Carol Small. Investigation of Algebraic Query Optimisation for Database Programming Languages. In *Proceedings of the 20th Int'l Conference on Very Large Databases (VLDB)*, pages 415–426, Santiago, Chile, September 1994.

14. Christian Rich, Arnon Rosenthal, and Marc H. Scholl. Reducing Duplicate Work in Relational Join(s): A Unified Approach. In *Proceedings of the Int'l Conference on Information Systems and Management of Data (CISMOD)*, pages 87–102, Delhi, India, October 1993.

15. Hennie J. Steenhagen, Peter M.G. Apers, Henk M. Blanken, and Rolf A. de By. From Nested-Loop to Join Queries in OODB. In *Proceedings of the 20th Int'l Conference on Very Large Databases (VLDB)*, pages 618–629, Santiago, Chile, September 1994.

16. Phil Trinder. Comprehensions, a Query Notation for DBPLs. In *Proceedings of the Third Int'l Workshop on Database Programming Languages (DBPL)*, pages 55–68, Nafplion, Greece, 1991.

17. Bennet Vance. Towards an Object-Oriented Query Algebra. Technical Report 91-008, Oregon Graduate Institute of Science & Technology, January 1992.

18. David A. Watt and Phil Trinder. Towards a Theory of Bulk Types. Technical Report FIDE/91/26, Computer Science Department, University of Glasgow, 1991.

19. Limsoon Wong. Normal Forms and Conservative Properties for Query Languages over Collection Types. In *Proceedings of the 12th ACM Symposium on Principles of Database Systems*, pages 26–36, May 1993.

Optimisation of Partitioned Temporal Joins

Thomas Zurek

Department of Computer Science
University of Edinburgh
Email: tz@dcs.ed.ac.uk

Abstract. Partitioning data for temporal join processing is not trivial because tuples have to be replicated between data fragments. This causes three types of overheads: (a) an overhead caused by the replication process itself, (b) a processing overhead caused by the additional joining that has to be done and (c) an overhead for removing duplicates in the result. Previous work has mainly concentrated on avoiding (a) but still suffers from the consequences of (b) and (c).

In this paper, we show how partitioned temporal joins can be optimised for sequential and parallel processing by reducing tuple replication, thereby reducing the total overhead. For that purpose, a new data structure, namely the IP-table, is introduced. The idea is to have IP-tables of individual temporal relations stored in the database system's catalog from which they can be retrieved for the optimisation process. IP-tables of two or more temporal relations might be required for optimisations, too. These can be created by merging IP-tables of individual relations at optimisation time – a fast and straightforward process.

IP-tables can be used for creating *and* analysing partitions over interval timestamps. Three strategies for partitioning interval data are presented, each of which can be easily and efficiently implemented using IP-tables. The performance determining parameters of a partition can also be derived from IP-tables.

Keywords: temporal join, parallel join, optimisation, interval partitioning.

1 Introduction

Recent years have seen a significantly increasing interest by the industrial and academic community in modeling and storing data that changes over time. One important example is trend analysis, e.g. in the context of data warehouses [7]. Temporal databases have also been the focus of a large number of research papers [9]. With this development comes a whole bunch of new problems: temporal data models, temporal query languages, temporal operators etc. are required. In this paper, we look at one particular performance-critical temporal operator, namely the temporal join, and ways in which temporal join processing can be optimised. We thereby concentrate purely on temporal-specific optimisation and regard our proposal as an enhancement of existing relational optimisation techniques.

In the past, very efficient algorithms have been developed for equi-joins, i.e. joins with an equality join condition. These are based on several forms of **partitioning** [5]. Explicit partitioning – as one form that is, for example, used in hash or parallel joins – breaks up the one 'big' join operation into several *smaller* and *independent* joins. This can be summarised in the following equation:

$$R \bowtie_C Q = R_1 \bowtie_C Q_1 \cup \cdots \cup R_m \bowtie_C Q_m \tag{1}$$

where the R_k and Q_k are referred to as *fragments* of the relations R and Q, respectively. C is a boolean expression and said to be the *join condition*.

(1) works very well for equi-joins because it is easy to create *disjoint* fragments $R_1, \ldots, R_m$ ($Q_1, \ldots, Q_m$ respectively). In practice, most join conditions in real queries are built on an equality predicate such as "key = foreign key" conditions, as in the case of a customers table being joined with an address table via equal name attribute values.

In the case of **temporal joins**, however, the join conditions are usually based on a non-equality predicate. We adopt the most frequently used temporal data model in which tuples of a temporal relation have an interval timestamp. Intervals have proved to be the most versatile representation of time: intervals and relationships between intervals can adequately express almost any time reference in natural language [1]. *Intersection* of two intervals is the most prominent and the most general join predicate in this case. It is a supertype of most other possible relationships between two intervals. Furthermore, it plays a similarly important role for interval data as equality for atomic data: it establishes the notion of *simultaneity* of two temporal objects.

A join condition based on intersection of two timestamp intervals, however, imposes a problem on partitioning temporal joins as in (1): it is usually impossible to create fragments $R_1, \ldots, R_m$ ($Q_1, \ldots, Q_m$ respectively) that are disjoint. Consider the example of figure 1. It visually describes the computation of a temporal join $R \bowtie Q$ that is partitioned into three partial joins. Tuples of R are put along a horizontal axis, tuples of Q along a vertical axis. R and Q are partitioned into three fragments respectively. Squares symbolise possible combinations of tuples of R and Q. The figure shows nested-loop computations for the partial joins $R_k \bowtie Q_k$, i.e. every tuple in R_k is compared with every tuple in Q_k. Tuple comparisons that are successful are shown in dark grey, comparisons that are performed in a preceding partial join are in black, unsuccessful comparisons in light grey. Figure 1 makes the following problems evident:

(a) Tuples have to be replicated between fragments. This causes an overhead (*replication overhead*). Figure 1 has a total of 13 tuple replications (5 for R, 7 for Q).

(b) As a consequence, the fragments grow. This implies more tuple comparisons (*processing overhead*). Figure 1 has a total of 132 comparisons. Using different breakpoints of the time domain, e.g. $\{5, 9\}$ instead of $\{4, 7\}$ as in figure 1, would lead to 156 comparisons, i.e. 18% more.

(c) Finally, the tuple replications cause duplicates in the result (see black squares). This contributes to the processing overhead but also causes an additional problem: duplicates might have to be removed from the result. This can be quite expensive (*duplicates overhead*).

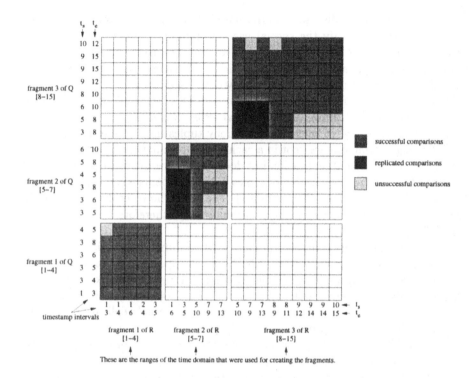

Fig. 1. Partitioned temporal join computation.

From the scenario of figure 1 we can conclude that badly chosen partitions can impose a significant overhead on the join processing costs. The major contribution of this paper is to show how the processing of partitioned temporal joins can be optimised by choosing an appropriate way of partitioning the temporal data. We will show which information about the temporal data has to be acquired in order to create *and* to analyse partitions (i.e. to predict their performance effects) and how this process can be done efficiently such that an optimisation decision can be taken before the join is processed.

First, we look at some previous work on partitioned temporal joins in section 2 and introduce the notations that are used throughout the paper in section 3. The structure of a temporal join optimiser is presented in section 4. Section 5 introduces the essential data structure, the *IP-table*[1], on which our proposal is based. Section 6 describes three partitioning strategies which can be easily and efficiently implemented using IP-tables. Finally, section 7 summarises and concludes the paper.

---

[1] IP = Interal Partitioning

2   Previous Work

Several authors have discussed temporal join processing based on explicit partitioning:

Leung and Muntz discuss partition-based temporal joins for parallel processing [3]. They identify the special cases of temporal intersection for which tuple replication can be (partially) avoided. We, however, concentrate on the cases in which replication *cannot* be avoided. Therefore, our work can be regarded as an enhancement of Leung and Muntz's approach.

Soo *et al.* propose a valid-time join algorithm which is based on a partitioning approach as in (1) [8]. However, the partial joins[2] $R_m \bowtie Q_m, \ldots, R_1 \bowtie Q_1$ are processed *sequentially* (in that order) whereby tuples that have to be present in the following partial join are kept in a cache. This technique avoids the overhead (a) caused by the actual replication but does not reduce the processing overhead (b) caused by the fact the number of tuples in the fragments is significantly higher for badly chosen partitions (see section 1). The latter, however, has proved to be the critical one [10]. Our optimisation techniques can therefore help to overcome this deficit.

Lu *et al.* map interval data to points in a two dimensional grid which is divided into disjoint fragments afterwards [4]. What appears to be an advantage at first sight is unfortunately built on the expense of a major drawback: a fragment R_k is not only to be joined with one corresponding fragment Q_k but with several others. As in the previous case, they can avoid the actual replication of tuples (a) but remain with the processing overhead (b).

Finally, two optimisations of partitioned temporal join processing are proposed in [13]. One reduces addition I/O cause by tuple replication, the other shows how duplicates can be avoided, thus reducing the processing overhead (b) and avoiding the duplicates overhead (c).

3   Notational Conventions

We adopt the following notations:

A *temporal relation R* is a relation in which each tuple carries one timestamp, the latter being represented as an interval. The restriction to one timestamp per tuple only simplifies the following notations. In general, two or more timestamps per tuple are possible. In this case, we concentrate on the one that is used for partitioning purposes.

Intervals are defined over a certain domain. For our purposes, we can assume the set of integers to be the domain. We assume that the left and right neighbours of a time point t can be referred to by $t-1$ and $t+1$ respectively given by the discreteness[3] of a total ordering defined on the domain. *Intervals* have the

---

[2] In the following we omit the reference to a join condition C and use $R \bowtie Q$ meaning a temporal intersection join between R and Q.

[3] Discreteness is merely used for simplifying the notation and does not represent a necessary precondition for the work presented in this paper.

following notations:

$$[t_s, t_e] = \{x : t_s \leq x \leq t_e\}, \qquad (t_s, t_e] = \{x : t_s < x \leq t_e\} = [t_s + 1, t_e]$$

The left delimiter, t_s, of an interval is called the interval's *startpoint*; the right one, t_e, is the *endpoint*. We use the first type in the timestamps of the temporal relations that are to be partitioned and the second type for the partitioning segments (see below).

In order to simplify expressions we use the shortcut notation $[t_s, t_e] \in R$ to express that $[t_s, t_e]$ is a timestamp of one or more tuples in R.

The *range* $T(R)$ of the intervals of a temporal relation R is the part of the domain covered by the intervals in R. The *lifespan* $L(R)$ of R is interval that contains every interval of R. $T(R)$ and $L(R)$ are defined as

$$T(R) = \{t : t \text{ is contained in some interval } [t_s, t_e] \in R\}$$
$$L(R) = [\min T(R), \max T(R)]$$

The lifespan may contain parts of the domain that are not covered by any interval and are therefore not included in the range $T(R)$. The sets of interval startpoints, $S(R)$, and endpoints, $E(R)$, are defined by

$$S(R) = \{t_s : \exists t_e \in T(R) \text{ such that } [t_s, t_e] \in R\}$$
$$E(R) = \{t_e : \exists t_s \in T(R) \text{ such that } [t_s, t_e] \in R\}$$

The following functions are defined on the time domain:

$s_R(t) =$ number of intervals in R that start at time point t

$e_R(t) =$ number of intervals in R that end at time point t

$i_R(t) =$ number of intervals in R that intersect with / contain time point t

$o_R(t) =$ number of intervals in R that overlap time point t

(i.e. intersect with t *but do not end at* t)

A *partition* P is an ordered set $\{p_1, \ldots, p_{m-1}\}$ of *breakpoints* that divide the lifespan and range into m segments $(p_{k-1}, p_k]$ for $k = 1, \ldots, m$ with p_0 and p_m being the left and right border of the plot, for example, $p_0 = \min T(R) - 1$ and $p_m = \max T(R)$.

4 Structure of the Optimisation Process

Figure 2 shows the dataflow in the optimisation process for a partitioned temporal join between two temporal relations R and Q. Data is represented as rectangles, computation as ovals. The entire process consists of four stages corresponding to the four grey boxes in figure 2:

1. Firstly, the temporal relations have to be analysed to acquire some information about the structure and characteristics of the temporal data. In its simplest form, this information can be represented by a data sample that has been drawn from the two relations. This approach has been taken in [8]. A second form is to get some meta-information on the data which might be stored in the database catalog. We follow the latter approach and define *IP-tables* for this purpose in section 5.

2. Based on the information acquired in stage 1 and the systems parameters (number of processing nodes, amount of memory etc. that are currently available) several strategies can be applied to find suitable partitions for the temporal data. Section 6 presents three such strategies.

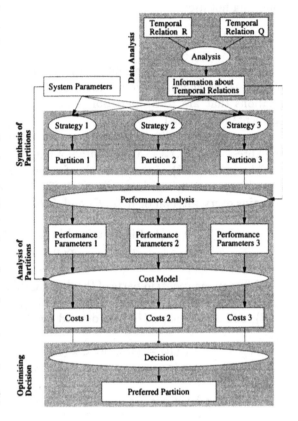

Fig. 2. Structure of the optimisation process.

3. Using the partitions and information on the temporal data, performance-determining parameters, such as the loads of the fragments R_k and Q_k, can be approximated (e.g. when using data samples) or exactly calculated (e.g. by our approach). These parameters are then fed into a cost model which derives the processing costs of the partitioned temporal join based on the respective partition and the current system parameters.

4. Finally, the cheapest partition is chosen.

5 IP-Tables

5.1 Motivation

Before defining IP-tables in the following section we want to make two observations which serve as a motivation:

① The most important parameters that determine the performance of a partitioned join as in (1) are the cardinalities $|R_k|$ and $|Q_k|$ of the fragments R_k and

Q_k. Imagine now a temporal relation R and a partition $\{p_1, \ldots, p_{m-1}\}$. Then the number $|R_k|$ of tuples in a fragment R_k can be determined by (i) the number of tuples that overlap from preceding fragments R_j $(j < k)$ plus (ii) the tuples that start in the time segment $(p_{k-1}, p_k] = [p_{k-1} + 1, p_k]$ that corresponds to R_k. Obviously (i) corresponds to the number of intervals which contain the first point in the time segment but start before, i.e. the number $o_R(p_{k-1})$, whereas (ii) can be determined by summing up the values $s(p_{k-1} + 1), \ldots, s(p_k)$. Thus

$$|R_k| \;=\; o_R(p_{k-1}) + \sum_{t=p_{k-1}+1}^{p_k} s_R(t) \tag{2}$$

Several other performance influencing parameters can be calculated in a similar way such as the following two:

$$\textit{number of overlapping intervals} \;=\; \sum_{k=1}^{m-1} o_R(p_k)$$

$$\textit{average interval length} \;=\; \frac{1}{|R|} \cdot \sum_{t=\min T(R)}^{\max T(R)} s_R(t) + o_R(t-1)$$

② For our purposes we require only the values $s_R(t)$ and $o_R(t)$ for those t at which at least one interval starts or ends: for all other time points t it is $s_R(t) = 0$ and $o_R(t) = o_R(t')$ with t' being the next start- or endpoint (of some interval) before t. It is only there where the sum (2) changes. This allows us to concentrate on the start- and endpoints of the intervals rather than the entire time span [11].

5.2 Definition

An IP-table for one or more temporal relations stores information about the temporal structure of the time intervals appearing in these relations; the IP-table is specific to those temporal relations. We now define an IP-table for a temporal relation R; the definition for two or more relations works accordingly. The IP-table for R consists of three columns, each with N entries. Initially, N is the number of distinct start- and endpoints used in intervals of R; in section 5.4 we show how N can be reduced if the IP-table gets too big:

- The first column contains the values

$$V(R) \;=\; S(R) \cup E(R) \;=\; \{t_1, \ldots, t_N\} \text{ such that } t_j < t_{j+1} \text{ for } j = 1, \ldots, N-1.$$

- The second column holds the values $s_R(t_j)$ for $j = 1, \ldots, N$.
- The third column holds the values $o_R(t_j)$ for $j = 1, \ldots, N$.

For each t_j we can derive the values $e_R(t_j)$ and $i_R(t_j)$ by using the following equations:

$$i_R(t_1) = s_R(t_1)$$
$$i_R(t_j) = s_R(t_j) + o_R(t_j - 1) \qquad \text{for } j = 2, \ldots, N$$
$$e_R(t_j) = i_R(t_j) - o_R(t_j) \qquad \text{for } j = 1, \ldots, N$$

Using these constraints it becomes obvious that we can alternatively store any pair of the values $s_R(t_j), e_R(t_j), i_R(t_j), o_R(t_j)$.

Figure 7(a) shows an example for timestamp intervals of a temporal relation R. Intervals are represented as bold bars connecting their start- and endpoint respectively. Figure 8 shows the IP-table for R (in bold typeface) plus the derivable values $e_R(t_j)$ and $i_R(t_j)$ for demonstration purposes.

5.3 Merging IP-Tables

Two (or more) IP-tables of two (or more) temporal relations can be merged into one IP-table that describes the characteristics of the union of the participating relations. This is very useful as we can precompute the IP-tables for individual relations and merge them when optimising a temporal join between those relations. This is only relevant for join algorithms that require two or more input relations to be partitioned along certain constraints. Partitioning then needs information on all these relations, thus we need the IP-table of the union of the relations.

The merging process is fairly straightforward: Imagine two IP-tables of two relations R and Q participating in a temporal join $R \bowtie Q$. They have time point sets $V(R)$ and $V(Q)$ and functions s_R, o_R and s_Q, o_Q respectively. These two tables can be merged into one IP-table with time point set

$$V(R \cup Q) = V(R) \cup V(Q)$$

and functions $s_{R \cup Q}, o_{R \cup Q}$ defined as

$$s_{R \cup Q}(t) = s_R(t) + s_Q(t)$$
$$o_{R \cup Q}(t) = o_R(t) + o_Q(t)$$

Please note that the IP-table of R might not hold values for all $t \in V(Q)$ and, similarly, the IP-table of Q not for all $t \in V(R)$. This is not actually a problem as these values can be derived by using the second observation made in section 5.1.

The correctness of the merge process as described should be obvious. We omit a formal proof due to the space restrictions for this paper. Figure 3 shows how the IP-table approach fits into the optimisation process as outlined in figure 2.

5.4 Condensing IP-Tables

In section 5.2, we assumed that the number N of entries in the IP-table equals the number of distinct interval start- and endpoints, i.e. $N = |S(R) \cup E(R)|$.

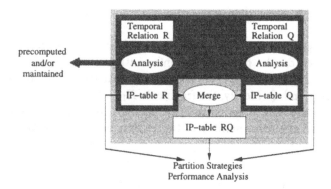

Fig. 3. Acquiring information about (temporal) characteristics of temporal relations by using IP-graphs

Critics might ·argue that – in the worst case – a temporal relation with one million tuples has an IP-table with two million entries and that this might cause the IP-table approach to be unusable. In the following, we want to address these concerns.

First, IP-table entries are very short: a time point or chronon, t_j, might be represented as 6 bytes, and the two integers, $s_R(t_j)$ and $o_R(t_j)$, say 4 bytes each. In total these are 14 bytes. Considering a typical tuple size of 500 bytes or more then an IP-table will still have only $\frac{2 \cdot 14}{500} = 5.6\%$ of the size of the originating relation.

Second, we analysed several real-world temporal relations[4] R and found ratios $\frac{|S(R) \cup E(R)|}{|R|}$ between 0.09 and 0.12, i.e. far away from the 2.0 for the worst case. If we assume a tuple size of 500 bytes then the IP-table would be less than 0.4% of the size of the originating relation. This is far below the 3% for data samples claimed in [8].

Third, IP-tables can be condensed (compressed). One possibility is to use only every a-th element of $S(R) \cup E(R)$. This results in values $t'_j, s'_R(t'_j), o'_R(t'_j)$ which can be derived according to the following equations for $j = 1, \ldots, N'$:

$$N' = \left\lfloor \frac{N}{a} \right\rfloor, \quad t'_j = t_{j \cdot a}, \quad s'_R(t'_j) = \sum_{l=(j-1)a+1}^{j \cdot a} s_R(t_l), \quad o'_R(t'_j) = o_R(t_{j \cdot a})$$

This process divides the size of the IP-table by a, thus the figure 0.4% obtained above is reduced to 0.04% for $a = 10$. Naturally, the IP-table becomes coarser and less precise. This decreases the quality of the resulting partitions but makes the process of deriving the partition more efficient. We conducted various experiments on this issue and found almost no drawbacks for $a \leq 10$.

---

[4] Login information to several computing clusters and airline timetables.

6 Partitioning Strategies

There are various ways to partition interval data. In this section, we present three strategies, all of which can be based on the information stored in an IP-table. They create partitions $\{p_1, \ldots, p_{m-1}\}$ for computing a partitioned temporal join (1) of two relations R and Q. Ideally, the fragments $R_1, \ldots, R_m$ and $Q_1, \ldots, Q_m$ are well balanced with respect to each other, i.e. the R_j and Q_j contain a similar number of tuples, and the total number of tuples that have to be replicated is as small as possible.

6.1 Uniform Strategy

This is the simplest strategy. It divides either the joint range $T(R \cup Q)$ – as in [8] – or the joint lifespan $L(R \cup Q)$ into m equally sized segments. As a third option we propose to divide the startpoints' span

$$SP(R \cup Q) = [\min S(R \cup Q), \max S(R \cup Q)]$$

for the following reason: after $\max S(R \cup Q)$ no more intervals start, i.e. no more intervals are added to the plot. If a breakpoint p_k was chosen after that point the fragments R_{k+1} and Q_{k+1} would hold only intervals that are already in R_k and Q_k and thus would already be joined in $R_k \bowtie Q_k$. Thus a join $R_{k+1} \bowtie Q_{k+1}$ would be without significance. It is therefore feasible to divide the startpoints' span rather than the lifespan in order to avoid such a situation.

The three different spans can be easily calculated by using the IP-table for $R \cup Q$. Let $V(R \cup Q) = \{t_1, \ldots, t_N\}$ with $t_j < t_{j+1}$.

- The lifespan $L(R \cup Q)$ is simply the span between the first and the last time point in the table, i.e. $[t_1, t_N]$.
- The range $T(R \cup Q)$ is the lifespan minus certain gaps. The latter can be simply identified because they are exactly those areas between a t_{j-1} and a t_j that are not overlapped by any intervals, i.e. $o_{RUQ}(t_j) = 0$. Thus all entries in the table with a 0 entry in the third column identify a gap.
- Finally, the startpoints' span is simply the interval between t_1 and the highest t_j entry such that $s_{RUQ}(t_j) > 0$.

If either the lifespan or the startpoints' span is used, a uniform partition $P = \{p_1, \ldots, p_{m-1}\}$ can be computed as $p_k = t_1 - 1 + \lceil k \cdot \frac{\text{length of the span}}{m} \rceil$ for $k = 1, \ldots, m - 1$. In the case of partitioning $T(R \cup Q)$ the gaps have to be considered as in the algorithm of figure 4. Figure 7(b) shows a uniform (lifespan) partition of the example of figure 7(a). Circled numbers show the number of intervals per fragment; numbers below the breakpoint lines show the number of overlapping intervals $o_R(p_k)$ at the respective breakpoint p_k.

It is obvious that a uniform strategy is liable to perform badly in the case of skewed, i.e. not uniformly distributed, data. There is hardly any control over the fragments' loads and thus over the load balance. There are, however, many examples for temporal relations that have periodically repeated patterns of tuple timestamps: imagine a relation logging the starting and ending times of calls made by customers of a telephone company. The distribution of phone calls over a daytime period will vary significantly with many calls during business hours and few in the early morning and late evening. Considering a long time period, however, a daily pattern is probably repeated periodically. Thus we can expect a poor partition result when uniformly partitioning a one-day-span but a much better one for a period comprising several days, in particular when m matches the number of days.

```
/* V(R ∪ Q) = {t₁,...,tₙ} with tⱼ < tⱼ₊₁ */

target  = ⌈ length of the range / m ⌉   /* target length of the segments */
k       = 1                             /* number of next pₖ to be computed */
length  = 0                             /* length of current segment */

for  j = 2 to N do              /* scans the IP-table for R ∪ Q */
   if  length > target then     /* current segment exceeds target length */
      pₖ      = tⱼ₋₁
      k       = k + 1
      length  = 0
   fi
   if  o_{R∪Q}(tⱼ) > 0 then     /* consider length only if there was no gap */
      length  = length + (tⱼ − tⱼ₋₁)
   fi
od
```

Fig. 4. Algorithm for partitioning $T(R \cup Q)$ uniformly.

6.2 Underflow Strategy

The goal of this strategy is to sequentially fill the fragments R_1, R_2, ... (Q_1, Q_2, ..., respectively) such that a given number X of tuples per fragment is 'underflowed', i.e. not exceeded. The IP-tables for the individual relations R and Q together with equation (2) can be used for this purpose. Figure 5 presents an algorithm that implements this strategy using the IP-tables of R and Q. Figure 7(c) shows the partition resulting from partitioning the example of figure 7(a) using the underflow strategy.

The advantage of this strategy is that the fragments' loads are well controlled and can be expected to be well balanced as long as the values $s_R(t_j)$ are relatively small in order to approach the limit X as close as possible (see if-condition in figure 5). There is, however, no control over the number of intervals overlapping the breakpoints. Incorporating a mechanism for this is the goal of the strategy discussed in section 6.3.

```
/* V(R ∪ Q) = {t₁,...,t_N} with t_j < t_{j+1} */

k     = 1           /* number of next breakpoint p_k to be computed */
load_R = s_R(t₁)     /* load of current fragment R_k */
load_Q = s_Q(t₁)     /* load of current fragment Q_k */

for j = 2 to N do
   if load_R + s_R(t_j) > X or load_Q + s_Q(t_j) > X then  /* |R_k| or |Q_k|      */
      p_k    = t_{j-1}                                      /* would exceed       */
      k      = k + 1                                        /* the max. load X   */
      load_R = o_R(t_{j-1})
      load_Q = o_Q(t_{j-1})
   fi
   load_R = load_R + s_R(t_j)
   load_Q = load_Q + s_Q(t_j)
od
```

Fig. 5. Algorithm for the underflow strategy using the IP-tables of R and Q.

6.3 Minimum-Overlaps Strategy

Similar to the underflow strategy the goal of this one is to create fragments R_1, R_2, ... (Q_1, Q_2, ... , respectively) such that a given number X of tuples is not exceeded *and* that the sum of intervals overlapping the breakpoints is minimal. This problem has a polynomial solution which is based on a dynamic programming approach [11]. Describing the algorithm in detail would go beyond the space limits of this paper. We therefore restrict ourselves to the following informal description:

The time points $t_1,...,t_N$ of the IP-table of $R \cup Q$ are processed from 1 to N. For each t_j a partition of the span $[t_1, t_j]$ is computed that has minimal sum of overlaps and has fragment loads less than X. More precisely, for each t_j a predecessor $pred(t_j)$ is determined which represents the preceding breakpoint that leads to this 'optimal' partition. The final minimising partition is then given by the sequence $pred(t_N)$, $pred(pred(t_N))$, ... (until a delimiting dummy point t_0 appears). Figure 6 summarises the algorithm. In figure 7(d) the partition is shown that results from partitioning the example of figure 7(a) using the minimum-overlaps strategy.

This strategy can be expected to perform at least as well as the underflow strategy. Its disadvantage, however, is its run time complexity of $O(N^2)$ compared to $O(N)$ of the underflow strategy which restricts its suitability to small IP-tables.

7   Summary and Conclusions

In this paper, we have shown how partitioned temporal joins can be optimised for sequential and parallel processing. For that purpose, a new data structure,

```
/* V(R ∪ Q) = {t₁,...,tₙ} with tⱼ < tⱼ₊₁ */
```

$$/* \ V(R \cup Q) = \{t_1,\ldots,t_N\} \text{ with } t_j < t_{j+1} \ */$$

$$t_0 = -\infty \qquad /* \text{ a dummy point } */$$

for $j = 1$ **to** N **do**

    among the points $t_0,\ldots,t_{j-1}$ choose a point, denoted as $pred(t_j)$, such that the numbers of intervals of R and Q that are respectively intersecting with the segment $(pred(t_j), t_j]$ does not exceed X *and* such that the total sum of overlaps $\sum o_R(pred^z(t_j)) + o_Q(pred^z(t_j))$ (with $z \geq 1$ and $pred^z(t_j) > t_0$) is minimal*.

od

The minimising partition is given by the sequence $pred(t_N), pred(pred(t_N)),\ldots$ (it stops before t_0 appears).

$$* \ \overline{pred^z(t_j)} = \underbrace{pred(\ldots pred}_{z}(t_j)\ldots)$$

Fig. 6. Algorithm of the minimal overlaps strategy for relations R and Q.

namely the IP-table, has been introduced. The idea is to have IP-tables of individual temporal relations stored in the database system's catalog from which they can be retrieved for the optimisation process. IP-tables of two or more temporal relations might be required for optimisations. These can be created by merging IP-tables of the individual relations – a fast and straightforward process – at optimisation time.

IP-tables can be used for creating *and* analysing partitions over interval timestamps. Creating such a partition is not trivial because it determines significant overhead costs caused by the necessary replication of tuples. Three strategies for partitioning interval data have been presented, each of which can be easily and efficiently implemented using IP-tables. The performance determining parameters of a partition can also be derived from the IP-tables of the relations that participate in the join, such as the fragments loads (2) or the total number of tuples to be replicated.

The IP-table approach has major advantages over alternative techniques such as optimisations based on data samples. Firstly, IP-tables can be precomputed and stored in the system's catalog or – in case of an IP-table for more than one relation – can be easily computed by using precomputed tables. Secondly, IP-tables are much smaller data structures than e.g. data samples. Thus they can be scanned and analysed much more efficiently. This accelerates the creation and analysis stages of the optimisation process. Thirdly, the information stored in IP-tables is precise. Information drawn from data samples, however, is only an approximation. In summary: the IP-table approach is faster and more precise.

In the future, we want to analyse the IP-table approach is some more detail. IP-tables are similar to histograms as used in join selectivity estimation [2], [6] and, in fact, can be used for this purpose as well [12]. We will investigate this relationship in more detail.

Acknowledgement

I would like to thank my department for their financial support for the publication of this paper.

References

1. J. Allen. Maintaining Knowledge about Temporal Intervals. *Communications of the ACM*, 26(11):832–843, Nov. 1983.
2. R. Kooi. *The Optimization of Queries in Relational Databases*. PhD thesis, Case Western Reserver University, Sept. 1980.
3. T. Leung and R. Muntz. Temporal Query Processing and Optimization in Multiprocessor Database Machines. In *Proc. of the 18th International Conference on Very Large Data Bases, Vancouver, Canada*, pages 383–394, Aug. 1992.
4. H. Lu, B.-C. Ooi, and K.-L. Tan. On Spatially Partitioned Temporal Join. In *Proc. of the 20th Internat. Conf. on Very Large Data Bases (VLDB), Santiago de Chile*, pages 546–557, Sept. 1994.
5. P. Mishra and M. Eich. Join Processing in Relational Databases. *ACM Computing Surveys*, pages 63–113, Mar. 1992.
6. V. Poosala, Y. Ioannidis, P. Haas, and E. Shekita. Improved Histograms for Selectivity Estimation of Range Predicates. In *Proceedings ACM SIGMOD Conference on Management of Data, Montreal, Canada*, pages 294–305, June 1996.
7. Red Brick Systems. The Data Warehouse. White paper, Red Brick Systems, Aug. 1995.
8. M. Soo, R. Snodgrass, and C. Jensen. Efficient Evaluation of the Valid-Time Natural Join. In *Proc. of the 10th International Conference on Data Engineering, Houston, Texas, USA*, pages 282–292, Feb. 1994.
9. V. Tsotras and A. Kumar. Temporal Database Bibliography Update. *SIGMOD Record*, 25(1), Mar. 1996.
10. T. Zurek. Parallel Temporal Nested-Loop Joins. Technical Report ECS-CSG-20-96, Dept. of Computer Science, Edinburgh University, Jan. 1996.
11. T. Zurek. Optimal Interval Partitioning for Temporal Databases. In *Proc. of the 3rd BIWIT Workshop, Biarritz, France*. IEEE Computer Society Press, July 1997.
12. T. Zurek. Parallel Processing of Temporal Joins. *Informatica*, 21, 1997.
13. T. Zurek. Parallel Temporal Joins. In *"Datenbanksysteme in Büro, Technik und Wissenschaft" (BTW), German Database Conference, Ulm, Germany*, pages 269–278. Springer, Mar. 1997. (in English).

Appendix: An Example Scenario

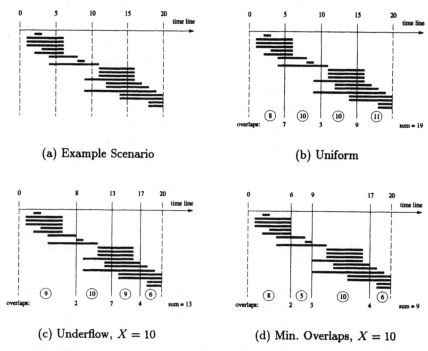

(a) Example Scenario

(b) Uniform

(c) Underflow, $X = 10$

(d) Min. Overlaps, $X = 10$

Fig. 7. Scenario for interval timestamps and the results of 3 partitioning strategies.

j	t_j	$s_R(t_j)$	$o_R(t_j)$	$e_R(t_j)$	$i_R(t_j)$	j	t_j	$s_R(t_j)$	$o_R(t_j)$	$e_R(t_j)$	$i_R(t_j)$
1	1	3	3	0	3	9	12	2	7	0	7
2	2	2	5	0	5	10	14	2	9	0	9
3	3	1	5	1	6	11	16	0	5	4	9
4	4	2	7	0	7	12	17	0	4	1	5
5	6	0	2	5	7	13	18	2	5	1	6
6	8	1	2	1	3	14	19	0	4	1	5
7	9	2	3	1	4	15	20	0	0	4	4
8	11	3	5	1	6						

Fig. 8. The IP-table (in bold) for the intervals in fig. 7 plus $e_R(t_j)$ and $i_R(t_j)$.

Maintaining Library Catalogues with an RDBMS: A Performance Study

O. Balownew[1], T. Bode[1], A.B. Cremers[1],
J. Kalinski[1], J.E. Wolff[1], H. Rottmann[2]

[1] Institute of Computer Science III, University of Bonn,
Römerstr. 164, 53117 Bonn, Germany
{ *oleg,tb,abc,cully,jw* } *@cs.uni-bonn.de*

[2] Hochschulbibliothekszentrum des Landes NW (HBZ),
Classen-Kappelmann-Str. 24, 50931 Köln, Germany
rottmann@hbz-nrw.de

Abstract. Our study [1] is the result of a cooperation with the University Library Center of the State of North-Rhine Westfalia (HBZ). The HBZ catalogue is a collection of data about (amongst others) documents, persons, keyword sequences and the relationships between them. As many of the HBZ data is data about well-structured entities, it is natural to ask whether a relational DBMS performs sufficiently powerful to meet the requirements of the HBZ with respect to retrieval and update operations.

The following tests are based on real catalogue data (comprising about 7.5 mio. document titles) and on librarians' real queries and updates. While part of the user transactions can be expressed by standard SQL queries and updates, special support is needed for keyword search.

The first test series took place at the SEQUENT test center in Munich.[1] Different loads with up to 50 new transactions per second have been generated (average load in the actual system: 5 transactions/second). In several hardware configurations standard SQL queries and updates could be answered in less than one second. These positive results are implications of the librarians' ability to specify their interests in a very concise way such that more than 99% of all SQL queries have less than 50 hits.

We then tested in how far ORACLE's TextServer3 supports the HBZ application in respect to keyword search. In TextServer3 word occurrence information is represented by bitvectors and stored in database tables in a compressed format. Our measurements show that this tool fails to meet the HBZ performance requirements: In a realization with so-called hitlist tables as well as in an API-based solution the first evaluation step (bitvector processing) already takes 3–5 seconds.

The promising performance of the DBMS server motivated us to dispense with bitlist encodings and to compare different realizations of keyword

---

[1] ORACLE DBMS Version 7.2, server: SEQUENT Symmetry 5000 SE 60 with 16 pentium CPU's and 1.5 GB main memory, clients: five SUN SPARCstation 20

search within standard SQL. We now represent every word occurrence by one tuple (word ID, document ID, title ID) stored in a database table having more than 48 mio. rows.[2] A thorough analysis of pure keyword queries reveals that, although entire queries specify a small set of document records (on average 76 hits), the single query words tend to have significantly more hits (on average: 29,636). But fortunately, every query also contains a very selective infrequent word (on average 524 hits). Using these specific characteristics of HBZ queries, a nested loop join can be made the best evaluation strategy (curve O in Fig. 1), but only after query words have been "manually" re-ordered according to their frequency values. Nested loop evaluation without re-ordering (curve N) and an INTERSECT-based solution (curve I) turn out to be significantly less efficient.

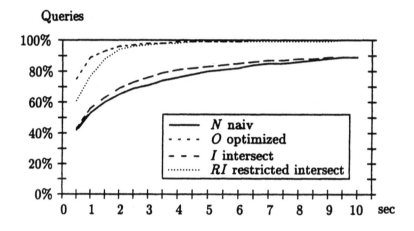

Fig. 1. Performance of evaluation strategies

As an alternative optimization Kaufmann and Schek [2] propose to ignore frequent words in the INTERSECT-step (see curve RI). But in the HBZ application a quarter of the intermediate results will then be incorrect (i.e. too large) requiring expensive post-processing in order to detect the *"false drops"*.

---

[2] Using ORACLE 7.3.2 on a SUN SPARCstation 10 with Solaris 2.5 at our institute.

References

1. O. Balownew, T. Bode, A.B. Cremers, J. Kalinski, J.E. Wolff, and H. Rottmann. Maintaing Library Catalogues with an RDBMS — A Performance Study —. Technical Report IAI-TR-96-13, University of Bonn, November 1996.
2. H. Kaufmann and H.-J. Schek. Text search using database systems revisited — some experiments —. In C.A. Goble and J.A. Keane, editors, *Proc. of the 13th British National Conf. on Databases*, pages 204–225. Springer, LNCS 940, 1995.

Merging an Active Database and a Reflective System: Modelling a New Several Active Meta-Levels Architecture

Laure Berti

Equipe Système d'Information Multi-Média,
Groupe d'Etude du Codage de Toulon,
Université de Toulon et du Var, B.P. 132,
F-83957 La Garde cédex, France
e-mail: berti@univ-tln.fr

Abstract. The complexity of implementing, debugging and maintaining large numbers of rules in active database systems and the need for understanding the behaviour of rules in spite of their non–deterministic execution make us suggest applying the reflective systems' approach to an active database system. The control of execution cycles, rule's flow and relating transactions processing can be made dynamically and introspectively by the active system which monitors itself [2].

Beyond actual debugging, visualisation and explanation tools – DEAR [4], REFLEX Visual Supervisor [7], Sentinel Debugger [3], OLAF [10] – our aim is to maintain consistency among ECA rules and recover the DBMS when it fails during rules execution (especially during the detection of composite events [11]) with the reflection concept. In the early stages on our research, we examine which malfunctions must be taken into account as specialized internal events in the several active meta-levels architecture we propose. Each active meta-level acts only on the level immediately below itself: the root level of the active reflective database recognizes specific situations and reacts to them without explicit user or application requests by means of ECA rules. The second active meta-level of the reflective database analyses and corrects malfunctions occuring in rules execution of the first active level.

We show how debbugging of ECA rules can be dealt with, as the reflective dimension is added to the active behaviour of the database. This dimension relates to the structure, execution model and management of active rules (indissociable with the extended transaction model [1] [5]). It enables distinctly but conjointly the concise expression, detection and consummation of:

– events which happen inside the root level of the active reflective database as specific events of the application

– and events (usually malfunctions) which occur during rules execution (cascading, looping or blocking rules...).

The greatest advantage is to separate these different kinds of events (or malfunctions) taking part (or occuring) in the execution of a set of ECA rules, in order to recommand specific recovery strategies and to modify dynamically events consummation contexts and coupling modes. The future concerns of our work will focus on implementing and validating reflective systems' principles in [9] [6] to an active database system architecture.

References

1. Barga, R., Pu, C. Reflection on a legacy transaction processing monitor. In *Proceedings of the ACM Reflection'96*, 1996.
2. Berti, L. Bases de donnés actives et systèmes réflexifs : de la convergence au fusionnement. *submitted to Inforsid'97*, 1997.
3. Chakravarthy, S., Tamizuddin, Z., Zhou, J. A visualisation and explanation tool for debugging ECA rules in active databases. In *Proceedings of the 2nd Intl. Workshop on Rules In Database Systems*, pages 197–209, 1995.
4. Diaz, O., Jaime, A., Paton, N. DEAR: a DEbugger for Active Rules in an object-oriented context. In *Proceedings of the Intl. Workshop on Rules In Database Systems*, pages 180–193, 1993.
5. Jawadi, R., Su, S. Incorporating flexible and expressive rule control in a graph-based transaction framework. Technical Report, Department of Computer and Information Sciences, University of Florida, *UF-CIS-TR-94-030*, 1994.
6. Kornman, S. Surveillance et réflexivité: présentation du système SADE. *Revue d'Intelligence Artificielle*, vol.7 (**3**),pages 295–327, 1993.
7. Naqvi, W., Ibrahim, M. The REFLEX active database system. Technical Report, Database Systems Research Laboratory, University of Greenwich, *TR-CIT-DB0692* , 1992.
8. Paton, N., Diaz, O., Williams, H., Campin, J., Dinn, A.,Jaime, A. Dimensions of active behaviour. In *Proceedings on Rules In Database Systems, Workshop on Computing*, pages 40–57,1994.
9. Smith,B. Reflection and semantics in a procedural langage. PhD Thesis, MIT, Computer Science Laboratory, *TR-272*, 1982.
10. Thomas, I., Jones, A. OLAF: the GOAD active database event/rule tracer. In *Proceedings of the 7th Intl. Conference of Database and EXpert systems Applications*,pages 436–445, 1996.
11. Zukunft, O. Recovering active databases. In *Proceedings of the 2nd Intl. Workshop on Rules In Database Systems*, pages 357–371,1995.

A Framework for Database Mining

Himanshu Gupta[1], Iain McLaren[2], Alfred Vella[1]

[1]Department of Computing, The University of Luton, Luton LU1, UK
{himanshu.gupta, alfred.vella}@luton.ac.uk

[2] Parsys Limited, Boundary House, London W7 2QE, UK
iain.mclaren@parsys.co.uk

Abstract. Data mining is an attempt to automatically extract useful information from passive data using various artificial intelligence techniques [2]. Conventional database systems offer little support for data mining applications. At the same time, statistical and machine learning techniques usually perform poorly when applied to large data sets. These twin limitations suggest the development of algorithms which extract useful knowledge from large data sets efficiently and within a reasonable time. These algorithms should be able to operate directly against data held in relational database systems and therefore no longer restrict the size of the data set which can be manipulated [5]. This abstract outlines a framework for implementing these *database mining* algorithms [3].

Early attempts at database mining are based on a loosely coupled architecture [1], where SQL commands are embedded within a host programming language. The machine learning algorithm retrieves records from the database in a tuple-at-a-time fashion, each time switching control to the database. Recent database mining systems have begun to integrate the machine learning and database components [4]. The machine learning algorithms are pushed into the execution engine of the database. This reduces execution time by avoiding context switching between the database and machine learning algorithm. The potential of this approach is enhanced by the fact that modern database packages allow user defined procedures to be written and stored in the database for execution. To implement these algorithms, sections of code need to be identified from standard algorithms and re-coded as user defined database functions.

Efficiently supporting the queries generated during the data mining process causes problems for conventional database systems. This is because their indices are designed to support predictable queries. However, it is impossible to predict the queries generated during data mining. Support for unpredictable queries is achieved by general purpose multi-dimensional indexing techniques found in spatial and advanced database systems. This type of index needs to be available if database mining algorithms are to be successful [6].

Extracting meaningful models from very large sets of data is a complex, and time consuming task. Most conventional artificial intelligence algorithms are unable to support these sizes of database. One technique which has been developed to overcome this problem is the use of incremental learning. This technique generates a model for an initial data set and updates this model as new records are added.

Iterative learning is also applicable in the data mining process. This is because models are generated over several iterations. Current database mining systems regenerate the whole model on each iteration. Iterative modelling techniques use the model generated from the previous pass as the starting point for generating the new model. By avoiding repetitive learning at each iteration, a more accurate model is produced in less time with each pass through the process.

Finally, to efficiently deploy any generated models in a conventional database, it is important that the model can be converted into the form of an SQL query.

This abstract has outlined a framework for database mining encompassing an integrated architecture which can support data mining within a database environment. Furthermore, this framework has introduced some issues which need to be addressed to efficiently perform database mining within this architecture. These issues include the use of incremental and iterative learning techniques on large data sets, and the conversion of the models produced into SQL queries. With this set of requirements, we are investigating approaches to data mining which fit the proposed framework.

References

1. R. Agrawal and K. Shim. *Developing tightly-coupled data mining applications on a relational database system.* In: Proceedings of the Second International Conference on Knowledge Discovery and Data Mining, Portland, USA, August 1996.

2. W. Frawley, G. Piatetsky-Shapiro and C. Matheus. *Knowledge discovery in databases: an overview.* In: G. Piatetsky-Shapiro and W. Frawley (eds.), Knowledge Discovery in Databases, The AAAI Press, 1991.

3. H. Gupta, I. McLaren and A. Vella. *A step beyond data mining: Database mining.* In: Proc. of Conference and Workshop on New Approaches in Computing, Coventry, UK, May 1997.

4. M. Holsheimer and M. Kersten. *Architectural support for data mining.* In: Proceedings of the AAAI Workshop on Knowledge Discovery in Databases, Seattle, USA, 1994.

5. T. Imielinski and H. Mannila. *A database perspective on knowledge discovery.* Communications of ACM 39, November 1996.

6. I. McLaren, E. Babb and J. Bocca. *DAFS: Supporting the knowledge discovery process.* In: Proceedings of First International Conference on Practical Applications of Knowledge Discovery and Data Mining, London, UK, April 1997.

Query Processing Techniques for Partly Inaccessible Distributed Databases

Oliver Haase and Andreas Henrich

Praktische Informatik, Fachbereich Elektrotechnik und Informatik,
Universität Siegen, D-57068 Siegen, Germany,
e-mail: {haase|henrich}@informatik.uni-siegen.de
WWW: http://www.informatik.uni-siegen.de/pi/

Abstract. One important characteristic of distributed database management systems (DBMS) is that due to network or machine failure the environment may become partitioned into sub-environments that cannot communicate with each other. However, there are various application areas where the individual sub-environments should remain operable even in such situations [2, 5]. In particular queries to the database should be processed in an appropriate way [4].

To this end, the final and all intermediate results of queries in distributed DBMS must be regarded as potentially vague or incomplete. As a consequence, we have to deal with vague values and vague collections during query processing. Whereas vague values have been addressed in various papers dealing with null values in the relational context [1, 3], vague collections stemming from inaccessibility represent a novel research topic. In this work we present suitable representations for vague sets, vague multisets and vague lists as well as appropriate adaptations of the usual query language operators for these representations.

Our representation for *vague sets* consists of an enumerating and a descriptive part: The enumerating part in turn consists (1) of the explicit part of a lower bound of the desired set and (2) the explicit part of an upper bound of the desired set. Elements in (1) are known to be surely contained in the desired query result while elements in (2) may be in the query result. The descriptive part is a three-valued logical predicate specifying the missing elements of the vague set. These elements complete the enumerating parts to actual bounds.

The descriptive part can be employed to check for potential candidates if they belonged to the desired query result. This is applicable, because in the case of inaccessibility not only inaccessible elements can be missing in the result of a query, but also accessible elements that could not be reached by the normal query evaluation. An example for such a situation may arise when we want to traverse a path built by a multi-step relationship which is disconnected due to inaccessibility.

The adaptations of the query operators to vague sets define the explicit parts of the vague result set as well as the descriptive part. This way we implicitly define how the descriptive part of the result of a query can be calculated. Furthermore the adaptations of the operators employ the descriptive parts of the operands to revise their enumerating parts during query processing. By that way our approach can significantly improve the correctness of the vague result set.

When we are concerned with *vague multisets*, there are not only missing elements, but also the number of occurrences of enumerated elements can be vague. In our approach the first kind of vagueness is dealt with quite analogously to vague sets, while the second kind of vagueness is treated as follows: the number of occurrences of each individual element is represented by a set of possible numbers of occurrences instead of a single number. The adapted query language operators have to combine these vague occurrences when computing a vague result multiset.

Vague lists are more complicated, because when sorting a vague set or a vague multiset, even the arising order can be vague. Our approach comprises an adequate representation for vague lists, too. Our representation of vague lists minimizes the vagueness in the order of the list by enforcing the typical requirements for an order such as irreflexivity, transitivity and trichotomy. The vagueness concerning the uncertain membership of elements of the vague lists is dealt with analogously to vague sets and vague multisets.

Additionally we consider *vague aggregate functions*. In the case of inaccessibility the evaluation of an aggregate function must also be done three-valued resulting in a set of possible aggregate values. In general this evaluation can cause considerable efficiency problems. To overcome these problems, we identify two special classes of aggregate functions, that can be computed efficiently even in the case of vagueness; these classes are called set-monotone aggregations and element-monotone aggregations.

Finally we describe how our hybrid representations for vague collections can serve as the basis for the implementation of a query language for a distributed database.

Compared to other approaches — e.g. in the field of null values — the main contribution of our approach is the use of a descriptive part which describes and restricts the missing elements in a vague collection. This descriptive part can be employed in various situations to improve the enumerating parts of the query result.

References

1. E. F. Codd. Extending the database relational model to capture more meaning. *ACM Transactions on Database Systems*, 4(4):397–434, December 1979.
2. European Computer Manufacturers Association, Geneva. *Portable Common Tool Environment — Abstract Specification (Standard ECMA-149)*, June 1993.
3. G.H. Gessert. Four valued logic for relational database systems. *ACM SIGMOD Record*, 19(1):29–35, March 1990.

4. O. Haase and A. Henrich. Error propagation in distributed databases. In *Proc. 4th Int. Conf. on Information and Knowledge Management (CIKM'95)*, pages 387–394. ACM press, November 1995.

5. A. Heuer and A. Lubinski. Database access in mobile environments. In *Proc. 7th Int. Conf. on Database and Expert Systems Applications*, volume 1134 of *LNiCS*, pages 544–553, Zürich, 1996. Springer.

Indexing Multi-Visual Features in Image Database

Rong Lei, Anne H. H Ngu and Jesse J. Jin

School of Computer Science & Engineering
University of New South Wales,
Sydney 2052 NSW, Australia
e-mail:{rlei, anne, jesse}@cse.unsw.edu.au

Abstract. Separate index structure for each image feature set such as colour, texture or shape can not support composite feature queries classes efficiently. To answer a query based on composite features, a hierarchical approach is often used where each component of a query is applied against an appropriate index. Then a higher layer merges results are presented to users. This method is inefficient in terms of storage utilization and system performance. Moreover, it also has a disadvantage in making a decision for complex visual scene, where visual features are weighted unequally. In this paper we have proposed an indexing scheme by combining various visual features in a unique space to support the composite multi-features queries.

There are two main problems to be addressed before combining different features into an integrated index structure. One is that the integrated feature generates a higher dimensional vector which can not be handled efficiently by existing spatial access methods. The other is how to measure the similarity in a unique feature space while visual features are not weighted equally in human visual perception.

The core of our schemes is to use hybrid dimension reduction by combining linear Principal Component Analysis (PCA) and nonlinear neural network to adjust the weighting for the integrate different visual features together with feature dimension reduction. After the image features dimension reduction, an existing spatial access method (SAM) can be used to index these compressed feature vectors.

The idea of this method is that training data set for the network is first analyzed using PCA. Then a new set of training data is selected based on the direction of major eigenvectors of the correlation matrix of training data set in their order of significance. Thus the new training set contains lower dimension than the original training set but keeps the maximum information about the training data. With this new training data set, the computation of non-linear dimension reduction can be reduction dramatically and the network learning rate is also improved.

The architecture of this method is in Figure. 1. The architecture of this method consists of two basic parts. At the bottom part of this structure, there are a number of boxes which contain the PCA analysis. The neural network in the top of box is a three-layer perceptron feedforward network to perform nonlinear dimension reduction (NLRD). First, PCA analysis is performed on the original image features separately for the whole image database. After PCA analysis, NLRD can be carried out on this intermediate representation of images. When the network training completed, the hidden layer of the neural network can be seen as the final lower dimension representation of the images. The training procedure is as following:

Step 1: Compute eigenvalues of correlation matrixes of the whole image database for each visual feature.

Step 2: Select the first m eigenvalues from each list of eigenvalues in Step 1 by using a cut-off values λ. This cut-off value account for the total variance of these m eigenvalues.

Step 3: Find the m eigenvectors of each correlation matrix and rearrange them based on the descending order of their corresponding m eigenvalues into the rows of the PCA transformation matrix T.

Step 4: Obtain the new representation Y_i for each image feature X_i by using PCA transformation.

Step 5: Select the training samples and classify them into different classes based on the human visual perception.

Step 6: Present the training samples to train the network with quickprop learning algorithms [1].

Step 7: Test the convergence of the network. If the condition of convergence of the network is satisfied, Stop training; Otherwise go back to step 6 and repeat the processing.

This method has been tested on 20 images with colour and texture feature. It has been show that this new method is more efficient than nonlinear -dimensionality-reducer (DR) and more accurate than linear-DR. An existing SAM such as R+tree [2] can be used to index these lower dimension representations of images.

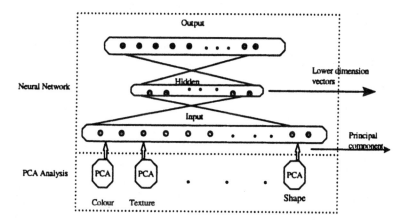

Fig. 1. Hybrid image feature dimension scheme

References

1. Fahlman, S. E. An empirical study of learning speed for Back-propagation networks. *Technical report CMU-CS 88-162*, Carnegie-Mellon University.
2. Sellis, T.; Roussopoulos, N.; and Faloutsos, C. The R+-tree: a dynamic index for multimensional objects. *Proc. VLDB, Brighton.* 1987.

Customisable Visual Query Interface to a Heterogeneous Database Environment: A Meta-Programming Based Approach

A.P. Madurapperuma, W.A. Gray and N.J.Fiddian

Department of Computer Science
University of Wales, Cardiff, UK
e-mail: {scmapm|wag|njf}@cs.cf.ac.uk

Abstract. Increasingly large numbers of users are gaining access to data sources stored in networked database environments which are characterised by the heterogeneous nature of the participant database systems and the varying frequency of access by users to the component databases. Visual query interfaces [1] to the participant databases can be used in such an environment to hide some of the heterogeneity due to the different database types, by using these interfaces to present conceptual visual models [2] of the data structures in the individual databases. Such visual models can be viewed and queried graphically to facilitate user interaction with the databases. However, not all the databases will have such an interface and within the environment there could be several different visual query interfaces [3].

We present a system that helps the users of such an environment interact with its varied component database sources. This is achieved by letting a user interact with all the data sources through a graphical interface which can represent all the associated conceptual models in the user's preferred visual paradigm. Consequently the interface to the environment must be able to map the conceptual model of any of its constituent databases into the user's preferred visualisation model and, conversely, map any queries prepared by a user against this model into a format appropriate to the target database's query processing sub-system.

The approach used in our system is based on employing: (a) an intermediate modelling system to reduce the required number of mappings between data models and visual models; (b) externally defined knowledge bases (specification schemes) to guide the processes involved in schema visualisation and graphical querying; and (c) meta-programming techniques to create a user-specific graphical interface.

The architecture of the system is shown in fig.1.

The use of this system involves four major stages: (a) a **definition** stage during which a meta-programmer can define new specification schemes or modify existing schemes to suit end-user requirements and/or preferences; (b) a **configuration** stage during which the end-user selects the necessary specification schemes depending on the target DBMS and the visual model to be used; (c) an **application** stage in which the user-selected specification schemes are used to capture the schema from the target database and present it to the user in a pictorial form; and (d)

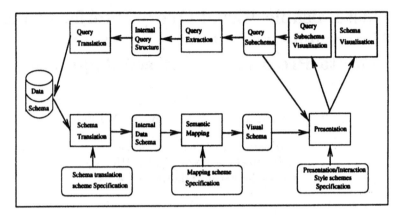

Fig.1. An Overview of the Architecture for a Customisable Visual Query Interface to a Heterogeneous Database Environment

a graphical querying stage in which the user interacts with the visualised schema to build queries graphically, to submit each formulated query to the target DBMS and to receive the results of the query.

This work has established a foundation for developing a visual interface that serves as a common front-end to a variety of data sources in heterogeneous database environments and that can flexibly evolve to deal with new DBMSs in the environment and new preferences for the visual model. Our prototype system is implemented in Quintus PROLOG release 3 using the MOTIF toolkit. Schema information extraction modules are developed in a query language embedded in C for each of the DBMSs supported. The retrieval of data from databases is through a query language interface embedded in C. Currently, facilities for interacting with the relational DBMSs INGRES and ORACLE, and the extended relational DBMS POSTGRES, are available. Visual model description files for EER, OMT and tabular form have been developed.

References

1. Batini, C., Catarci, T., Costabile M.F., Levialdi, S., (1994), On Visual Representations for Database Query Systems, *Proceedings of the International Conference on Interfaces to Real and Virtual Worlds.*

2. Chen, P., (1976), The entity-relationship model: Towards a unified view of data, *ACM Transactions on Database Systems* 1(1).

3. England D., Cooper, R., (1992), Reconfigurable User Interfaces for Databases, *Proceedings of the International Workshop on Interfaces to Database Systems.*

Automatic Web Interfaces and Browsing for Object-Relational Databases

Mark Papiani, Alistair N. Dunlop, and Anthony J. G. Hey

Department of Electronics and Computer Science,
University of Southampton, Southampton SO17 1BJ, UK,
e-mail: {mp|and}@ecs.soton.ac.uk

Abstract. Reformatting information currently held in databases into HTML pages suitable for the Web requires significant effort both in creating the pages initially and their subsequent maintenance. These costs can be avoided by coupling a Web server to the source data within a database. The purpose of this research is to generate automatically Web interfaces to object-relational databases using metadata from the database catalogue. A prototype system has been developed to provide automatic Web interfaces employing a graphical means of specifying queries. Hypertext browsing of object-relational databases is made possible by creating dynamic links that are included automatically within the query results. These links are derived from relationships inferred by referential integrity constraints defined in the metadata.

The aim of our work is to allow databases to be placed on the Web with virtually no programming effort. The HTML pages that provide the query interface to the database are generated automatically. Web access to a database can be provided without any interference to the existing database. Rather, our method uses the structure and information contained in the database to generate HTML pages and links when the data is accessed. Because HTML is not stored, no separate maintenance of the HTML pages and database source data is required. Any changes made to the database are reflected the next time the data is accessed. By connecting to the database in real-time we make use of the sophisticated search engine provided by the database management system (DBMS). Our system differs from many commercial offerings which require programming effort to define screen input and output formats and pre-defined queries for hypertext links.

In a tutorial on database research directions opened by the Web, Manber [1] states, "Finding ways to include browsing in even relational databases would be a great step". The system we have developed addresses this problem by supporting both direct querying of the database and browsing via dynamic hypertext links.

Object-relational databases are the main focus of our work for a number of reasons. Firstly, they can store large and complex data types (such as images, drawings, audio and video). Second, the Standard Query Language (SQL) can be used on these databases. We make use of metadata that can be extracted from the catalogue using SQL. This is used to provide the automation in our system. We extract metadata describing the complete database schema, for example, table names, attribute names and attribute types (both standard and user-defined), primary keys and foreign keys. To access data initially from the database the user is presented with a query form interface similar to Query By Example. To use the query form, users are required to select the fields to be returned by the query, and optionally, they can restrict the data returned by placing selection conditions on one or more fields. The query result is a table consisting of the requested columns, and rows that meet the selection conditions.

To add a browsing facility on the data we exploit the existence of foreign keys in the database. Most databases used in industry contain foreign keys because of the need to maintain referential integrity. Foreign keys effectively define the relationships between tables in the database. The database system tables identify the primary and foreign keys in all relations. When a user requests data from the database, the system table is examined to see if the requested table columns participate in referential integrity constraints. The system tables are also queried to identify any columns containing Large OBject (LOB) data. For both these cases the data returned from the database is modified so that the attributes within these columns are "selectable". The resulting HTML page thus contains a table with hypertext links. These links provide the capability of browsing the database for information without the need for the user to explicitly submit further database queries. When the user selects a dynamic link a CGI program is invoked to generate the new query based on the selection. Currently, the following types of links are included.

1. A single foreign key value will link to a row of a table in which the value appears as a primary key. This is a specialising link and will always return a single row.
2. A single primary key value may link to rows in a table which contain the value as a foreign key. This is a generalising link. The user may have a choice of tables to link to, and for the selected table, one or more rows may be returned.
3. Any fields which contain a LOB type will display the size of the LOB in bytes. This can be selected to retrieve the actual LOB from the database. A LOB field could, for example, contain image, audio, video or character data.

On-going work includes a new implementation using Java Database Connectivity. The extensive metadata classes and URL based database naming provide a means for extensions such as multidatabase browsing.

References

1. Manber, U., Future Directions and Research Problems in the World Wide Web. In *Proc. 15th ACM SIGAT-SIGMOD-SIGART Symposium on Principles of Database Systems*, pages 213–215, Montreal, Canada, June 3-5, 1996.

A Mechanism for Automating Database Interface Design, Based on Extended E-R Modelling

S R Rollinson and S A Roberts

School of Computer Studies, University of Leeds
Leeds, LS2 9JT, UK

Abstract. This work sets out to examine the nature of the correspondence between the E-R model of an application domain and the interface structures that would support maintenance of the application's data. It is shown that this correspondence can be exploited during database application development to aid user interface construction, including the possibility of automatic interface generation. Other work has used the E-R model as the basis for automating the interface design process [2, 3]. However, our work differs from these in that it uses a richer set of interface structures than [3], and it generates the interface layout from a single model, rather than the two preferred by Janssen et al. in [2]. The main objective of this work was to investigate the feasibility of mapping relationship-types from the underlying model to the interface. We concentrate on relationships rather than attributes as many DBMSs already provide tools that automate the placement of attributes on forms. Two key concepts feature in our approach, familiarity and simplicity. Using the entity-relationship model provides a technique that is used in methodologies such as SSADM [1] and is thus familiar to developers. Simplicity is achieved by adding only a minimal set of extensions to E-R notation.

A methodology was adopted to ensure sound conclusions could be drawn. The first stage is to generalise from case-studies of existing information systems. The output of this stage is a set of rules that map from relationship-types to interface structures, and a set of extensions required to the E-R model. The next stage is to check for consistency and completeness. By consistency we mean that rules derived from different case-studies produce mappings that are consistent with each other. By completeness we mean that every relationship type in the E-R model maps to an interface structure. The third step is to test the rules on an "unseen" application and evaluate the resulting interface. Evaluation has only been completed by the authors to date. This is sufficient to determine whether the mechanism leads to a sound interface. The final stage is to implement a software tool to generate interfaces automatically. Generation is a two stage process, mapping and construction. Mapping is achieved using Prolog to implement the rules, this outputs an interface specification. To demonstate the construction phase Microsoft Access is used to convert the specification into a physical interface.

The rules have proved successful for the automatic and semi-automatic (i.e. with user intervention) generation of a first-cut user interface from an extended E-R model. The interfaces, are able to cater for all the data management tasks required. During testing some important lessons were learnt. Firstly the discipline of extending the E-R model forces the analyst to question the modelling that led to the diagram. Two small omissions to the diagram used in testing were discovered this way. Secondly the determing of user keys highlights the need for unique identification of entities through attributes that are familiar to the end-user. A third result relates to the comparison between automatic and semi-automatic generation strategies. The two interfaces differed in only one respect and were both usable, but the fact that a difference existed supports the case for some user intervention in the interface design process.

The main contribution of this work is the identification of a set of rules, and a minimum set of extensions to the E-R model for automatic interface generation. The extensions are minimal in the sense that any fewer concepts would lead to ambiguity in the choice of interface structures. The extensions are sufficiently small and clear to be both managable and useful. The work has also shown there to be scope for automating the construction of data entry/update interfaces. Although Microsoft Access has been used as a vehicle for testing our approach the results, in terms of extensions to the E-R model and Prolog rules, are more widely applicable. Issues that have not been addressed in this work are the ordering or grouping of fields in the interface, and where the automation might take place. We believe the first issue could be dealt with using views as in [2]. Our preference for the second issue is to give the designer tools for automatically generating interface elements rather than attempting to generate the whole interface automatically. A final issue which needs to be addressed in future work is a more comprehensive user evaluation of the generated interfaces.

References

1. Downs, E., Clare, P., Coe, I., (1991) Structured Systems Analysis and Design Method: Application and Context, 2nd Edition, Prentice Hall.
2. Janssen, C., Weisbecker, A., Ziegler, J., (1993) Generating User Interfaces from Data Models and Dialogue Net Specifications in *Proceedings of InterCHI'93, S. Ashlund, K. Mullet, A. Henderson, E. Hollnagel, T. White (eds.), ACM Press*, pp. 418-423
3. Petoud, I., Pigneur, Y., (1990) An Automatic and Visual Approach for User Interface Design in *Engineering for Human-Computer Interaction, North-Holland*, pp. 403-420

Exploration of the Requirements in a Visual Interface to Tabular Data

Ian Taylor and Steve Benford

Department of Computer Sciencce
The University of Nottingham, Nottingham. NG7 2RD, UK
http://www.crg.cs.nott.ac.uk/ imt/iviz.html

Abstract. This document summarises the use of a three-dimensional scatter plot system in which graphical attributes may be dynamically mapped to data attributes and image re-generation performed instantly. A key part of this work was in the application of this system to a commercial dataset. The ease of use and versatility of the visualisation enabled hitherto un-noticed trends to be revealed.

The 2-D scatter plot has shown itself to be effective in revealing implicit information in large datasets. It exploits the human visual system's ability to isolate groups of points based on position, colour, size and shape [1]. Trends and anomalies are easily identified which may confirm or contradict our perception of the data. Like others, we suspect that a 3-D plot may allow additional expressiveness by notionally increasing the number of variables on view Recent research has examined the effectiveness of abstract three dimensional visualisations of large datasets. Examples include VR-VIBE [2] and QPIT [3]. The second of these systems adopts an approach described by Michael Benedikt [4]. Benedikt described the generation of information landscapes by mapping data attributes to graphical attributes. Here we describe one such system in which a dataspace is generated from tabular information. There are three key features to this system; instant image re-generation, dynamic filtering/data space adjustment and instant switching between scatter or geographic plots. These are intended to allow users to quickly experiment with any combination of attribute mappings and permit flexible control over the dataspace. This exercise used real world data and development and evaluation was performed in conjunction with industrial collaborators. Following discussion a suitable dataset was located in the form of Gas Demand Forecast data for the past three years. Simultaneous comparison of several variables was required to spot any new trends and anomalies in their data and so this seemed at be an ideal test case for our visualisation tool. The software was then used by BG employees who were familiar with the data and had already used other data mining tools with it. During the sessions the users gained rapid familiarity with the interface. Six degrees of navigation was often disorienting and object centred movement or automated transitions would have been desirable. Colour was found to be a powerful communicator of trends. Spin was suited to boolean or similar types as small variations were difficult to perceive. Shape did well as a loose indicator of value Size was rarely used in a 3-D plot as it was subject to perspective distortion. Filtering was frequently used as it was often the case that outlying values were of interest. It also meant a lower machine load which allowed faster navigation. Instant regeneration was the system's key strength and graphs were generated as thoughts arose and avenues pursued. The dynamic features supported a tendency to develop ideas during use. Users praised the versatility of the system in encouraging spontaneity and allowing gradual refinement of queries. By gradual mapping, the users saw the evolution of the graph and did not have to deal with a sudden barrage of information. This allowed the users to exploit the third dimension without confusion. The significant result of the session from a data point of view was the discovery made in the performance of one predictive model. Error values for different models were successively mapped against date. By repeated regeneration it was seen that one model had shown a particularly noticeable number of relatively higher error values for the past year.

Our experience suggests that offering the user a large degree of control over the definition of an image and responding quickly to preferences is crucial in effective visualisation. Users must be able to dynamically interact and experiment with the image. This is a strong argument in favour of the use of virtual reality type technology, which enables interaction with 3-D graphics, as opposed to just 3-D imaging of datasets. We must ensure that the users receives an awareness of their viewing position within the context of the entire dataspace and so graphical keys and position indicators are essential. The available set of data types were limited and failed to exploit an environment in which expression of semantics is well accommodated e.g. shapes could closely symbolise a fields nature. Also, by allowing many-to-one mappings, the system could use composites of attributes in the visualisation process thereby allowing more variables to be expressed in a single image. Ultimately, this work has demonstrated the examination of a single table. By traversing the data hierarchy, a more complete environment and associated guidelines will be produced. We wish to thank BG plc who provided funding and assistance.

References

1. Csinger, Andrew: The Psychology of Visualization (Technical Report), no.TR-92-28, University of British Columbia, Nov 1992.
2. Benford, S., Snowdon, D., Greenalgh, C., Ingram, R.,and Knox, I: VR-VIBE: A Virtual Environment for Cooperative Information Retrieval, Proc. Eurographics '95.
3. Steve Benford, David Snowdon and John Mariana: Populated Information Terrains: first steps. In R. A. Earnshaw, J. A. Vince, H. Jones (ed),Virtual Reality Applications, pp 27-39. Academic Press, 1995.
4. Benedikt, M: Cyberspace: Some proposals. In M. Benedikt (ed.) Cyberspace: The first steps. Cambridge, MA: MIT Press 1991.

DOA – The Deductive Object-Oriented Approach to the Development of Adaptive Natural Language Interfaces

Werner Winiwarter and Yahiko Kambayashi

Department of Information Science, Kyoto University,
Sakyo, Kyoto 606-01, Japan,
e-mail: {ww|yahiko}@kuis.kyoto-u.ac.jp
WWW: http://www.isse.kuis.kyoto-u.ac.jp/Welcome-e.html

Abstract. We present the Deductive Object-oriented Approach (DOA), a new framework for natural language interface design. It uses a deductive object-oriented database (DOOD) for developing the interface as component of the database system. This provides the basis for a consistent and efficient mapping of the user input to the target representation. Furthermore, we propose adaptive techniques to deal efficiently with the difficult task of dynamic knowledge engineering. As first feasibility test we have developed an adaptive interface for Japanese, which is applied to the question support facility of a collaborative education system.

Despite the long tradition of the research field of natural language interfaces, we have to face the situation that natural language interfaces are still far away from widespread practicable use [1]. One of the main responsible factors for this is *missing integration*, which results in insufficient performance and wrong interpretations. Therefore, we define a new framework for natural language interface design in which the interface constitutes a component of the DOOD *ROCK & ROLL* [2]. Especially its inheritance mechanisms make it possible to structure the linguistic knowledge hierarchically to guarantee a compact representation.

Another main difficulty for natural language interfaces is the high amount of necessary manual knowledge engineering. For each portation to a new application this elaborate process has to be repeated. Furthermore, the interfaces are often part of dynamic environments with constant changes concerning topics and user population. Therefore, we apply linguistic resources and methods from machine learning to the automatic acquisition of linguistic knowledge.

The applied interface architecture consists of the two main parts lexical and semantic component. The *lexical component* possesses three central modules: morpho-lexical analysis, unknown value list (UVL) analysis, and spelling error correction. *Morpho-lexical analysis* performs the *tokenization* of Japanese input, i.e. the segmentation into individual input words. By accessing a domain-independent lexicon the module transforms the input into a *deep form list* (DFL), which indicates for each token its surface form, category, and a set of associated deep forms. During *UVL analysis* we deal with domain-specific terms in the input and we also support *spelling error correction* of those terms. Besides this, we apply the following three *adaptive techniques*: (1) the use of the

Japanese-English dictionary *EDICT* as secondary lexicon for the retrieval of information about unknown words and the automatic generation of new lexical entries, (2) the semi-automatic extraction of domain-specific terms from domain-specific documents, and (3) the application of pronunciation data from the Japanese character file *KANJIDIC* to improve the precision of spelling error correction.

The *semantic component* generates the semantic representation of the input sentence. For this purpose the semantic analysis accesses a semantic application model. It contains *activation rules* to choose the correct semantic category based on the information in the DFL and the UVL [5]. The use of *syntactic analysis* is restricted to situations in which it is necessary for disambiguation. Finally, *pragmatic analysis* extends the scope of analysis from the isolated sentence by keeping track of the current focus to deal with missing information due to input referring to previous sentences. As powerful adaptive technique we have developed an *incremental learning module* that learns a consistent set of activation and syntactic disambiguation rules for selecting the correct semantic category based on past input data. The module is an adaptation of the *SE-tree approach* [3]; a generalisation of decision trees especially well suited for domains with few training examples and noisy environments.

As first test of the feasibility of our approach we have used the interface architecture successfully for the question support facility of the collaborative hypermedia education system *VIENA Classroom* [4]. The semantic representations of questions are applied either to the retrieval of corresponding answers from a FAQ knowledge base or to the gathering of new questions. We believe that the deductive object-oriented approach will become a valuable paradigm for the development of successful natural language interfaces with broad user acceptance.

References

1. I. Androutsopoulos, G. D. Ritchie, and P. Thanisch. Natural language interfaces to databases – an introduction. *Journal of Natural Language Engineering*, 1(1):29–81, March 1995.
2. M. L. Barja et al. An effective deductive object-oriented database through language integration. In *Proc. 20th Int. Conf. on Very Large Data Bases (VLDB'94)*, pages 463–474, September 1994.
3. R. Rymon. An SE-tree-based characterization of the induction problem. In *Proc. Int. Conf. on Machine Learning (ML'93)*, pages 268–275, June 1993.
4. W. Winiwarter et al. Collaborative hypermedia education with the VIENA Classroom system. In *Proc. 1st Australasian Conf. on Computer Science Education (ACSE'96)*, pages 337–343, July 1996.
5. W. Winiwarter, O. Kagawa, and Y. Kambayashi. Applying language engineering techniques to the question support facilities in VIENA Classroom. In *Proc. 7th Int. Conf. on Database and Expert Systems Applications (DEXA'96)*, pages 613–622, September 1996.

An Efficient Indexing Scheme for Objects with Roles

F. M. Lam , H. Lewis Chau , Raymond K. Wong *

Department of Computer Science
Hong Kong University of Science and Technology
Clear Water Bay, Hong Kong

Abstract. Indexing schemes for traditional Object-Oriented Databases (OODBs) are divided into two catalogues: *class hierarchy indexing* and *nested indexing*. Since most of these systems are static in nature, dynamic operations like class versioning and role playing are not supported by traditional indexing schemes. In order to support these dynamic query operations, a more sophisticated indexing scheme is needed. In this paper, we present the *Double Signature Indexing Scheme (DSIS)* for a dynamic object-oriented database programming language with role extension, called *DOOR*. It supports retrievals of a large range of queries including class relation queries, nested queries as well as queries that exist only in dynamic environments like qualification and versioning queries. Query relaxation and specification are also supported by the index structure. We describe the index structure of the indexing scheme and show how the index structure supports dynamic operations as well as static operations. In addition, we present the operations of the indexing scheme and demonstrate how the operations of the new indexing mechanism handle different kind of queries.

Keywords : *Indexing techniques, objects with roles*

1 Introduction

Object-oriented databases have gained wide attention in the last few decades because their greater modeling power on structurally complex data compared to relational database systems. Recent advances in semantic data modeling have driven the development of systems requiring encapsulation, extensibility and manipulation of complex relationships among data. These applications, benefited by the object-oriented approach, require a high quality of performance on data manipulation. Indexing is one common technique to increase the performance of an object-oriented system.

Although many indexing techniques were proposed in the past, their approaches only support queries on inheritance relations [2, 7] or nested relations

---

* Current address: Department of Computing, School of MPCE, Macquarie University, Sydney, NSW 2109, Australia

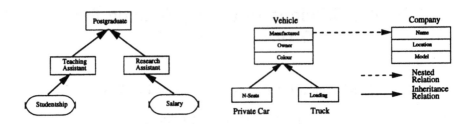

Fig. 1. Sample object-role organization

Fig. 2. Sample aggregation and class hierarchy

[3]. Queries on relations among classes over the whole class hierarchy like superclass and sibling relations cannot be evaluated efficiently by these indexing techniques. For example, in Fig. 1, queries like *"Retrieve all counterparts of class TA with salary over 14,390"* are difficult to be answered by traditional indexing schemes since the complete class hierarchy is not considered by index structure. As a result, the querying capacities of the database systems are seriously affected.

Moreover, most of these indexing schemes proposed in the past cannot keep track of the object-class relations when the systems are running. The reason for this weakness is the static nature of the systems or the programming languages underneath. Systems built on traditional object-oriented languages like C++ usually do not preserve the concept of class after the compilation of the program. Without the present of class hierarchy, advanced query operations like query relaxation [6] and specification are difficult to achieve.

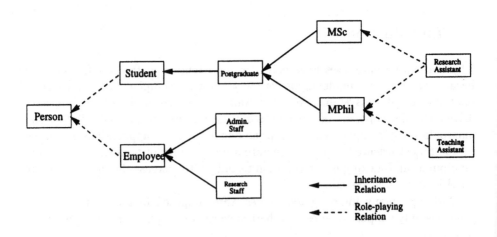

Fig. 3. Sample object-role schema

Besides, in many class-based object-oriented systems the association between an instance and a class is exclusive and permanent. Thus these systems have serious difficulties in representing objects taking on different roles over time. Such systems are called *static object-oriented database systems*. Querying on dynamic objects is infeasible in these systems. For instance, in Fig. 3, the role Research Assistant can be played by both MSc and MPhil students in certain time periods. The *role-playing* relation allows objects to behave differently or evolve over time. Queries like *"Find all research assistants who are studying in MPhil programmes at time t"* cannot be answered by static OODBs.

In this paper, the Double Signature Indexing Scheme (DSIS) is proposed to provide a more flexible index structure for the dynamic object-oriented database systems which support role-playing mechanism and allow class relations to be changed while the system is running. The scheme also maintains the object-class information in order to solve queries stated above. The object-class information is important for facilitating query generalization and specification. Moreover, our implementation supports class versioning, which allows dynamic changes of class definitions or method implementations of a class without affecting the object instances created before. Class versioning is an essential property for dynamic object-oriented programming languages. For example, a class Computer has an member function called *Printing* which simulates the printing of documents using a dot-matrix printer. Let PC_1, PC_2 be instances of this class. If now the printing technology is advanced and the *Printing* function of the class Computer is updated to simulate the printing of documents using a laser printer, let PC_3 is an instance of this new Computer class. Class versioning allows systems to model this situation and treat PC_1, PC_2 and PC_3 as the same class. At the same time, PC_1, PC_2 and PC_3 are different in the printing method.

2 Related Works

2.1 The DOOR Model

Traditional object-oriented data models are based on the concept of class. Real world entities with similar behavior and properties are represented as object instances of a specific class. The association between instances and classes are exclusive and permanent. However, objects usually behave differently over time. The most illustrative example is people. The concept of roles was realized in work on semantic modeling [11] and object-oriented modeling [12]. Object-oriented language with role extension were proposed recently [1] in order to represent objects evolving over time. A role extends an object with additional behavior and properties. Thus, the behavior of an object is defined by the class to which the object belongs, as well as, the roles being referenced by the object. A dynamic object-oriented database programming language called DOOR [13] has been developed in Hong Kong University of Science and Technology. The language is built based on the concept of meta-object protocol (MOP) such that various dynamic features are rapidly prototyped and can be easily extended.

Besides general OODB constructs and versions, in particular, DOOR supports the dynamic role playing which solves the problems in traditional class-based object-oriented systems caused by a permanent and exclusive link between an instance and a class. Role classes are defined to complement object classes. An object of an object class can play zero or more roles, and a role of a role class can only exist by being associated with an object. Moreover, a role can also play roles. The *played-by* relationship is defined between a role player and the roles being played by means of delegation. Through delegation, a unique object can be accessed through different roles (i.e., different perspectives), which have different types and can answer in different ways to a message. Furthermore, the player qualification feature models the fact that not every object qualifies to play a particular role. That is, to qualify as a player of a particular role, a player must be an element of the extension of one of the classes specified in the player qualification of the role classes.

2.2 Indexing Techniques

Indexing techniques for object-oriented databases were introduced in the recent years after object-oriented techniques were widely accepted as tools for advanced computer systems. The basic idea of indexing techniques is to provide an indexing structure to avoid inspection of non-interesting objects in the retrieving process since traversal of intermediate objects involves costly overhead. An indexing scheme is feasible if the cost of traversing the non-interesting objects is higher than the cost of using indexing structure to skip this traversal. Although most indexing schemes can improve the performance on retrieval of objects, they also introduce a net storage overhead and high maintenance cost. To get around with the overheads, most indexing schemes build their indexing structure only on a limited set of attributes which are frequently asked.

Indexing Nested Hierarchy. Indexing schemes for nested queries in OODBs in earlier days were based on extending operations in relational database systems. Indexing techniques specific for OODBs were first studied by Kim and Bertino [3]. They proposed three indexing schemes: *Nested Index*, *Path Index* and *Multi Index*. The nested index defines the direct association between the attribute values and the objects containing these values. As path information is ignored, maintenance and updating is costly since all indices of objects along the nested path need to be retrieved. The path index defines indices along the path from the root class to the target class. Retrieval on nested queries takes only one lookup of the path index. The multi index defines indices on attributes of every nested class. Evaluation of a nested queries may involve several lookups of the multi index along the path.

Recently, the *Path Dictionary Index Method* was proposed by Lee [10, 9] which combines the *path dictionary* and the *s-expression* scheme. Although the path dictionary index can support fast retrieval on queries like nested equality and range queries, its storage overhead is tremendous due to the large number of additional index structures introduced.

Indexing Class Hierarchy. Retrievals in relational database systems are mainly based on join and selection operations applied to different tables. However, in OODBs, the hierarchy of classes makes these operations very complex. For example, if the querying class is a sub-class, selection of objects with a specific attribute value needs to examine all objects in that sub-class and all its parent classes. Thus, new indexing schemes are needed in order to answer queries efficiently.

The indexing scheme on class hierarchy was studied in [8]. A class index is built on attributes of a class associated with a list of OIDs pointing to objects of the class as well as its sub-classes with the indexing values. The *Single-class index* maintains an index for each class whereas *class-hierarchy index* introduces an index on an attribute of all sub-classes rooted at a particular class.

2.3 Signature File Techniques

Signature File Technique [5] is a widely used text retrieval tool by its limited storage overhead compared with other indexing techniques like inverted files. A *signature* is a bit string containing the abstracted information of a data object in the database. In processing a query, a query signature is created to hold the query values. If an object signature does not match with the query signature, the object is eliminated as it does not contain the required values. Objects which pass the test are called *drops*. Next, the candidate objects are tested by actually accessing them and checking whether the query values are matched. Matched objects are reported and the rest are called *false-drops*. Thus, signature files can be viewed as a powerful filtering tool to filter out objects that are not qualified.

3 Double Signature Indexing Scheme

3.1 Signature Path Vector

In this section we present the signature path vector that captures the relations and connections among classes and objects. The signature path vector is also the basic index structure of DSIS.

Objects in an object-oriented database can be clustered in different groups according to different aspects. Class can be viewed as one kind of clustering scheme used in OODBs. However, in order to achieve efficient indexing in OODBs, object clusters must be organized in a structured way. For example, inheritance and nested hierarchies cluster classes according to the super/sub-class relation and aggregation relation respectively. In a dynamic environment, more relations can be defined. For example, Type Abstract Hierarchy (TAH) [4] specifies relations among classes for query relaxation and specification and the qualification relation reflects the role-playing order among classes. The indexing scheme for such a dynamic environment must support different class structures for efficient retrieval for specific queries. Signature path vectors in DSIS store the path information for special relations among classes in the database. Since path information is stored in the form of signatures, access and retrieval of a node are much faster. In our implementation, each signature path vector represents one relation on the class hierarchy. Besides, in order to facilitate class versioning in DSIS, two additional attributes are included in the signature path vector:

- **Local version number**: The local version number defines the version status of a class locally. It records the number of changes of a class and the version information which is local to the class.
- **Global version number**: The global version number defines the version status of the whole hierarchy. It records the total number of versions created in the hierarchy. Each signature path vector has its own global version number in order to maintain the versioning sequence of the indexing hierarchy.

Definition 1. A signature path vector with versions is defined in the form of $GVerC_1C_2\cdots C_n$ where $GVer$ is the global version number of the current signature path vector and C_i:

1. is null, or
2. is in the form of $\langle Sig_i, EID, PVer, LVer, \Theta (C_i) \rangle$ where EID is the entity identity, $\Theta(C_i)$ is either null or a list of signature path vectors with versions where the entity relates to and Sig_i is the signature of the entity which is composed by superimposing the signatures of the entities in $\Theta(C_i)$. If there is no entity in $\Theta(C_i)$, a random bit string is created and assigned to it. $LVer$ and $PVer$ are the local version number and the global version number of the previous local version respectively.

Since the signature of an entity class is formed by superimposing the signatures of its children's classes, the signature can also be viewed as superimposing signatures of all leave nodes of the tree rooted at that entity class. EID can be the name of the class or other distinct identity key. By the recursive definition of the signature path vector, all classes in the database can be organized in a structural hierarchies representing different class relations.

In the indexing scheme we implemented, signature path vectors are generated for the class hierarchy, role hierarchy, role qualification hierarchy and nest hierarchy. Class hierarchy is based on the "is_a" relationship among the classes. Nested hierarchy is based on the "part_of" relationship among objects. Role hierarchy, similar to class hierarchy, expresses the super/sub-class relationship among role classes. Role qualification hierarchy presents the order sequences on how roles can be played by the objects. For example, an object of class **Person** must play the role **MPhil** before playing the role **Teaching Assistant**. This kind of role playing requirement provided by the DOOR programming language introduces a more powerful modeling feature over other dynamic object-oriented programming languages. Our implementation also allows additional relations to be added to the indexing scheme to facilitate faster retrieval on special sets of queries and objects.

For example, with the signatures for the role classes shown in Fig. 4, and no version is created (i.e., global version number is 1), the signature path vector with versions for the role hierarchy in the object-role schema defined in Fig. 3 is shown in Fig. 5.

Class Name	Signature
Admin. Staff	00100100
Research Staff	10010010
MSc	00001011
MPhil	01010001
Research Assistant	01110110
Teaching Assistant	10011001

MSc	00001011
∨ MPhil	01010001
Postgraduate	01011011
Student	01011011

Admin. Staff	00100100
∨ Research Staff	10010010
Employee	10110110

Fig. 4. Sample class signatures

$(1, \langle 01011011, Student, 0, 1, (\langle 01011011, Postgraduate, 0, 1, (\langle 00001011, MSc, 0, 1, nil\rangle,$
$\langle 01010001, MPhil, 0, 1, nil\rangle))\rangle)\rangle,$
$\langle 10110110, Employee, 0, 1, (\langle 00100100, Admin.\ Staff, 0, 1, nil\rangle,$
$\langle 10010010, Research\ Staff, 0, 1, nil\rangle)\rangle,$
$\langle 01110110, Research\ Assistant, 0, 1, nil\rangle,$
$\langle 10011001, Teaching\ Assistant, 0, 1, nil\rangle)$

Fig. 5. Sample signature path vector with versions

3.2 Implementation of Double Signature Indexing Scheme

Data Structure of the Signature Path Vector. The data structure of the signature path vector is illustrated in Fig. 6. Each signature path vector is composed of a list of cells. Each cell represents the data structure of an entity class in the corresponding hierarchy. A cell is headed by the signature of the entity class, Sig_i, described in the previous section. Following the signature is the key or the name of the entity class. *LVer* stores the local version number that is used to identify the local version status of the entity class. *PVer* gives the global version number of the previous local version of that entity class. The two version numbers provide efficient access on retrieving objects of a particular version of a particular class. In order to allow multiple inheritance in the class level, *Parent* is defined as a list of pointers which point to the cells of its parent entities in the hierarchy. The root entity will have this field null. *Next* is a pointer which point to the sibling entity cell. It is set to null if no sibling entity is defined. *Child_pt* is defined as a list of pointers which point to its succeeding classes according to the relation the signature path vector expresses. *Obj_file* is a pointer which points to a memory storage located in either main memory or secondary organization called object file. The structure of the object file is presented in the next section.

The advantage of this representation is the fast retrieval of any entity class along the entire entity hierarchy. Since each cell in the vector corresponds to one entity of the hierarchy and the storage cost of a cell is fixed, the storage overhead is proportional to the number of entities in the hierarchy. Since the

\<SIG\>	Entity Name	PVer	LVer	Parent	Next	Child_ptr	Obj_file	\<SIG\>	Entity Name	PVer	LVer	Parent	Next	Child_ptr	Obj_file	....

Fig. 6. Data structure of signature path vector

storage overhead is relatively small and predictable, the signature path vectors can either be located in the main memory or secondary organizations.

With this data structure, the abstract information of each class and the whole class hierarchy can be expressed in the signature path vector. As the class relation is stored, class relation queries like *"Find all counterparts MPhil students who are taking the course 'Introduction to dynamic OODBs'"* or *"Find all students who are qualified to play the role Research Assistant"* in Fig. 3 can be evaluated by traversing along the corresponding signature path vector. Besides, as signature file technique is used and the size of signature path vector is relatively small, the traversal along the signature path vector requires relatively fewer page accesses. As a result, the evaluation of queries can be more efficient.

In addition, the present of class hierarchy makes intelligent operations like query relaxation and specification possible. Query relaxation enlarges the scope of queries if the answer for the original query is unsatisfactory or too specific. On the other hand, query specification reduces the scope of queries. For example, if the query *"Retrieve all MPhil students who have CGA over A"* cannot provide a satisfactory result, the system may relax the query to *"Retrieve all Postgraduate students who have CGA over B+"*. The relaxation or specification can be achieved by traversing either upward or downward the class hierarchies (represented by signature path vectors) to locate the corresponding object files.

Moreover, classes can be evolved frequently. When a class evolves, a new version is created. A new version expresses a new class structure and results in a new signature path vector. The small storage cost of signature path vectors can help reduce the overall storage overhead due to additional versions created.

As described in the above section, the signature of an entity class is formed by superimposing all the leave nodes of the tree rooted by that class. Signatures of higher level nodes suffer the problem of superimposing too many signatures of its descendants and result in a decrease of the filtering power of the signature. One way to solve the problem is to increase the size of signatures for higher level entity classes so the average bit-set ratio can be restored.

Object Files. OID's and their signatures are stored in the object file of the corresponding entity class. The object file is composed of two structures: the *object expression* and the *signature table*. Figure 7 shows the data structure of the object file.

Object expression is a modified signature path vector specific for a nested relation. The object expression captures the class-attribute hierarchy rooted at a specific class. The head of the expression is the entity cell of the corresponding

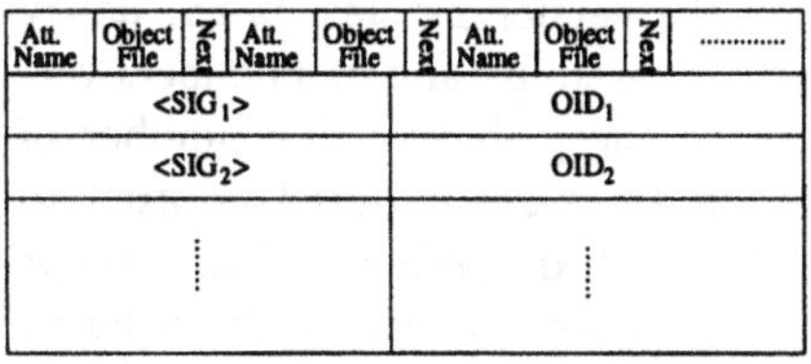

Att. Name	Object File	Next	Att. Name	Object File	Next	Att. Name	Object File	Next	....
$\langle SIG_1 \rangle$						OID$_1$			
$\langle SIG_2 \rangle$						OID$_2$			
⋮						⋮			

Fig. 7. Data structure of object file

Object C1 of class Company :

Attribute Name	Value	Signature
Name	Honba	01101100
Location	Hong Kong	00100110
V Model	PG 50	01000111
Object signature of C1		01101111

Fig. 8. Sample object signature of class Company

class or role class. Since changing information in the object expression is equivalent to creating a new version, versioning information such as local and global version numbers is not included in the object expression. Moreover, since the nested relation is one-direction relationship among classes, the *Parent* field can be ignored. Besides, each object expression contains only one entity cell and a set of pointers to the objects expressions of the nested classes. This approach can minimize the storage overhead of the object expressions.

The signature table contains entries in the form of $(\langle SIG \rangle, OID)$ where $\langle SIG \rangle$ is the signature of the object pointed by OID which is created by superimposing all the primary attribute values of that object. For example, if C1 is an instance of class Company in Fig. 1, the object signature of C1 is shown in Fig. 8. The storage overhead of an object file is proportional to the number of classes in the object expression and the number of objects in the class. Thus, the object files are usually stored in the secondary organizations. However, they can also be located in the main memory if the number of objects and classes are relatively small.

The signature path vector is focused on maintaining the class organization. On the other hand, the object file is focused on maintaining the object organization. Since classes are changed frequently in a dynamic object-oriented environment, the separation of class and object organizations makes the independent indexing of classes and objects possible in order to reduce the maintenance cost for the whole index structure. For example, when a class migrates or moves along the class hierarchy, traditional indexing schemes usually require rebuilding the whole index structure. In our scheme, only a new signature path vector for the corresponding class relation is required to be built. The object indices for all instances in these two classes are not affected.

Version Implementation. Class versioning is achieved by adding version information in the signature path vector. A global version number is added to the signature path vector. When a version is created, a new signature path vector is produced by copying the path vector from the old version. Since the two versions are the same, their structures, including the object file pointers, are the same. The global version number of the new vector is then increased by one. The cell of the versioning class is also modified. In signature path vectors for inheritance, role and role qualification relations, a new object file is created and pointed by the object file pointer in the cell of the versioning class in the newly created path vector in order to store the newly created instances. The local version number is updated and the *PVer* is set to the global version number of the old path vector. The version pointers in the front are updated in order to provide flexible retrieval along the versions. The indexing scheme always keeps an environment pointer which points to the most updated version in order to capture the current information of the database. Figure 9 illustrates the data structure of signature path vector with a previous version. Since class versioning only occurs in class hierarchies, an object expression in object files do not contain any version information.

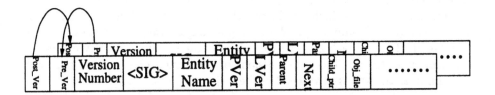

Fig. 9. Data structure of signature path vector with versions

Overall Data Structure in DSIS. As mentioned above, the DOOR programming language introduces three relations among classes. These are the inheritance relation, role relation and the role qualification relation. Our indexing scheme supports all three kinds of the above relations by applying three signature path vectors with versions for each of these relations. Each class instance or role instance has pointers which point to the corresponding entity cells in the signature path vectors. Thus, a class instance contains a pointer to a cell in the class signature path vector. A role instance has two pointers, one points to the role signature path vector and the other points to the qualification signature path vector. This arrangement is used because our implementation supports queries starting with objects that are frequently asked for in a programming language rather than queries starting with a class or an attribute value in traditional database. For example, queries like *"Find all students who take courses with Eric"* are evaluated starting from the class instance.

Although there are three signature path vectors, the object file pointers of the same class in different vectors linked to one object file only. This is because the path vectors give only different partitioning schemes on the same set of classes. However, the situation may apparently fail if versions are created. Since our indexing scheme allows the creation of versions in any combination of the three relations, introducing new versions on some signature path vectors creates new object files for updating the path vectors only and the rest preserve the old ones.

Object expression, on the other hand, is not pointed directly by any class or role instance. The vectors are indirectly pointed by the object file pointers in the signature path vectors in order to support queries involving both nested objects. Nested queries are answered by first retrieving the object file of the querying class. The nested signature path vector in the object file is then traversed to locate the object file of the particular class. Since the DOOR programming language has a special feature in which every nested object has a pointer pointing back to the calling object, after retrieval of the nested object with matched attributes, the rest of the querying process is simply the backward traversal through the path up to the top level object. Figure 10 illustrates the overall structure of DSIS.

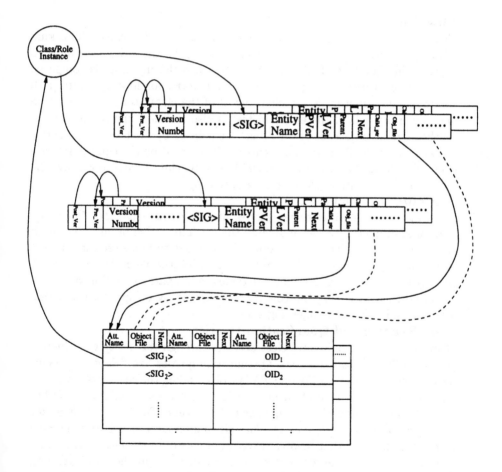

Fig. 10. Overall index structure of DSIS

4 Operations of DSIS

The introduction of dynamic object-oriented programming language enhances the modeling power of traditional static object-oriented programming languages and the databases built on such languages. Accompanying the increase of modeling power of the language is the increase of the complexity and variety of queries. The double signature indexing scheme is created to deal with such queries on the dynamic language platform.

4.1 Retrieval

DSIS supports fast retrievals on class related queries and nested queries. It also supports queries on retrieving objects with different versions.

- **Class Queries**
  Class queries answer queries like *"Find all students in the school"*. This kind of query is executed by first executing a lookup on the class hash table to retrieve the signature of the class **Student**. Then the signature is compared with the signature of the root entity of the corresponding signature path vector. If the signature is satisfied, the id of the class **Student** is compared and the entity cell. If the entity id test is also satisfied, the target class is reached and all object ids of the object file pointed by the target class entity cell are retrieved. Otherwise, the entity cells pointed by the child points are compared. If the entity cell has no child or all its children fail to retrieve the target class, the entity cell is called a false drop.
- **Attribute Value Queries**
  Attribute value queries answer queries like *"Find all students of age 13"*. This kind of query involves matching the attribute value of an object with the querying value. The sample query is executed by first executing a class query on the class **Student**. After retrieving the object file of the target class, the object signatures in the signature table are compared with the hash value of *13*. Objects satisfying the condition are tested by comparing the actual attribute value with the querying value.
- **Class Relation and Qualification Queries**
  Class relation queries involve class accesses through the entity class hierarchies of different class relations. Qualification queries like *"Find all persons who are qualified to play the role TA"* involve finding the role class TA in the qualification signature path vector and traverse to its super-classes. Other examples on class relation are queries like *"If class 'TA' and 'RA' have the same parent class 'Postgraduate', find all counterparts of TA with research interest 'Indexing'"* that involve traversal of classes in the class hierarchies. In order to answer the above queries, the entity cell in the corresponding class signature path vector is first retrieved. Then from the entity cell, the target entity cell is retrieved by using the parent class pointers and child class pointers. After the interested object file is found, the resulting objects are retrieved using the method stated above to solve attribute value queries.

- **Nested Queries**

Nested queries involve access to the class-attribute hierarchy expressed in the nested signature path vector in the object file. For example, the class Student contains an attribute called *book_list*, which is an object of the class Book. One example nested query is *"Find all students who have the Bible"*. This query is executed by first getting the entity cell of the class Student in the corresponding signature path vector. Then the object expression is searched and the target nested entity cell is retrieved. The object file pointed by the entity cell is scanned and qualified objects are reported. Since in the implementation of DOOR, each nested object has a pointer which links back to its parent object. The rest of the query is done by traversing back to the top level calling objects and return them as the result.

- **Versioning Queries**

The versioning mechanism is one special type of query which is supported only by dynamic object-oriented database systems since traditional static object-oriented database systems do not allow changing of the class definition at any time. The versioning queries are divided into two types: global versioning queries and local versioning queries. Local versioning queries retrieve objects with a version local to a special class. One example is *"Find all cars of previous version of 'Corolla' manufactured by 'Toyota'"*. Global versioning queries consider the overall versioning status within the system. Queries are like *"Restore all cars of the earliest model of 'Corolla'"*. Executing the global versioning queries involves forward tracing of the signature path vectors to locate the vector with the particular global version number and to continue the retrieval within the selected path vector. Local versioning queries are executed by locating the entity cell in the current signature vector and checking its local version number. Since the global version number of the previous local version is stored in the entity cell, the previous local version can be retrieved using this global version number. The search continues recursively until the interested local version is retrieved.

- **Complex Queries**

DSIS also supports complex queries which are any combination of the queries stated above. Since each kind of queries above is executed in different level of the indexing scheme, complex queries can be solved by first solving the versioning part. The class relation part can be executed next. After the target object file is retrieved, the nested part of queries can be solved. Finally the attribute value part can be executed.

4.2 Insertion

Insertion in DSIS is divided into two parts: insertion of an entity class in signature path vectors and insertion of an object in the particular object file. Insertion of a new class involves creation of a new entity cell and a new object file of the inserting class. After retrieving its parent classes, the entity cell and the object file are inserted and the corresponding pointers are updated. Besides, the signatures of all ancestor entity cells along the path are re-calculated. Insertion of an object in an object file involves creation of the object signature by super-imposing all the signatures of the primary attribute values of the object. Then the $(\langle SIG\rangle, OID)$ pair is inserted into the signature table of the corresponding object file.

4.3 Deletion

There are two approaches for deleting a class in a class hierarchy. One approach is to delete a class and at the same time delete all its sub-classes in the sub-tree rooted at the deleting class. The other approach is deleting a class and at the same time promoting its sub-classes to links to its parent. Our implementation uses the latter approach since in many cases the sub-classes need to be preserved. For example, if Person ←— Graduate ←— Postgraduate is a class hierarchy rooted at Person , deletion of class Graduate should not affect the existence of the class Postgraduate since Postgraduate is still a Person.

The deletion of a class involves locating the parent and children classes of the deleting class. Then the children classes are promoted up one level. The signatures of all ancestor entity classes along the path are updated. Deletion of an object in the object file involves only the deletion of the corresponding $(\langle SIG\rangle, OID)$ pair in the corresponding object file.

4.4 Version Operation

Version operation is different from other operations that version can only be created and cannot be deleted and updated. The creation of version involves duplication of the current signature path vector. The *pre_ver*, *post_ver*, global version numbers and the local version numbers of the corresponding entity class are updated. Moreover, the $PVer$ pointer is updated to point to the old signature path vector.

5 Conclusion

Indexing schemes proposed in the past have focused mainly on object-oriented databases which did not support dynamic operations like role-playing mecha-nism. The static nature of these systems, not only restricted the modeling of data, but it also limited the querying power of the databases. In this paper, we presented the double signature indexing scheme (DSIS) for the dynamic object-oriented database language called DOOR. We described the signature path vectors used in DSIS and showed how abstract information of different class hierarchies was stored in the vectors in order to maintain the dynamic class structure. We also presented the object files which stored the attribute information of objects. The separation of class and object structures reduced the maintenance cost of the whole index structure in a dynamic environment. With the implementation of the signature path vectors and the object files, we described how our index structure supported different types of class hierarchies for modeling dynamic objects and how class versioning was achieved by DSIS. In addition, we presented the operations of the indexing scheme to demonstrate how DSIS handled different kinds of queries which were difficult to be answered by static object-oriented databases and maintain the index structure.

We have finished the prototype for the indexing scheme. The retrieval cost model and storage cost model are also developed. We are going to have the full scale implementation. We also plan to study the consistency issues on the multi-user DSIS platform.

References

1. Antonio Albano, Giorgio Ghelli, and Renzo Orsini. Fibonacci: A programming language for object databases. In *Proceedings of the Eleventh International Conference on VLDB*, pages 403–443, 1995.
2. E. Bertino. An indexing technique for object-oriented database. In *Proceedings of the Seventh International Conference on Data Engineering*, pages 160–170, Kobe, Japan, 1991.
3. E. Bertino and W. Kim. Indexing techniques for queries on nested objects. In *IEEE Transactions on Knowledge and Data Engineering*, volume 1, June 1989.
4. Wesley W. Chu, Hua Yang, and Gladys Chow. A cooperative database system (cobase) for query relaxation. In *Proceedings of the Third International Conference on Artificial Intelligence Planning Systems*, May 1996.
5. C. Faloutsos and S. Christodoulakis. Signature files: An access method for documents and its analytical performance evaluation. In *ACM Trans. Database System*, pages 267–288, Oct 1984.
6. T. Gaasterland, P. Godfrey, and J. Minker. Relaxation as a platform for cooperative answering. In *Journal of Intelligent Information Systems*, 1993.
7. E. Gudes. A uniform indexing scheme for object-oriented databases. In *Proceeding of the Twelfth International Conference on Data Engineering*, pages 238–246, 1996.
8. W. Kim, K.C. Kim, and A. Dale. *Indexing techniques for Object-Oriented Databases*, chapter 15, pages 371–394. ACM Press, 1989.
9. W.C. Lee and D.L. Lee. Combining indexing technique with path dictionary for nested object queries. In *Proceedings of the 4th International Conference on Database Systems for Advanced Applications (DASFAA 95')*, pages 107–114, Singapore, April 1995.
10. W.C. Lee and D.L. Lee. Path dictionary: A new approach to query processing in object-oriented databases. In *IEEE Transactions on Knowledge and Data Engineering*, July 1996.
11. Q. Li and F. H. Lochovsky. Roles: Extending object behavior to support knowledge semantics. In *International Symposium on Advanced Database Technology and Their Integration*, pages 314–322, Japan, 1994.
12. M. P. Papazoglou. Roles: A methodology for representing multifaceted objects. In *Proceedings of the International Conference on Database and Expert Systems Applications*, pages 7–12, 1991.
13. R. Wong, H. Chau, and F. Lochovsky. A data model and semantics of objects with dynamic roles. In *Proceedings of the Thirteenth International Conference on Data Engineering*, pages 402–411, Birmingham, UK, 1997.

A Prefetching Technique for Object-Oriented Databases

Nils Knafla

Dept. of Computer Science
University of Edinburgh
United Kingdom
Email: nk@dcs.ed.ac.uk

Abstract. We present a new prefetching technique for object-oriented databases which exploits the availability of multiprocessor client workstations. The prefetching information is obtained from the object relationships on the database pages and is stored in a *Prefetch Object Table*. This prefetching algorithm is implemented using multithreading. In the results we show the theoretical and empirical benefits of prefetching. The benchmark tests show that multithreaded prefetching can improve performance significantly for applications where the object access is reasonably predictable.

Keywords: prefetching, object-oriented databases, distribution, performance analysis, multithreading, application access pattern, storage management

1 Introduction

Two industry trends in the performance/price ratio of hardware systems have implications for the efficient implementation of object-oriented database management systems (OODBMSs) in a client/server computing environment. Firstly, the continuing fall in price of multiprocessor workstations means that such machines are cost effective as client hosts in OODBMSs. Secondly, although the performance/price ratios of both processors and disks are improving, the rate of improvement is greater for processors. Hence, the disk subsystem is emerging as a bottleneck factor in some applications. Recent advances in high bandwidth devices (e.g. RAID, ATM networks) have had a large impact on file system throughput. Unfortunately, access latency still remains a problem due to the physical limitations of storage devices and network transfer latencies.

In order to reduce access latency database systems cache pages in the buffer pools of both the client and server. Prefetching is an optimisation technique which reads pages into the database buffer before the application requests them. A successful prefetching technique is dependent on the accuracy of predicting the future access. If accuracy is high, performance can be improved since the penalty of waiting for the completion of a page fetch is so high. If accuracy is poor, the performance can actually decrease due to cache pollution, channel congestion and additional workload for the server.

The fate of OODBMSs will largely depend on their performance in comparison to relational databases. The simple tabular structures of relational databases and the set-at-a-time semantics of retrieval languages such as SQL make it easy to parallelise relational database servers. However, in an OODBMS the structures are complex and typically the retrieval chases pointers. Furthermore, in most OODBMSs the bulk of the processing occurs on the client: the server merely serves pages.

In this paper, we present a new prefetching technique for page server systems. The prediction information is obtained from the object structure on the database pages and is stored in a *Prefetch Object Table* (POT) which is used at run time to start prefetch requests. Our technique is different from existing techniques in the fact that we use an adaptive mechanism that prefetches pages dependent on the navigation through the object net. We implemented this technique in the EXODUS storage manager (ESM) [1]. We also incorporated Solaris threads into ESM to have the application thread and the prefetching thread running on different processors in the client multiprocessor.

In section 2 we give an overview of the related work in the area of prefetching. How we predict pages to prefetch and store this information is described in section 3. The prefetching architecture is explained in section 4. In section 5 we present the theoretical results and the performance measurements. Finally, in section 6 we conclude our work and give an idea of future work.

2   Related Work

The concept of prefetching has been used in a variety of environments including microprocessor design, virtual memory paging, compiler construction, file systems, WWW and databases. Prefetching techniques can be classified by many dimensions: the design of the predictor, the unit of I/O transfer in prefetching, the start time for prefetching or the data structures for storing prediction information. According to [7] predictors can be further classified as *strategy-based*, *training-based* or *structure-based*.

Strategy-based prefetching has an explicit programmed strategy which is used internally (One Block Lookahead [9]) or by a programmer's hint [14]. In the Thor [12] database, an object belongs to a *prefetch group*. When an object of this group is requested by the client, the whole object group is sent to the client.

Training-based predictors use repeated runs to analyse access patterns. For example, Fido [13] prefetches by employing an associative memory to recognise access patterns within a context over time. Data compression techniques for prefetching were first advocated by Vitter and Krishnan [17]. The intuition is that data compressors typically operate by postulating a dynamic probability distribution on the data to be compressed. If a data compressor successfully compresses the data, then its probability distribution on the data must be realistic and can be used for effective prediction.

Structure-based predictors obtain information from the object structure. Chang and Katz's technique [3] predicts the future access from the data semantics in terms of structural relationships, e.g. inheritance, configuration and version history. They prefetch the immediate component object or immediate ancestor/descendent in a version history. An assembly operator for complex objects to load sub-objects recursively in advance was introduced by Keller [10]. The traversal was performed by different scheduling algorithms (*depth-first* and *breadth-first*). Our prefetching technique [11] also belongs to the *structure-based* approach.

In object-oriented databases the unit of I/O is an object (*Object Server*) or a page (*Page Server*) or a larger conglomeration, e.g. a segment. An object server prefetches an object or a group of objects [5] and a page server prefetches one or more pages ([4], [8]). Another possible classification of prefetching is the time factor. Smith [16] proposed two policies: (a) prefetch only when a buffer fault occurred (*demand prefetch*), (b) prefetch at any time (*prefetch always*).

3 The Prefetching Design

3.1 Prefetch Object Table

OODBMSs can store and retrieve large, complex data structures which are nested and heavily interrelated. Examples of OODBMS applications are CAD, CAM, CASE and Office automation. These applications consist of objects and relationships between objects containing a large amount of data. A typical scenario is laid out by the OO7 benchmark [2]. It comprises a very complex assembly object hierarchy and is designed to compare the performance of object-oriented databases.

In a page server, like ESM, objects are clustered into pages. Good clustering is achieved when references to objects in the same page are maximized and references to objects on other pages are minimized. In our benchmark we use a *composite object clustering* technique.

The general idea of our technique is to prefetch references to other pages in a complex object structure net (e.g. OO7). We obtain the prefetch information from the object references without knowledge of the object semantics. Considering the object structure in a page, we identify the objects which have references to other pages (*Out-Refs*). One page could possibly have many *Out-Refs* but sometimes it is not possible to prefetch all pages because of time and resource limitations. Instead, we observe the client navigation through the object net. We know which objects have *Out-Refs* and when we identify that the application is processing towards such an *Out-Ref-Object* (ORO) the *Out-Ref* page becomes a candidate for prefetching.

The prefetch starts when the application encounters a so-called *Prefetch Start Object* (PSO). Although the determination of OROs is easy, determining PSOs is slightly more complicated. There are two factors that complicate finding PSOs:

1. Prefetch Object Distance (POD)
   For prefetching a page it is important that the prefetch request arrives at the client before application access to achieve a maximum saving. The POD

defines the optimal distance of n objects from the PSO to the ORO object which is necessary to provide enough processing to overlap with prefetching. Let C_{pf} denote the cost of a page fetch and let C_{op} denote the cost of object preparation. The cost of object preparation is the ESM client processing time before the application can work on the object[1]. Then POD is computed as follows:

$$POD = \frac{C_{pf}}{C_{op}}$$

If the prefetch starts before the POD, a maximum saving is guaranteed, however, if it starts after the POD, but before access, some saving can still be achieved (see section 5.2).

2. Branch Objects

   A complex object has references to other objects. The user of the application decides at a higher level the sequence of references with which to navigate through the object net. We define a *Branch Object* as an object which has at least two references to other objects. Objects that are referenced by a *Branch Object* are defined as a *Post-Branch Object*. For example in fig. 1 we have a complex object hierarchy. The object with the OID[2] 1 would be defined as a *Branch Object* because it contains a branch in the tree of objects. Objects with OID 2, OID 7 and OID 12 would be defined as *Post-Branch Objects* because they are the first objects de-referenced by a *Branch Object*.

For every identified ORO in the page we compute the PSO by the following algorithm:

1. Retrieve the OID of the ORO and of the object in the next page referenced by the ORO.
2. Compute the POD to define the distance of n objects from PSO to ORO.
3. Determine the PSO by following the object reference n objects backwards from the ORO. If there are not enough objects in the reference chain before the ORO, then we will identify the first object in the page from the reference chain to achieve at least some saving.
4. If the object is already identified as a PSO and the previously identified PSO has a different *Post-Branch Object* then we would identify the *Post-Branch Objects* of the object as PSOs[3].

Defining *Post-Branch Objects* as PSOs can improve the accuracy for the prediction and reduces the number of adjacent pages to prefetch. For example in fig. 1 we would identify OID 5, OID 10 and OID 15 as OROs. In this example we assume a POD of 4 objects. On analysing page 2 we would identify OID 5 as an ORO. From OID 5 we would go through the chain backwards by 4 objects and identify OID 1 as a PSO. Then we would do the same for the OROs OID 10

---

[1] Additionally we could use the expected amount of processing from the application.
[2] OID = Object Identifier
[3] This step is executed after we have defined all PSOs from the OROs in a page.

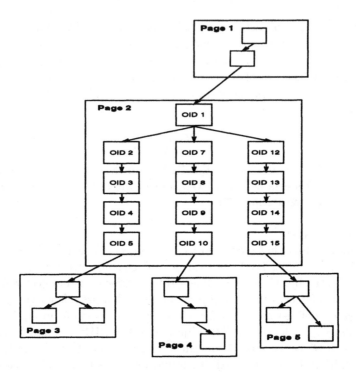

Fig. 1. Object relationship

and OID 15 and identify OID 1 as the PSO for both. After analysing the whole page we would find out that OID 1 has three PSOs with different *Post-Branch Objects*. In this case we would identify the *Post-Branch Objects* of OID 1 (OID 2, OID 7 and OID 12) as PSOs instead of OID 1.

The novel idea about our technique is to make prefetching adaptable to the client processing on the object net. Because the cost of a page fetch is high we try to start the prefetch early enough to achieve a high saving but not too early to prefetch inaccurately. In contrast to the work of [10], we do not prefetch all references recursively; instead we select the pages to prefetch, dependent on the client processing. Recursive object prefetching has also the problem that prefetched pages can be replaced again before access. Adaptive object prefetching limits the number of prefetch pages to the adjacent pages. In contrast to [3], we look further ahead for objects to prefetch than the immediate object.

Each page of the database is analysed off-line. The Analyzer stores this information in the POT for every database root[4]. The overhead for this table is quite low as it only contains a few objects of the page.

At run time, the information from the POT is used to start the prefetch requests. The run time system allocates enough threads for prefetching. If essential pointers for the navigation are updated in a transaction we would invalidate the POT for this page and modify it after the completion of the transaction.

---

[4] This is important because objects on the same page could belong to different roots.

This prefetching technique is not only useful for complex objects, it can also be used for collection classes (linked list, bag, set or array) in OODBMSs. Applications traverse an object collection with a cursor. With PSO and ORO it would be possible to prefetch the next page from a cursor position. In the description of our technique, the object size is assumed to be smaller than the page size. If the object is larger than a page, prefetching can be used to bring the whole object into memory.

In future work we want to investigate performance and behaviour when the POT predicts a large number of pages. For this case we could use a multiple page request. To further reduce the number of pages, we could maintain information about a frequency count on how often the referenced page is accessed from this ORO. The total frequency count for a page would be computed by adding up all frequency count values of the OROs having the same referenced page. This total frequency count combined with a threshold makes the prefetch decision. Another possibility is to declare special data members of the object which are as important for prefetching.

3.2 Replacement Policy

In the ESM client it is possible to open buffer groups with different replacement policies (LRU and MRU). Freedman and DeWitt [6] proposed a LRU replacement strategy with one chain for demand reads and one chain for prefetching. We also plan to use two chains with the difference that when a page in the demand chain is moved to the top of the chain the prefetched pages for this page are also moved to the top. The idea of this algorithm is that when the demand page is accessed, it is likely that the prefetched pages are accessed too. If a page from the prefetch chain is requested it is moved into the demand chain.

4 System Architecture

4.1 The EXODUS Storage Manager

For the evaluation of the prefetching technique we chose the EXODUS storage manager to implement this idea. The EXODUS Client/Server database system was developed at the University of Wisconsin. The basic representation for data in the storage manager is a variable-length byte sequence of arbitrary size. Objects are referenced using structured OIDs[5]. On these basic storage objects, the storage manager performs buffer management, concurrency control, recovery, transactions and a versioning mechanism.

4.2 The Prefetching Architecture

In this section we describe how prefetching is incorporated into ESM. For the concurrent execution of the application and the prefetch system we use the Solaris thread interface. As depicted in fig. 2, the database client is multithreaded.

---

[5] Object identifier containing a physical and logical component (in ESM page number and slot number)

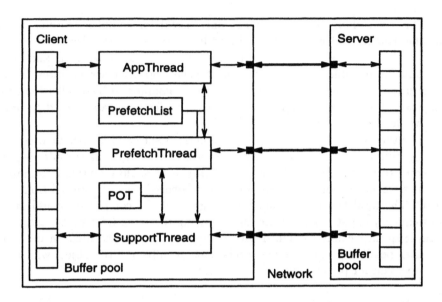

Fig. 2. Architectural Overview

The *AppThread* is responsible for the processing of the application program and the *PrefetchThread* is responsible for fetching pages in advance into the buffer pool. A *SupportThread* has the same task as the *PrefetchThread* with the only difference being that it is scheduled by the *PrefetchThread*. Each thread has one associated socket. The POT informs the *PrefetchThread* which pages are candidates for prefetching from the current processing of the application. The *Prefetch List* is a list of pages which are currently prefetched. The ESM server is not multithreaded[6].

At the beginning of a transaction the *AppThread* requests the first page from the server by a demand read. The *PrefetchThread* always checks which objects the *AppThread* is processing. Having obtained this information, it consults the POT for a page to prefetch and checks if this page is not already resident. If not, the page is inserted in the *Prefetch List* and the request is sent to the server. The server responds with the demanded page and the client inserts the page in its buffer pool. Eventually the page is removed from the *Prefetch List* and inserted into the hash table of the buffer pool.

If the POT predicts multiple pages, *SupportThreads* help the *PrefetchThread*. The number of *SupportThreads* is determined by the number of simultaneous prefetch requests. Each *SupportThread* runs on its own LWP[7] and while one *SupportThread* blocks on I/O, another *SupportThread* insert its page into the buffer pool.

---

[6] But ESM runs many tasks, as concurrent processes, on one processor

[7] Lightweight process (LWP) can be thought of as a virtual CPU that is available for executing code

When the *AppThread* requests a new page, it first checks if the page is in the buffer pool. If the page is not resident then it checks the *Prefetch List*. If the page has been prefetched the *AppThread* waits on a semaphore until the page arrives, otherwise it sends a demand request to the server.

5 Performance Evaluation

5.1 System Environment

For the ESM server we need a machine (called Dual-S[8]) configured with a large quantity of shared memory and enough main memory to hold pages in the buffer pool. To take full advantage of multithreading we chose a four processor machine (called Quad) for the client. Table 1 presents the performance parameters of the machines. Dual-C and Uni are also used as database clients. The network is Ethernet running at 10Mb/sec. The disk controller is a Seagate ST15150W (performance parameters in table 2).

Parameter	Dual-S	Quad	Dual-C	Uni
SPARCstation	20 Model 612	10 Model 514	20 Model 502	ELC (4/25)
Main Memory	192 MB	224 MB	512 MB	24 MB
Virtual Memory	624 MB	515 MB	491 MB	60 MB
Number of CPUs	2	4	2	1
Cycle speed	60 MHz	50 MHz	50 MHz	33 MHz

Table 1: Computer performance specification

Parameter	Disk controller
External Transfer Rate	9 Mbytes/sec
Average Seek (Read/Write)	8 msec
Average Latency	4.17 msec

Table 2: Disk controller performance

5.2 Theoretical Results

The success of prefetching is dependent on the completion of the prefetch request before access. We define the cost of object processing to be C_o. Let C_{op} denote

---

[8] The names of the machines indicate the number of processors

the cost of preparing one object for application access and let C_{oa} denote the cost of processing on the object from the application plus waiting time. C_o is calculated by:

$$C_o = C_{op} + C_{oa} \tag{1}$$

The saving for one out-going reference S_{or} is dependent on the number of objects between the start of the prefetch and application access to the prefetched object (N_o) and the cost of prefetching a page (C_p):

$$S_{or} = \begin{cases} C_p & \text{if } (C_o \cdot N_o \geq C_p) \\ C_o \cdot N_o & \text{otherwise} \end{cases} \tag{2}$$

If there is enough processing $(C_o \cdot N_o)$ to overlap then the saving is the cost of a page fetch. If not, there is also a lower saving of the amount of processing from prefetch start to access $(C_o \cdot N_o)$. Pages normally have many out-going references. The number of references to different pages is denoted by n. S_p, the saving for a whole page, is given by:

$$S_p = \sum_{i=1}^{n} S_{or}(i) \tag{3}$$

Finally, the saving of the total run is defined by S_r which is influenced by the cost of the thread management (C_t), by the cost of the socket management (C_s) and by the number of pages in the run (q):

$$S_r = (\sum_{j=1}^{q} S_p(j)) - C_t - C_s \tag{4}$$

In our performance test we measured the elapsed times for the demand version (RT_d) and for the prefetching version (RT_p). The savings are computed as follows:

$$savings = \frac{RT_d - RT_p}{RT_d} \cdot 100 \tag{5}$$

But the percentage of savings is always dependent on the amount of processing required on the page. For example in table 3 a page fetch costs 2 time units. With 10 CPU time units the saving is only 16 % but with 2 CPU time units the saving is 50 %. Therefore we plan to use a more accurate formula to

CPU	Page Fetch	Savings in percent
10	2	16 %
2	2	50 %

Table 3: Savings in percent

compute savings in percent. T_{sp} is the saved time with prefetching and T_p is the total time of all page fetches:

$$savings = \frac{T_{sp}}{T_p} \cdot 100 \qquad (6)$$

We did not use this formula because it requires a more complicated measurement technique.

5.3 Performance Measurements

For the evaluation of the prefetching technique we created a benchmark with complex objects. The structure of the benchmark should be complex with many relationships between objects, but not too complex for comprehension. Every object in the data structure has two pointers to other objects. Most of the objects point to another object in the same page; only one object in a page has two pointers to two different pages. Having this object structure, the pages are connected like a tree. The size of one object is 64 bytes which gives space for 101 objects in one 8K page. In one run 200 pages are accessed (equal to the size of the buffer pool at the client and server). The application reads only one object from the first faulted page and then all objects from the second faulted page. Every object is fetched into memory with no computation or waiting time on the object.

Although the tests were made in a multi-user environment the workload of the machines and the network was low. The results of the benchmark are dependent on the workload of the machines: using busy machines and networks would increase the page fetch latency. Since there were different workloads during the tests, it is not possible to compare the absolute times in different tests. In figures 4b to 8 the savings in percent are the savings of the prefetching version compared with the Demand version (application with no prefetching) elapsed times.

In fig. 3 we compared the cost of one prefetch request to processing 101 objects in a page. The processing time of 61 milliseconds is about 5 times higher than the time to prefetch one page which took 11 milliseconds. Most of the processing is due to an audit function that calculates the slot space of the page.

In fig. 4a and 4b we present the results of our benchmark. The prefetching version is always faster than the Demand version. The best result was made on the slow Uni machine because of its longer network connection and slower access to the socket. Quad has the same cycle speed as Dual-C but a higher saving. Dual-C and Quad have, in contrast to Uni, two processors or more, allowing threads to run on different processors concurrently. This would be more beneficial with more prefetch requests at the same time. In this test every prefetch is done with 100% accuracy to see the maximum speedup of prefetching.

As mentioned in section 5.2 the saving of prefetching is dependent on the percentage amount of processing of the application. Having 101 objects on one page, we compared the elapsed-time savings under varying object access rates from the application (from 10 objects to 100 objects accessed). Fig. 5 shows the highest saving is with an object access of 20 because the object processing cost is almost equal to the page fetch cost. For the access of 10 objects there is not enough CPU overlap for prefetching. Increasing the number of objects gradually decreases the savings.

When two pages have to be prefetched under strong time restrictions such that there would only be enough time to prefetch one page successfully, we use *SupportThreads* to prefetch simultaneously. We compared different prefetch cb-ject distance parameters to see under which conditions more *SupportThreads* are useful. In fig. 6 Prefetch1 means a prefetching version with just one *Prefetch-Thread* and Prefetch2 means a version with one *PrefetchThread* and one *SupportThread*. Above the distance of 40, both prefetching versions perform equally well. Then Prefetch2 can improve performance and, even at a distance of 1, is better than Demand (Prefetch1 is worse than Demand at a POD of 1).

The application fetches all objects by OID into memory without any processing on the objects or any waiting time. Also a pointer swizzling technique is necessary for real applications to translate the OID into a virtual memory pointer. All this would produce more processing overhead for the client. We simulate this overhead with a loop after every object fetch and called it Inter-Reference Time (IRT). The results in fig. 7 show that with more processing the savings in percent get smaller. This is because the application is more and more dominated by CPU processing (as explained in section 5.2).

In this test we studied the impact of wrong prefetches. We fetched 100 wrong pages from 200 page fetches. The other important parameter is the prefetch object distance. We used the distances of 1, 20 and 100. Recall that we always fetch 2 new pages from one page (one correct and one incorrect page). The distance of 100 is sufficient to do a wrong prefetch, the distance of 20 is critical to do one prefetch right on time and with the distance of 1, the prefetch is always late. Fig. 8 shows the best result of 27 percent savings with a distance of 100, but even with a distance of 1 there is still a saving albeit of only 4 percent.

The last test measures the effect of additional clients on the Demand and the prefetching versions. In general each additional client increases the workload of the server and the network. If the prefetch request is completed before access, prefetching should improve performance even more with additional clients. If the server becomes a bottleneck and prefetch requests have to queue up at the server, prefetching can actually decrease performance. Fig. 9 shows that Demand decreases performance significantly with 4 clients and the prefetching versions decrease performance with 7 clients.

6 Conclusions and Future Directions

In this paper we presented a prefetching technique for complex object relationships in a page server. The object structure of the database is analysed and stored in a *Prefetch Object Table*. During the run time of the application this table is consulted to make the right prefetches on time. We used the object pointers to make predictions for future access. If the application follows such an object reference chain, we know the object that points to an object in the next page therefore making this page a candidate for prefetching. We also use the branch information of the complex relationships to predict the next pages as accurately as possible. If there are more prefetches to do at the same time we use more threads to get all prefetches before the application requires access.

In the implementation and performance tests we evaluated the prefetching technique. The prefetching version was 14% faster on the Quad machine, nearly 9% faster on Dual-C and 18% faster on Uni. Reducing the number of accessed objects in a page increases the savings. With an access of 20 objects in a page we achieved a saving of 45%.

This work will be continued in several directions. Firstly, we will look at the object structure of real applications to see how our technique will perform. We will test different levels of complexity with varying numbers of *Out-Refs*. If the application makes many updates of pointer references we will evaluate how this effects the performance of POT. Also, we will implement our buffer management algorithm to test repeated access to pages. Another possibility is to make the ESM server multithreaded.

References

1. M.J. Carey, D.J. DeWitt, G. Graefe, D.M. Haight, J.E. Richardson, D.T. Schuh, E.J. Shekita, and S.L. Vandenberg. The EXODUS Extensible DBMS Project: An Overview. In S.B. Zdonik and D. Maier, editors, *Readings in Object-Oriented Database Systems*, pages 474–499. Morgan Kaufmann, 1990.
2. M.J. Carey, D.J. DeWitt, and J.F. Naughton. The OO7 Benchmark. In SIGMOD [15], pages 12–21.
3. E.E. Chang and R.H. Katz. Exploiting Inheritance and Structure Semantics for Effective Clustering and Buffering in an Object-Oriented DBMS. In *Proc. of the ACM SIGMOD Conference on the Management of Data*, pages 348–357, Portland, Oregon, June 1989.
4. K.M. Curewitz, P. Krishnan, and J.S. Vitter. Practical Prefetching via Data Compression. In SIGMOD [15], pages 257–266.
5. M.S. Day. *Client Cache Management in a Distributed Object Database*. PhD thesis, Massachusetts Institute of Technology, Laboratory for Computer Science, 1995.
6. C.S. Freedman and D.J. DeWitt. The SPIFFI Scalable Video-on-Demand System. In *Proc. of the ACM SIGMOD/PODS95 Joint Conf. on Management of Data*, pages 352–363, San Jose, CA, May 1995.

7. C.A. Gerlhof and A. Kemper. A Multi-Threaded Architecture for Prefetching in Object Bases. In *Proc. of the Int. Conf. on Extending Database Technology*, pages 351–364, Cambridge, UK, March 1994.
8. C.A. Gerlhof and A. Kemper. Prefetch Support Relations in Object Bases. In *Proc. of the Sixth Int. Workshop on Persistent Object Systems*, pages 115–126, Tarascon, Provence, France, September 1994.
9. M. Joseph. An analysis of paging and program behaviour. *The Computer Journal*, 13(1):48–54, February 1970.
10. T. Keller, G. Graefe, and D. Maier. Efficient Assembly of Complex Objects. In *Proc. of theACM SIGMOD Int. Conf. on Management of Data*, pages 148–157, Denver, USA, May 1991.
11. N. Knafla. A Prefetching Technique for Object-Oriented Databases. Technical Report ECS-CSG-28-97, Department of Computer Science, University of Edinburgh, January 1997.
12. B. Liskov, A. Adya, M. Castro, M. Day, S. Ghemawat, R. Gruber, U. Maheshwari, A.C. Myers, and L. Shira. Safe and Efficient Sharing of Persistent Objects in Thor. In *Proc. of the ACM SIGMOD/PODS96 Joint Conf. on Management of Data*, pages 318–329, Montreal, Canada, June 1996.
13. M. Palmer and S.B. Zdonik. Fido: A Cache That Learns to Fetch. In *Proc. of the 17th Int. Conf. on Very Large Data Bases*, pages 255–264, Barcelona, Spain, September 1991.
14. R.H. Patterson and G.A. Gibson. Exposing I/O Concurrency with Informed Prefetching. In *3rd Int. Conf. on Parallel and Distributed Information Systems*, pages 7–16, Austin, Texas, September 1994.
15. *Proc. of the ACM SIGMOD Int. Conf. on Management of Data*, Washington, USA, May 1993.
16. A.J. Smith. Sequentiality and Prefetching in Database Systems. *ACM Transactions on Database Systems*, 3(3):223–247, September 1978.
17. J.S. Vitter and P. Krishnan. Optimal Prefetching via Data Compression. In *Proc. 32nd Annual Symposium on Foundations of Computer Science*, pages 121–130, San Juan, Puerto Rico, October 1991. IEEE Computer Society Press.

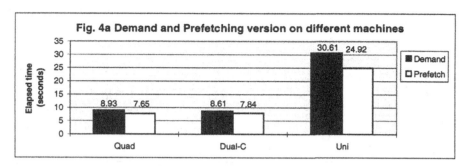

Fig. 4a Demand and Prefetching version on different machines

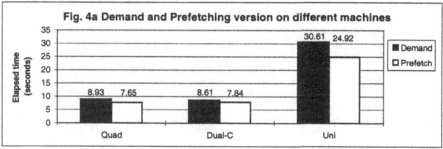

Fig. 4a Demand and Prefetching version on different machines

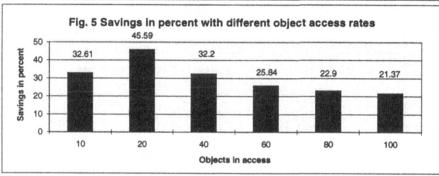

Fig. 5 Savings in percent with different object access rates

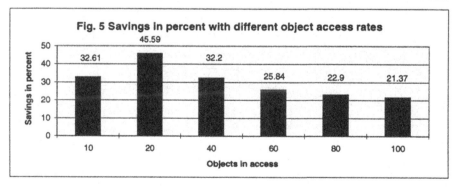

Fig. 5 Savings in percent with different object access rates

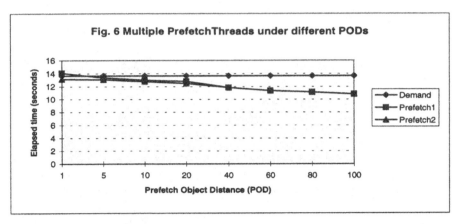

Fig. 6 Multiple PrefetchThreads under different PODs

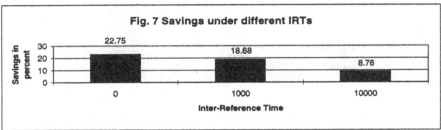

Fig. 7 Savings under different IRTs

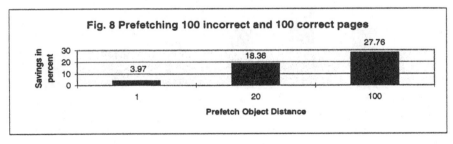

Fig. 8 Prefetching 100 incorrect and 100 correct pages

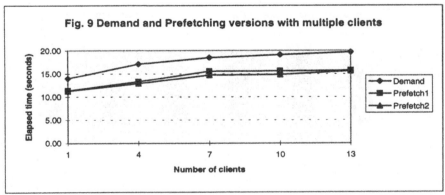

Fig. 9 Demand and Prefetching versions with multiple clients

WIND: A Warehouse for Internet Data

Lukas C. Faulstich[1],Myra Spiliopoulou[2],Volker Linnemann[3]

[1] Institut für Informatik, Freie Universität Berlin,
http://www.inf.fu-berlin.de/~faulstic
[2] Institut für Wirtschaftsinformatik, Humboldt-Universität zu Berlin,
http://www.wiwi.hu-berlin.de/~myra
[3] Institut für Informationssysteme, Medizinische Universität zu Lübeck,
http://www.ifis.mu-luebeck.de/staff/linneman.html

Abstract. The increasing amount of information available in the web demands sophisticated querying methods and knowledge discovery techniques. In this study, we introduce our architectural framework *WIND* for a data warehouse over a domain-specific *thematic section* of the Internet. The aim of *WIND* is to provide a partially materialized *structured view* of the underlying information sources, on which database querying can be applied and mining techniques can be developed.
WIND loads web documents into several complementary local repositories like OODBMSs and text retrieval systems. This allows for a combination of attribute and content-oriented query processing. Special interest is paid to domain-specific document formats. To support conversion between (semi-)structured documents and database objects, we consider a technique for the generation of format converters based on the notion of object-grammars.

Keywords: data warehouse, web, information retrieval, format conversion, grammars

1 Introduction

The Internet forms a large source of data in which users are looking for useful information. Access is mostly by browsing, supplemented by keyword searches on index servers like Lycos, Galaxy or Altavista. However, their coverage is not complete and results are often outdated. Also, a structured presentation of verified query results would be better than an unreliable and redundant hit list.

Integration of Information Systems. Among the numerous projects dealing with the integration of information systems, we mention TSIMMIS [7] and Information Manifold [17]. TSIMMIS wraps each information source in a "translator" that translates both queries and results. However, the *OEM* tree data model used is not well suited for complex objects, needed to model e.g. cyclic relationships in typical collections of web documents. The Information Manifold models each information source as a set of supported relational queries.

The issue of querying and updating text files integrated into a database is discussed in [2,3]. Generic storage methods to integrate SGML documents in the VODAK OODBMS are presented in [1].

Document transformations and unparsing. Syntax trees of structured documents can be processed using tree transformations [16,12,4]. These models do not support text generation (*unparsing*) though. An unparsing algorithm is given in [3]. An object-oriented data model based on attributed syntax trees is proposed in [19]. Most approaches to object-oriented attribute grammars aim at compiler construction [18] though. To our knowledge, there exists no general methodology for text representations of objects yet.

Mining and Data Warehouses. Data Warehouses [13,15] were originally considered to integrate data from "Legacy Systems" in a large database for mining. Inmon stresses that the ideal environment for data mining is a data warehouse [14]. Hence, organizing web data in a data warehouse offers a high potential for knowledge discovery. Web miners using domain-specific knowledge can discover valuable information [8]. Since the web is potentially unlimited and contains mostly unstructured documents, it is important (a) to restrict the warehouse to a single domain of information in order to exploit domain-specific knowledge [8], and (b) to preprocess the data for the application of mining strategies [11].

The WIND Model. We propose a model for the organization of domain-specific Internet information in a data warehouse and for the retrieval of this information with querying techniques, on top of which data mining can be implemented. The *WIND* architecture for a *W*arehouse on *IN*ternet *D*ata, aims at integrating structured and unstructured documents imported from the web both in advance and on demand, i.e. during query processing.

In order to support information extraction from data in different forms, *WIND* considers many repositories, including databases, text archives, media servers and file systems. Their respective query facilities are integrated in a uniform query language, *WINDsurf*, which is transparent to storage and access methods and to data formats. Format conversion is essential for *WIND*. The vast number of existing formats forbids ad hoc methods, so we propose the general concept of *object-grammars* for declarative specification of format transformations.

This article is organized as follows: in the next section we present our running example. In sections 3 to 5 we describe *WIND* and apply it on our running example. Emphasizing the problem of format conversion, we introduce our concept of object-grammars in section 6 and demonstrate in section 7 the usage of object-grammars in our running example. The last section concludes the study.

2 The Internet Movie Database

We use the *Internet Movie Database* (IMDB) as a running example to show how an information retrieval service can be enhanced by remodelling it as a *WIND* instance. IMDB is a public domain data set describing movies. The data are maintained in simple records on ASCII files as shown in Fig. 1.

Access to IMDB is provided via FTP, eMail and WWW servers mirroring the IMDB data. The web interface offers a number of query templates. From the

```
Allen, Weldon    Dolores Claiborne (1994)  [Bartender]  <13>

Allen, William Lawrence   Dangerous Touch (1994)  [Slim]  <3>
                          Sioux City (1994)  [Dan Larkin]  <11>

Allen, Woody     Annie Hall (1977) (AAN) (C:GGN) [Alvy Singer] <1>
                 Bananas (1971)  [Fielding Mellish]  <1>
                 ...
                 Zelig (1983)  (C:GGN)  [Leonard Zelig]  <1>
```

Fig. 1. A part of the list of actors in the IMDB.

query results, HTML pages are generated on the fly. However, ad hoc queries like *"which actors appeared in films of both Jim Jarmusch and of Aki Kaurismäki?"* are not supported.

HTML forms are offered for insertions and updates. However, a more intuitive solution would allow client side editing and uploading of IMDB pages.

IMDB offers a few links to other web resources on cinema (home pages of artists and studios, video clips, magazines, etc.), but cannot use them for answering queries like *"who plays the main character in 'The 3rd Man' and on which channel can he be seen next week?"*.

The *WIND* architecture is intended as a framework to meet these demands.

3   The WIND Architecture

Our *WIND* model gathers information on a given topic from different information sources in the web and organizes them in *Data Repositories* (DRs). A *WIND* instance is administered by a *WIND*-Server, which interacts with each DR via a WIND-*Wrapper* module. As illustrated in Fig. 2, the *WIND*-Server has the following components: (i) an *Internet Loader* importing data from external information sources, (ii) a *Repository Manager* (RM) processing transactions and queries at the server level and delegating subtransactions and subqueries to the DRs, (iii) a *View Exporter* responsible for the interaction with the clients.

3.1   The Interfaces to the Outer World

The Internet Loader. The Internet Loader gathers information from Internet sources like WWW-servers, news-servers, database servers, file systems etc. Also, for resource discovery, it interacts with meta-information providers, such as WWW search engines. The Internet Loader loads an initial document set into the data warehouse and extends it on demand, as discussed in the next section. Moreover, it must regularly update the contents of *WIND* by periodical polling and on update requests from the Repository Manager.

The View Exporter. The View Exporter offers interfaces to clients, such as web browsers, file-based legacy applications, database applications etc. Those interfaces translate the client requests (queries and updates) into the internal

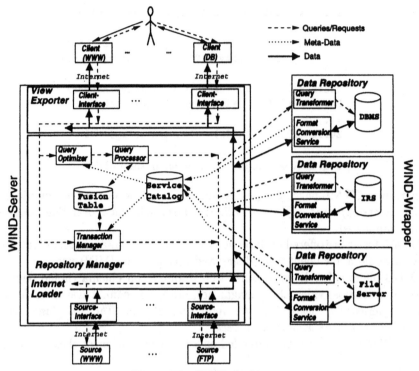

Fig. 2. The *WIND* Architecture

WINDsurf query language, forward them to the Repository Manager, and return the results to the clients. HTTP interfaces for the View Exporter are discussed further in [10].

3.2 The Inner World

The Data Repositories. *WIND* stores objects according to their structure in one or more specialized "Data Repositories" (DRs), such as databases, text retrieval systems, multimedia managers, file repositories etc. The *WIND*-Server interacts with the DRs via the *Query Transformer* and the *Format Conversion Server* (FCS) submodules of the *WIND*-Wrapper. The *WIND*-Wrappers are responsible for presenting the different schemata and data retrieval facilities of the DRs in a uniform way to the *WIND*-Server.

The View Exporter forwards a client query to the *WIND*-Server where the Query Optimizer transforms it into query subplans for the DRs. To each query subplan, a list of argument objects and an output format specification are attached. As shown in Fig. 3, the query is translated by the Query Transformer, while its arguments are converted by Format Converters (FC-1,...,FC-n) of the FCS in a format supported by the DR. The query results are converted into the desired output format and returned to the client.

For the generation of converters for the FCS we mainly consider *Object-Grammars*, although the FCS is open to other types of converters, too, e.g. for

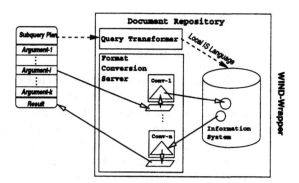

Fig. 3. Querying a Data Repository

picture and audio formats. Object-grammars (as described in Section 6) allow the specification of domain specific document formats in a concise and elegant way. Moreover, they can support both the translation of structured text into objects (parsing) and vice versa (unparsing).

The Repository Manager. The Repository Manager administers the Data Repositories. Its "schema" is the union of the DR schemas. The objects it "sees" are those stored in the DRs. Those objects are not necessarily distinct: the same entity may appear in more than one DR, e.g. a HTML-page may be also retained as a database object in an OODBMS and as a file in a text archive. So, it can be accessed by multiple retrieval mechanisms. We call those multiple representations of the same entity "sibling(s)". In the *Fusion Table*, the Repository Manager keeps track of those siblings, their source, locations, and conversions applied to them during query processing. The *Service Catalog* lists formats and converters available in the FCS of the *WIND*-Wrappers.

Query Language. The query language of *WIND*, *WINDsurf*, must support: (i) object-oriented database queries, (ii) predicates for information retrieval from multimedia archives, mainly based on pattern matching, (iii) format conversion requests and (iv) document updates.

Since those additional operations can be implemented as object methods, *WINDsurf* can adopt the syntax of OQL[5]. However, a *WINDsurf* query is executed against multiple DRs. There might even be several DRs which could be used to execute a certain subquery, as the same object appears in several DRs under different formats. The Query Optimizer of *WIND* must therefore incorporate techniques of distributed and federated query optimization to decide on the most appropriate DR to process each subquery.

Update Mechanism. The *Transaction Manager* of *WIND* controls updates of the DRs. Updates occur when the Internet Loader detects changes in the information sources, and on request of authorized clients. Updates must be propagated to *all* siblings of the same object, as registered in the Fusion Table. This implies translating the original request to commands understandable by each involved Data Repository. Our initial approach simply generates the siblings anew from the updated object.

4 Querying the Internet

4.1 The Contents of an WIND instance

WIND uses two groups of information sources: subject-related well known information sources that are tightly integrated and form the data core of the *WIND* instance, and unknown sources which complement this core with potentially relevant information. We use web search engines to discover such sources. For documents of known structure, converters generated from object grammars can extract information into the DRs. Web documents of unknown type must be processed by a generic converter which extracts at least the HTML structure and stores it in the OODBMS; the text parts can be extracted by another generic converter into a text archive. Media objects will be stored in specialized DRs.

4.2 Querying the DRs of WIND

A query towards the DRs is issued from a client of the *WIND*-Server and must be expressed in *WINDsurf*. The Query Optimizer decomposes it into subqueries towards the individual DRs. The optimizer also decides on use and creation of siblings depending on the formats required for query arguments, intermediate and final results. The output of the Query Optimizer is an execution plan consisting of subplans and conversion requests for the DRs. The Query Processor assigns the subplans and requests to the DRs involved, controls the transfer of intermediate data and merges the results. The result lists from text retrieval DRs are normally ranked by proximity, while the results of an OODBMS may or may not be ranked. Merging result lists ordered by different ranking criteria goes beyond standard query postprocessing. Advances on the processing of ranking predicates [6,9] will be considered in this context.

4.3 Dealing with insufficient information

The data retained in the *WIND* instance may be insufficient to answer a query, i.e. the result list is too small or contains many, but irrelevant results. We consider the design of a "sufficiency metric" modelling the ideal answer and the distance of the actual answer from it in terms of size and ranking of objects.

Once an answer is termed insufficient, the Query Processor asks the Internet Loader to import additional data, on which the query will then be executed again. To retrieve those additional data from well known sources in the web, the Internet Loader only needs a set of *acquisition plans* specifying how the sources should be accessed.

If these sources do not contain the requested information, generic acquisition plans must be used. They should contain search terms extracted from the *WINDsurf* query and domain-specific terms, in order to focus the search on domain-relevant documents. The resulting hit lists from the activated search machines must be merged into one list and reranked by the Internet Loader. This postprocessing is similar to that of **MetaCrawler**, but we expect that a most sophisticated reranking scheme will be necessary. Links to documents with high scores are traversed and the documents are fetched into the *WIND* instance. There, pattern and structure matching operators are applied in the respective DRs in an attempt to process the original query anew. Even though this might not suffice to answer the query exactly, at least a list of relevant documents can be returned as a provisional result.

5 Modelling the IMDB as an **WIND** Instance

The IMDB has several mirror sites in the Internet. We discuss the modelling of a movie database in *WIND* as a functionality enhanced IMDB mirror.

5.1 Structure of the IMDB-WIND

For reasons of brevity we consider a minimally equipped *WIND* instance. It consists of an OODBMS, a text archive and a HTML-page repository; the Internet Loader has http and ftp interfaces; the View Exporter supports a web interface. Additional repositories, such as a video archive, can obviously be added. The OODBMS repository is organized according to the schema in Fig. 4. This schema is a simplified version of the IMDB schema, allowing us to concentrate on the aspects of the movie database important for our study. The Format Conversion Server of the OODBMS is equipped with object grammars that can transform the IMDB files into objects, and with object grammars for the conversion of database objects into HTML pages.

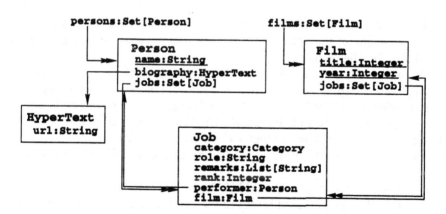

Fig. 4. The schema of the movie database

5.2 An Example Query on the IMDB

In the *WIND* -IMDB, let us retrieve *all persons (in alphabetical order), whose biography contains the words "neurotic" and "New York" or "New Yorker", and who appear in Woody Allen movies,* by the following *WINDsurf* -query:

```
1     sort p in (
2         select person
3         from person in persons
4         where person.biography.match("neurotic NEAR New York*")
5         and   exists film in
6                 (   select job.film
7                     from job in person.jobs
8                     where job.category = cast):
9                 (   exists director in
10                    (   select directing.person
11                        from directing in film.jobs
12                        where directing.category = direction):
13                    director.name = "Allen, Woody")
14        ) by p.name
15    ) @ HTMLDoc[UnorderedList[Link]]("Query result")
```

This query selects all persons with a biography matching the pattern ''neurotic NEAR New York*'' (line 4), for which there is a movie listing them as members of the cast (lines 6-8: category = cast) with a director category = direction named ''Allen, Woody'' (lines 9-13). The results are sorted alphabetically by name (line 14). In line 15 the format HTMLDoc is chosen, with title ''Query result'' and the body formatted as an UnorderedList of hyperlinks (format Link) to pages for the mentioned persons.

The predicate on line 4 is a pattern matching operation to be executed in the text archive. The other predicates must be processed in the OODBMS. The Query Optimizer produces the following execution plan:

1. The predicates of the original OQL query are executed in the OODBMS, with the exception of the NEAR predicate. The result is a list of cast members of all Woody Allen movies.
2. For each such person, the text is extracted from the person's biography page and stored in the text archive, where the pattern matching predicate is applied to it. For this extraction, a HTML-to-text converter is needed, belonging to the FCS of either the OODBMS or the text archive.
3. The persons filtered by the text archive are sorted by name.
4. The FCS of the OODBMS is used to transform the list of results in the format
   HTMLDoc[UnorderedList[Link]](''Query result'').
5. The HTML-page produced is sent to the web interface of the View Exporter

Format conversions are necessary in steps 2(a) and 4. Converters can be generated from object-grammars, which are introduced in the next section.

6   Object-Grammars

An *Object-Grammar* describes type dependent textual formats for objects. We discuss object-grammars only briefly. The full formalism can be found in [10].

6.1 Specifiying HTML Pages by an Object-Grammar

We show the use of object-grammars, by specifying simple web pages for persons in the movie database. A person's web page contains his/her name and links to all movies (s)he has been involved in. Variable parts are in *italics*:

```
<HTML><HEAD> <TITLE>Allen, Woody</TITLE> </HEAD>
    <BODY> <H1>Allen, Woody</H1>
        <OL>
            <LI><A HREF="/cache/title-exact/10478">Ants (1998)</A>
            ...
            <LI><A HREF="/cache/title-exact/55552">Laughmaker, The (1962)</A>
        </OL>
    </BODY></HTML>
```

A Person's HTML Page. The following object-grammar provides the SimpleHTML format representing persons as HTML pages.

```
1    Person @ SimpleHTML -->                    % Rule 1
2        "<HTML><HEAD><TITLE>" self.name "</TITLE></HEAD>"
3            "<BODY><H1>" self.name "</H1>"
4                self @ Films
5            "</BODY></HTML>"
```

Rule 1 describes the skeleton of a person's HTML page with **self** being bound to an object of class **Person**. The person's name occurs in the title (line 2) and the headline (line 3). The nonterminal expression **self@Films** in line 4 expands to the movie list of the person. This movie list is computed from the person's jobs by the query in lines 7–10 of rule 2 and formatted as **OrderedList**.

```
6    Person @ Films -->                         % Rule 2
7            (sort film in (
8                    select distinct job.film
9                    from job in self.jobs
10                   ) by -film.year, film.title) @ OrderedList
11   List[Film] @ OrderedList -->               % Rule 3
12           "<OL>" self @ Sequence "</OL>"
```

Rule 3 defines an OrderedList in HTML as a Sequence of elements enclosed in a pair of <OL>...</OL> tags. Format Sequence is defined in rule 4 as a wrapper for the recursive format From(.) defined by rule 5. It consists of two alternatives, selected by the constraints given in curly brackets. The first one (line 15) is empty and terminates the recursion, the other one (lines 16–18) represents the current element self[i] as ListItem and the list tail by recursion.

```
13   List[Film] @ Sequence --> self @ From(0)   % Rule 4
14   List[Film] @ From(i: Integer) -->          % Rule 5
15           { i >= self.count }
16         |   self[i]@ListItem
17             self@From(i+1)
18           { i < self.count }
```

Each film-list element is represented according to rule 6 by prepending a <LI> tag and then applying format Link as defined in rule 7 to provide a link to this film.

```
19    Film @ ListItem --> "<LI>" self@Link           % Rule 6
20    Film @ Link -->  % Rule 7
21       "<A HREF=" self.url ">" self.title "(" self.year ") </A>"
```

HTML links are specified using <A> elements. The destination URL (self.url) is given as HTML attribute HREF. The link is labeled with movie title and year.

Generalisation. The rules described above do not make use of modern software engineering concepts. By generalizing the formats OrderedList, ListItem, Sequence and From(.), we obtain generic, reusable formats:

In Rule 3 that defines format OrderedList, we generalize the type from List[Film] to the generic type List[G] and introduce a format parameter EltFormat, to be replaced with a format for the actual value of G.

```
22    List[G] @ OrderedList[EltFormat->G] -->        % Rule 3'
23          "<OL>" self @ Sequence[ListItem[EltFormat]] "</OL>"
```

Each list element in format OrderedList is represented as ListItem containing the element formatted in EltFormat. Hence ListItem takes EltFormat as a generic parameter. All list items are concatenated according to format Sequence, used for the list itself. The rules for Sequence, From and ListItem are generalized by making the object type generic and adding a format parameter:

```
24    List[G] @ Sequence[EltFormat->G] -->           % Rule 4'
25          self @ From[EltFormat](0)
26    List[G] @ From[EltFormat->G](i: Integer) --> % Rule 5'
27          { i>=self.count }
28       |  self[i] @ EltFormat
29          self @ From[EltFormat](i+1)
30          { i< self.count }
31    G @ ListItem[ItemFormat->G] -->               % Rule 6'
32          "<LI>" self @ ItemFormat
```

The generic formats described above can now be included in a standard library and used in other grammars, as well. In our case, the format Links in line 16 must be replaced by OrderedList[Link]. Rules 3–6 can then be omitted.

Example: Picasso's HTML Page. We now generate a filmography page for Pablo Picasso by applying format SimpleHTML to the object Person1 depicted in Fig. 5, which also contains the film objects "Le Testament d'Orphee" (1959) and "Le Mystere Picasso" (1956). The derivation tree is shown in Fig. 6. After each node, we indicate the rule used to expand this node.

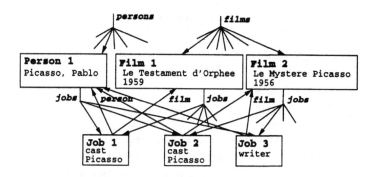

Fig. 5. Film projects of Picasso

6.2 The Formal Components of Object-Grammars

Formats are *described* by *format names* with an optional list of formal parameters attached to it. We define an actual *format* as a format name supplied with actual arguments. For representation of generic types, a *generic format* is described similarly by a *generic* format name supplied with actual parameters.

A *nonterminal* in an object-grammar is a pair $\tau@\phi$, where τ is a type and ϕ a format name. A grammar rule may be defined for any nonterminal $\tau@\phi$, and is inherited by all subtypes of τ unless it is redefined.

On the right hand of an object-grammar rule, we have *nonterminal expressions* instead of simple nonterminals. A nonterminal expression is a pair $t@f$ representing an object expression t in a format f (with format name ϕ). Different nonterminals and rules correspond to the actual type τ of the value of t. We call these nonterminals $\tau@\phi$ *potential nonterminals* of $t@f$.

By replacing all nonterminal expressions by potential nonterminals, we obtain for each object-grammar rule an equivalent, but arbitrarily large set of standard context free productions. This demonstrates the conciseness of object-grammars in comparison with standard context free grammars.

Object-grammars support queries in nonterminal expressions and constraints. This is a powerful feature: (i) Queries allow textual representations to be based on database views. (ii) Constraints can be used to determine the applicability of a rule and to bind variables. Parsing means solving these constraints and finding a new consistent database state containing the parsed information.

6.3 Using Object-Grammars in WIND

In the *WIND* architecture, object-grammars are used for both query *and* data translation. Incoming queries (coded for instance as URLs) must be translated by the View Exporter into *WINDsurf* queries. Subquery execution plans are sent to the DRs as objects and translated into the local query language by the query transformer. Object-grammars can generate converters to handle both types of translation.

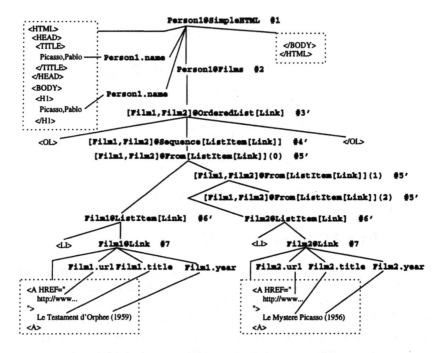

Fig. 6. Derivation of Picasso's HTML page

Arguments and results of subqueries towards a DR are translated to/from the repository internal data representation using format converters provided by the format conversion services of the *WIND*-Wrapper, as shown in Fig. 3. Object-grammars are developed against some DR schema and feeded into a converter generator as shown in Fig. 7. The converters thus generated are then used in the *WIND*-Wrapper.

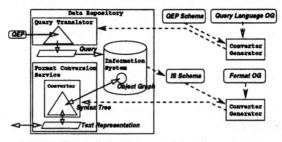

Fig. 7. Generation and use of format converters

7 Object-Grammars for the Internet Movie Database

We continue the example of modelling IMDB as a *WIND* instance by specifying the translation of the `actors.list` source file into database objects. The file contains one record per actor, as shown in Fig. 1.

Rule 1. The format Actors for a person set is based on all persons having a Job of category cast in some film. Lines 2–7 show a query specifying a sorted list of these persons. This list is expected in format Sequence (see section 6.1) with each Person formatted in the Actor style (see Rule 2). To import `actors.list` into the database, we parse it with start symbol persons @ Actors, updating the subset of all actors in persons with the actor descriptions from the file.

```
1    Set[Person] @ Actors -->                        % Rule 1
2           (sort actor in (
3                   select distinct person
4                   from person in self
5                   where exists job in person.jobs:
6                         job.category = cast
7                   ) by actor.name) @ Sequence[Actor]
```

Rule 2. The constraint of the rule (line 17) requires an actor to be member of persons. An existing Person object with primary key name is selected from this set. Otherwise, a new Person object is inserted and self is bound to it.

Each person's record begins with her full name. A list of appearances in films follows. It consists of the person's acting jobs sorted by film title and year formatted as a Sequence of Appearances:

```
8    Person @ Actor -->                              % Rule 2
9           self.name
10          (sort appearance in
11             (  select job
12                from job in self.jobs
13                where job.category = cast
14             ) by       -appearance.film.year,
15                         appearance.film.title
16          ) @ Sequence[Appearance(self)]   "\n"
17          { self in persons }
```

Rule 3. Each appearance of a person in a film consists of the MovieTitle of the film, optional remarks, the role name and optionally the person's rank in the credits. When parsing a Job in format Appearance, the respective attributes are set; person is set to actor and category is set to the constant cast:

```
18   Job @ Appearance(actor: Person) -->      "\t"    % Rule 3
19          self.film @ MovieTitle
20          self.remarks @ Sequence[Remark]
21          "[" self.role "]"
22          self.rank @ Rank          "\n"
23          { self.person = actor, self.category = cast }
```

Rules 4–6. In format `MovieTitle`, a film is represented by its title, followed by its production year. The constraint requires this film to be an element of `films`. The primary key formed by title and year selects an existing film from this set; otherwise a new `Film` object will be inserted. Rules 5 and 6 describe the `Remark` format for strings and a format for an optional integer rank.

```
24    Film @ MovieTitle --> self.title "("self.year")" % Rule 4
25           { self in films }
26    String @ Remark --> "(" self ")"                  % Rule 5
27    Integer @ Rank -->              { self = 0 }      % Rule 6
28               | "<" self ">"       { self != 0 }
```

8 Conclusions

Information from the Internet is retrieved mainly by browsing and searching on index servers. Database-like queries are supported only to a limited extent because most web documents lack an explicit schema and the Internet is practically unlimited. Another problem is to support user-specific views with respect to both the content and the format of the presented data.

In this work, we presented the *WIND* architecture offering solutions for both aspects of Internet data retrieval. We focus on domain-specific information integration. A core of domain-relevant information is loaded in advance, additional information is retrieved on demand. Data can be maintained in multiple presentations in different Data Repositories. The *WIND*-Server queries and updates the Data Repositories in a uniform manner. Translation of queries and postprocessing of the results for each Data Repository is performed by its *WIND*-Wrapper.

A key to our methodology for a flexible view of the Internet is the generation of format converters from object-grammars, as opposed to ad hoc solutions. For transformations between documents and objects, we propose the *object-grammar* formalism and show its appropriateness by examples.

The implementation of the *WIND* components poses several challenges like the automatic generation of format converters, the optimization of processing requests comprised of conventional subqueries and format conversion requests, and update propagation from the Internet sources to local representations. The aims of our current research cover three orthogonal issues: (x) For the support of different representations and querying mechanisms over documents we focus on the development of efficient parsing and unparsing algorithms for object-grammars and on the implementation of a format converter generator. (y) To establish a working *WIND* prototype, we focus on the crystallization of the *WINDsurf* syntax and on the development of some example Query Translators. (z) For the support of information extraction using domain-specific knowledge, we focus on the design of an information retrieval mechanism in the Internet Loader, in which descriptors of domain information are exploited for filtering and ranking.

References

1. K. Aberer, K. Böhm, and C. Hüser. The prospects of publishing using advanced database concepts. *Electronic Publishing*, 6(4):469–480, dec 1993.
2. S. Abiteboul, S. Cluet, and T. Milo. Querying and updating the file. In *19th VLDB Conf.*, volume 19, pages 73–85, 8 1993.
3. S. Abiteboul, S. Cluet, and T. Milo. A database interface for file update. In *SIGMOD '95*, pages 386–397, 1995.
4. S. Abiteboul, S. Cluet, and T. Milo. Correspondence and translation for heterogeneous data. In *ICDT '97*, number 1186 in LNCS, pages 351–363, 1997.
5. R. Cattell. *The Object Database Standard, ODMG-93*. Morgan Kaufmann, 1994.
6. S. Chaudhuri and L. Gravano. Optimizing queries over multimedia repositories. In *SIGMOD'96*, pages 91–102, Montreal, Canada, June 1996. ACM.
7. S. Chawathe, H. Garcia-Molina, J. Hammer, K. Ireland, Y. Papakonstantinou, J. Ullman, and J. Widom. The TSIMMIS project: Integration of heterogeneous information sources. In *Proc. of the 100th Anniv. Meeting*, pages 7–18. Information Processing Society of Japan, 1994.
8. O. Etzioni. The World-Wide Web: Quagmire or gold mine? *CACM*, 39(11):65–68, Nov. 1996.
9. R. Fagin. Combining fuzzy informationm from multiple systems. In *PODS'96*, pages 216–226, Montreal, Canada, June 1996. ACM.
10. L. Faulstich, V. Linnemann, and M. Spiliopoulou. Using object-grammars for internet data warehousing. Technical report, Institut für Informationssysteme, Med. Universität Lübeck, 1997. <http://www.inf.fu-berlin.de/~faulstic/wind.ps>.
11. U. Fayyad, G. Piatetsky-Shapiro, and P. Smyth. The KDD process for extracting useful knowledge from volumes of data. *CACM*, 39(11):27–34, Nov. 1996.
12. A. Feng and T. Wakayama. SIMON: A grammar-based transformation system for structured documents. *Electronic Publishing*, 6(4):361–372, Dec. 1993.
13. W. Inmon. EIS and the data warehouse: a simple approach to building an effective foundation for EIS. *Database Programming & Design*, 5(11):70–73, nov 1992.
14. W. Inmon. The data warehouse and data mining. *CACM*, 39(11):49–50, Nov. 1996.
15. W. Inmon and C. Kelley. *Rdb/VMS: Developing the Data Warehouse*. QED Publishing Group, Boston, Massachusetts, 1993.
16. E. Kuikka and M. Penttonen. Transformation of structured documents with the use of grammar. *Electronic Publishing*, 6(4):373–383, Dec. 1993.
17. A. Y. Levy, A. Rajaraman, and J. J. Ordille. Querying Heterogeneous Information Sources Using Source Descriptions. In *22th VLDB Conf.*, pages 251–262, 1996.
18. J. Paakki. Attribute grammar paradigms: A high-level methodology in language implementation. *ACM Computing Surveys*, 27(2):196–255, June 1995.
19. U. Stutschka and V. Linnemann. Attributierte grammatiken als werkzeug zur datenmodellierung. In G. Lausen, editor, *BTW'95*, pages 160–178, 1995.

An Object Versioning System to Support Collaborative Design within a Concurrent Engineering Context*

I. Santoyridis[1], T.W. Carnduff[2], W.A. Gray[1] and J.C. Miles[3]

[1] Department of Computer Science, University of Wales–Cardiff, UK
[2] University of Wales–Institute Cardiff, UK
[3] Cardiff School of Engineering, University of Wales–Cardiff, UK

Abstract. Engineering design is a collaborative and evolutionary process, involving designers from many disciplines. It is traditionally performed as a series of consecutive tasks, with any failures causing control to be passed back to the preceding task. If some or all of the design phases are able to be executed concurrently instead of sequentially, major improvements can be achieved. This approach is called Concurrent Engineering. This paper defines an object Versioning System to Support Collaborative Design within a Concurrent Engineering context. An initial model of this system based on a three-level hierarchical partition of the engineering database and five different version states of design artefact, was tested in a collaborative bridge design experiment. The results of the experiment showed that this model was useful, but several improvements were needed. The presented version of this system is the initial model augmented with extra functionality identified by the experiment. The implementation of this system in an OODBMS is discussed.

Keywords : object–oriented databases, versioning, configuration management, engineering design, concurrent engineering

1 Introduction

Engineering design is a process involving people from many disciplines (e.g. mechanical, electrical etc.), dealing with the project in hand from different perspectives. A common practice is to decompose the design of the targeted product into several well-defined subcomponents, which may be then further decomposed recursively into other subcomponents, whose design is assigned to groups of designers. As Rosenman [1] argues, any object which is not treated as a single element can be decomposed along structural lines into other objects. The nature of engineering design, as described above, means it must utilise the best possible coordination of the activities of participants coming from different disciplines or designing different subcomponents, hence making it a *collaborative* effort. A

---

* The work reported in this paper, is part of the DESCRIBE project, and is partially supported by EPSRC.

design process is also *evolutionary*, as designers generate several refinements and alternatives of the artefacts they design before they finally develop the desired solution [2].

This paper presents an *Object Versioning Support System for Collaborative Design* (VSSCD), which uses an *Object Oriented Database Management System* (OODBMS) to support the design process. Database support for the engineering design process has been an important area of research during the past decade, resulting in the emergence of several research prototypes as well as commercially available design support database tools [3][4]. Their main functionality is based on the provision of a *versioning scheme*, reflecting the collaborative and evolutionary nature of design. We review these systems in Section 2. This led to our initial conceptual model of VSSCD which was evaluated in an experiment we conducted. A brief description of the experiment and its results is given in Section 3. In Section 4 we describe the revised conceptual model of VSSCD resulted from this experiment. Implementation issues concerning the development of VSSCD are discussed in Section 5, while Section 6 concludes the paper and outlines our future plans.

2 Related Work

Traditionally engineering design is performed as a series of consecutive tasks (e.g. requirements definition, conceptual design, detailed design, construction/manufacturing, marketing). If inconsistencies or failures are detected during one task's execution, caused by insufficient or incorrect information from the previous task, control is passed back, thus creating an iterative mode of operation where the subsequent task is suspended until the preceding one is finished. This process, known as *Sequential Engineering* (SE), can be extremely time–consuming and expensive. If design phases are able to be executed in parallel, using well–founded assumptions about the other designers' perception of the problem in hand and means of communication, major improvements can be achieved in key areas like development time, number of design changes, product quality, time to market and return on assets. This approach is called *Concurrent Engineering* (CE) and its essence is defined as the merging of the efforts of design engineers, manufacturing engineers, marketing and service personnel, and all other people involved in the product and manufacturing process improvement [5].

The collaborative and evolutionary nature of the earlier stage of the design process within the CE environment results in several refinements and alternatives of the product and its parts, until the achievement of the desired design. These intermediate stages of the product and its parts, referred to as *versions* in the literature, have to be stored and managed by a database management system as their use facilitates the engineering design process. A comprehensive analysis of the terminology and the various aspects of database version management is provided by Katz in [3].

Our work concentrates on the development of a database tool, based on a versioning scheme, to support collaborative design within the context of CE.

Most of the researchers in the area point to the suitability of OODBMSs as the storage and management tool to model a design artefacts' versioning, and to support CE in general, because of the tight integration of data and process they provide. In [6] an analogy between the object–oriented and engineering design concepts is provided. A detailed comparison of such systems, regarding the support they provide for engineering design, can be found in [4].

Design artefacts are usually structurally complex as they are composed of other artefacts which in turn may recursively consist of others. This makes version management more complicated as it has to provide for the *configuration management* of the *composite* artefacts and their *components*, i.e. it has to determine which version of each component belongs to which version of the composite artefact.

One method for versioning support found in the literature, is based on a *three–level hierarchical division* of the engineering database, with a different type of version residing at each level. In the *Version Server* proposed in [7] a new version is generated by a designer checking an existing version from his(her) group's *shared workspace* into his(her) *public workspace* by copying it, and after the required modifications checking it out back to the shared one in order for it to be accessible by the other group's members. An *archive workspace* is used to store finished designs and is accessible to all the project's designers. A three–level engineering database hierarchy is presented in [8] with the *public* database at the highest level holding versions which are in the *released* state (non–updatable and accessible to all designers), the *project* databases at the middle level holding versions which are in the *working* state (stable but not validated and accessible only to the corresponding subproject's designers) and the *private* databases at the lower level holding versions which are in the *transient* state (updatable and accessible only by the corresponding owner designer). A new version is created by means of *check-in/check-out*, *derivation* from another version in the same state and *promotion* from a version in a lower state to a version in a higher one. Composite–component references are handled either *statically* by the user defining which component object belongs to which composite or *dynamically* in which case the reference resolves to the component's *default* version (usually the most recent one).

A more open and flexible database architecture is proposed in the *Distributed Version Storage Server* (DVSS) [9] and in the *Environment for the Design of Control System* (EDICS) [10]. DVSS provides distributed access to distributed objects with partition transparency and mainly deals with the support of storage requirements. In EDICS the design database architecture can be thought of as a three–layered structure where objects are arranged into hierarchies of *project*, *version* and *component* nodes. Composite objects are treated as the basic elements of the version derivation process while *incremental behaviour representation* records, created for each component that has been altered, are used to define its actual behaviour. Nevertheless, none of these systems provide a clear database and version classification reflecting the project's organization.

A rather different approach is presented in [11] where versioning is performed at the database granularity. A *multiversion database* is defined as a set of logically independent database versions while *database version stamps* are used to identify which version of each object belongs to which database version. Composite–component references are resolved dynamically using a *relationship table* for each object where each one of its versions is associated with the database versions to which it belongs. All these rather complex relationships between the database versions and the object versions impose a substantial maintenance overhead. Another approach to engineering data versioning is based on the provision of *predefined system classes* which are used to provide the necessary functionality to the design objects [12][13]. However, these systems do not provide the means for cooperative design as they do not deal with database partitioning.

The model proposed in [2] aims to support version management in a CE environment. Depending on the ability of an application to modify the contents of a version its state can be *active, suspended, declared* or *removed*, while based on status and access rights it could be *frozen, published, archived* or *persistent*. An *assembly* is a complex entity resulting from a composite modelling operation on a set of component instances, thus developing a component hierarchy. It can be *total*, describing a complete design from a particular discipline including at least one instance of each entity in that discipline, or *partial*, allowing it to be combined with other assemblies to form more complex ones. A *configuration* is a set of total assemblies, one from each discipline, and a set of constraints.

We believe that an engineering design support tool has to model the way that designers actually design. As Oxman argues in [14], experimentation can be employed as a means to develop a theoretical framework of the design process which can guide the development of design tools. We didn't find in the literature, experimental evaluation of any of the versioning systems presented above. In contrast with the other systems, VSSCD's functionality is based on the results of an experimental engineering design project.

3 Testing a Versioning System with an Experimental Bridge Design

In this section we present the conceptual model of our VSSCD as it was formed initially. It is based on a three–level hierarchical division of the engineering database and has been influenced by the versioning systems described in references [7] and [8]. We also briefly describe an experiment we conducted to evaluate the working of this model. A more detailed description of the experiment and its results can be found in [15] and [16].

3.1 Initial Conceptual Model of VSSCD

The design effort of an engineering project can be split into several subprojects according to the targeted product's structural and functional specifications. The structure of a project and its supporting database, as it was simulated in the experimental bridge design, is illustrated in Fig.1. A group of *individual designers*

(IDs) is allocated to each one of the subprojects in order to accomplish the design of the specified subcomponent of the product. Each one of the IDs works with his(her) own *private* database. Apart from the IDs each group is linked to a *subproject manager* (SM) who is responsible for the subproject's progress. Each SM owns a *subproject* database which is accessible by all the corresponding group's IDs and is used to store information relevant to the subproject's task. The whole project is administered by the *project manager* (PM), who is in contact with the SMs in order to pass any new major design decisions to them. The PM owns the *project* database, which is accessible by all the SMs and IDs and holds information relevant to the whole project.

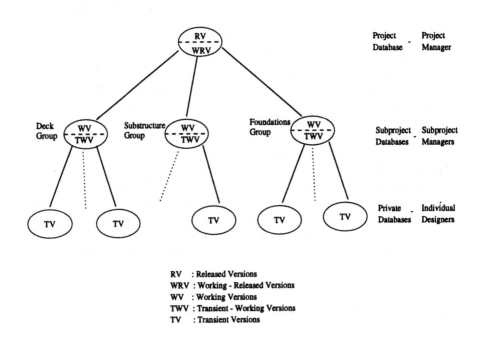

RV   : Released Versions
WRV : Working - Released Versions
WV   : Working Versions
TWV : Transient - Working Versions
TV   : Transient Versions

Fig. 1. Experimental project and database three–level hierarchy

Versions of design artefacts can be in one of five different states depending on which database level they reside in and their read–write permissions. These states are (from the lowest to the highest) *transient* (TV), *transient–working* (TWV), *working* (WV), *working–released* (WRV) and *released* (RV). The semantics of TVs, WVS and RVs are similar to the corresponding version states described in [8]. TWVs, residing in the subproject databases, and WRVs, residing in the project database, are added as a means of intra-group and inter-group communication respectively, before a version's promotion.

New versions are created by making a copy of another version of the same artefact, in one of three ways :

- by *deriving* a new version from another being in the same state
- by *checking–out* a version from a higher database level to a lower one
- by *promoting* a lower state version to a higher one by *checking* (copying) it from a lower level database *into* a higher level one

Fig.1 shows the different states of versions and the database level where they reside. Version evolution is modelled using *version creation graphs* (VCG) with arcs pointing from the *parent* version to the one(s) created from it, called its *child(ren)* (see Fig.2).

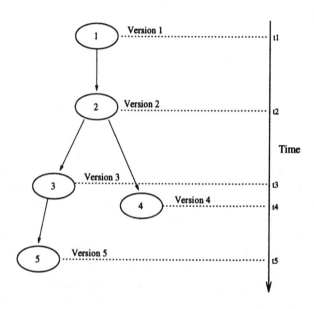

Fig. 2. Example of a version creation graph

Configuration management of structurally complex design artefacts is performed by the IDs in their private databases. This means that *component* objects can only have TVs, as the IDs are only allowed to promote to a TWV those versions of artefacts not belonging to any *composite*. Complex artefacts are modelled using *composition graphs* (CGs), with arcs starting from the composite and ending at its components (see example in Fig.3). It is the ID's responsibility to decide if a new TV of the composite will be created or not, when new TVs of its components are created.

3.2 The Experiment

We conducted an experiment where the model described in Sub-section 3.1 was simulated. The design task of the experiment was to prepare the conceptual

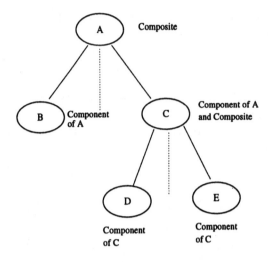

Fig. 3. Composition graph for artefact A

design of a road bridge crossing a dual two–lane highway. The designers (final year, undergraduate, civil engineering students) were divided into three groups designing the *deck* (4 IDs), the *foundation* (3 IDs) and the *substructure* (3 IDs). Each group of IDs had a postgraduate research student playing the role of the SM while one of this paper's authors was the project's PM.

The experiment took place in one room with the three groups working around three different tables. The participants' interactions were recorded by means of *forms*, which had to be filled in by the person initiating the interaction and then passed to the receiver, accompanied by any other documents (e.g. sketches, results of calculations). This gave us a record of all interactions. There was a form for each type of version derivation and promotion. Configuration management of composite artefacts had to be performed solely by the IDs.

It should be mentioned at this point that we consider the results of the experiment as only an indication of how team design is performed. The fact that we used undergraduate students as the IDs, having to produce the design of a bridge within three hours, obviously had an impact on the experiment's "realism".

After analysing the forms filled in by the participants, we came to some very interesting conclusions. The results showed that the initial model was in the right direction. Nevertheless, several deficiencies also emerged, the most important of which were :

- The fixed three–level hierarchy with versions being in five different states proved (as one might expect) to be rather inflexible. The IDs tended to neglect filling in the TWV and WRV version promotion forms, an indication that they considered them to be rather unnecessary and counterproductive to their work. This led us to the conclusion that a more flexible structure is needed.

- Instead of designing in isolation they tended to design together with their fellow group members, including their SM. The main reason for this communication were the artefacts' *interface attributes* and *constraints*, which determine the way a composite artefact interacts with its components as well as how the components interact among themselves.
- Configuration management could not be restricted to the IDs, as in some cases the other interested parties needed information about one of its components or even about an attribute and not the whole artefact.

4 Conceptual Design of VSSCD

The database and versioning support for engineering provided by VSSCD is an amalgamation of our initial version and extra functionality which the experiment showed is necessary.

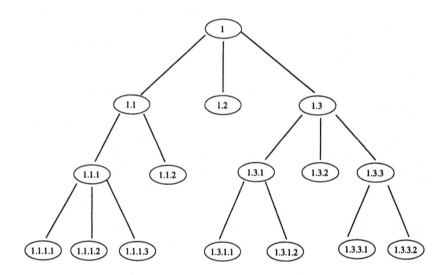

Fig. 4. Composition graph of targeted product

Assume that the CG for the targeted product, is the one depicted in Fig.4. The examples in the rest of this paper, refer to this figure. We assume that every node with no 'children' cannot be decomposed any further i.e. it represents a *non-composite* artefact (e.g. nodes 1.2, 1.1.2, 1.3.2). The project is partitioned into a number of *sub-projects* (a sub-project can be further partitioned into sub-sub-projects and so on) designing well-defined sub-components of the targeted product. Each of these sub-projects has a group of designers assigned to it, with one or more of them being the group's *local administrator(s)* (LA). An LA, apart from designing the artefacts assigned to him(her), supervises the progress of the task undertaken by his(her) group. Each artefact is assigned to one or more designers and each designer works on one or more artefacts. One or more designers are the *project administrators* (PA) and apart from being responsible for the top level artefact of the CG, supervise the whole project's design process.

4.1 Version States

VSSCD supports only three of the original version states (TVs, WVs and RVs), which have different semantics. The use of TWVs and WRVs was proved by the experiment to be redundant. A new version state, *working–abstraction* (WAV), has been introduced, to provide for inter-disciplinary communication in a CE context.

Transient Versions When designers are experimenting with the artefacts assigned to them they create TVs. Their semantics are :

- They are visible only to the owner designer and if requested to other group members. The granting of conditional read access rights to TVs designed by other group members has been added to VSSCD because during the experiment, we observed that designers of the same group were communicating before publishing their designs.
- TVs of non-composite artefacts are created by copying another TV of the same artefact, and after making changes.
- TVs of composite artefacts are created by changing the versions of their components. The component versions must be WVs and if owned by the composite's owner, they may also be TVs (see example in Fig.6). Versions of components not owned by the composite's owner may be TVs as well, provided that their owner has granted access to them.
- TVs of both non-composite and composite artefacts can be created by checking out a WV or RV (i.e. by copying it).
- They can be updated or deleted by the owner designer.

Working Versions WVs of artefacts are used to publish designs of artefacts considered as stable by their designers. The WVs' semantics are :

- They are visible to all designers of a discipline. This is another important difference with the initial model where WVs of an artefact were only visible to the members of the group designing it. If the artefact in question is composite, containing TVs of one or more of its components, they are also promoted to WVs
- They can be created in one of three ways :
  - by promoting a TV of the corresponding artefact, in which case a new copy of the corresponding version is created

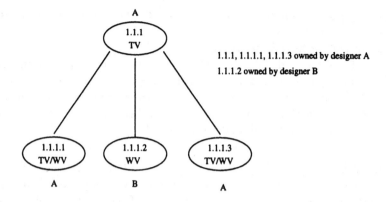

Fig. 5. Transient version of a composite artefact

- by changing a components' version (only for composite artefacts). The component's versions must be WVs (see Fig.7) and
- by demoting an RV of the corresponding artefact

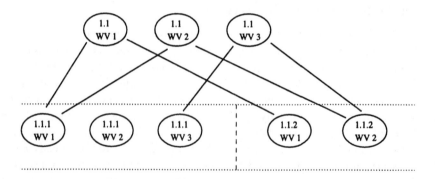

Fig. 6. Creation of a new composite WV by changing the components' versions

– They can neither be updated nor deleted.

Released Versions RVs represent artefacts which are in an accepted state. Their semantics are :

– They are visible to all designers.
– They are created by promoting a WV of the corresponding artefact (no copying takes place). If the artefact in question is composite, containing WVs of one or more of its components, their owners are asked to promote them to RVs. As a result of this, an RV of a composite may have one or more

of its components missing, when there is not a WV of it mature enough to be promoted to an RV.

- RVs can neither be deleted nor updated.
- At any time, only one RV of each artefact may exist, representing its development phase at that time. The current RV of an artefact may change either by creating a new RV and making it current, or by repromoting a WV which was RV at some earlier stage, but had been demoted. At that point, the current RV is demoted, and becomes a WV.

Working–Abstraction Versions WAVs are used to share information between designers from different disciplines. Before a WV is promoted to an RV, it is important to assess whether the change will affect other disciplines. Their semantics are as follow :

- They are visible to all designers.
- They are created by promoting a WV of the corresponding artefact, in which case a new copy of the corresponding version is created.
- They cannot be updated but they may be deleted by the owner of the corresponding artefact.

4.2 A Collaborative Design Scenario

The design of the product is split into well-defined subcomponents, by the PA(s), and are assigned to groups of designers each of which has its own LA(s). The subcomponents may be further decomposed by the owner LAs and this decomposition may proceed recursively, depending on the project's size. At any level, the interface between a composite artefact and its components, as well as between the components is initially specified. This interface, which consists of a set of constraints, has to be well-defined. At the end of this process, the first WVs for every composite and component artefact are created, mainly specifying all the necessary initial interfaces and perhaps some initial parameter values. Nevertheless, some interfaces between artefacts may remain unspecified until later stages of the design process when more information will become available.

The designers then start designing the artefacts assigned to them, by creating TVs, which are visible only to the owner designers. However, read access of interface parameters of TVs (or even of the whole TVs) may be granted to other designers designing components of the same composite or the composite itself, so that they can examine whether the designs are consistent with the specified interface. This communication may result in the definition of a different interface, specified in new TVs for the artefacts involved.

When a TV of an artefact is consistent with all the specified interfaces and its owner designer believes that it is a stable design, it is promoted to a WV. At that point, every designer of the specific discipline is enabled to read the WV and use it in any designs and calculations.

When a designer considers a WV of an artefact he(she) designs, to be in a generally accepted state, he(she) may promote it to an RV. At that point, the owners of WVs of components participating in that design, are asked to promote them to RVs. Note that the RV of the artefact may not be complete i.e. it might have some components missing if they have no WVs which are interface consistent or mature enough at that time (e.g. there may exist an RV of artefact 1 missing an RV of component 1.3). Before the promotion to RV, WVs of the the whole artefact or of some of its components, may be promoted to WAVs and sent to the other disciplines involved in the project, so that their design consistency can be checked.

If the design is considered unsatisfactory, the RV is demoted back to a WV, and redesigning of the whole product or parts of it (e.g. by changing the interfaces or other attributes of the components) takes place in the same fashion as described above. This process may be repeated many times until the resulting design satisfies the desired requirements.

5 Implementation Issues

VSSCD will be implemented using the C++ interface library of the ObjectStore OODBMS [17]. A detailed description of the ObjectStore functionality can be found in [18][19]. The main reason behind this OODBMS choice, is the facilities it offers to support collaborative groupwork. This functionality is mainly provided via the following two library classes :

os_workspace : provides for both shared and private work. Instances of this class form a parent/child hierarchy of arbitrary depth, so there can be many degrees of sharing and privacy.

os_configuration : serves to group together objects that are to be treated as a unit for the purposes of versioning. Instances of this class are the versioning units.

However, ObjectStore's versioning scheme has features not suited to our model, the most important ones being that (a) all workspaces in a hierarchy store versions of objects residing in the same database and (b) each workspace provides access to only one version of each object. In VSSCD each designer has his(her) own database where all versions of the artefacts he(she) designs are stored. We tackle this problem by creating two classes *versioned_database* and *versioned_artefact*, which inherit from the system classes *os_database* and *os_configuration* respectively and hide the functionality of class *os_workspace*.

5.1 Database Structure

Designers at all levels store the versions of the artefacts they design in their databases (one database for each designer). Each designer's database has a *private* part, storing TVs, and a *public* part, storing WVs, WAVs and RVs. However, as mentioned above, access to specific TVs stored in the private partitions of the databases may be granted, when necessary. The database model is illustrated in Fig.8. The public partitions of all the designers' databases may be thought of as a distributed database providing read access to the designs stored in it, to all designers of a discipline. ObjectStore's *cross-database pointers*, which are pointers from one database to another, are utilised to provide for access between the designers' databases.

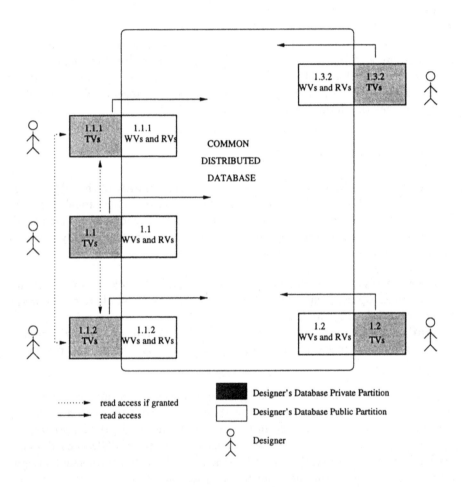

Fig. 7. Engineering design project database model

5.2 Implementation of Version States

Version evolution is often implemented by using VCGs, as shown in Fig.3, exploiting the *parent–child* relationship between nodes, that such a data structure offers. However, the definition of several version states makes such a representation unsuitable for all types of version in VSSCD, apart from the TVs of non-composite artefacts. Representing TVs of composite artefacts, and WVs of both non-composite and composite ones with VCGs is problematic. In the first case the fact that the component versions may be of arbitrary order, makes unclear which version of the composite has been derived from which (see example in Fig.9), while in the second, the fact that any TV may be promoted to a WV, makes the maintenance of the parent–child relationship for the WVs very difficult (see example in Fig.10). In both these cases, the artefact versions can be ordered at the time of their creation, and hence a *list* data structure is suitable for their implementation.

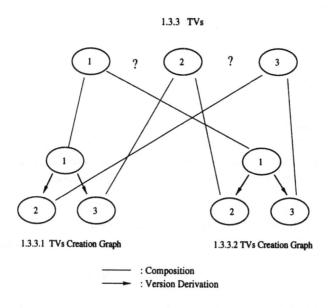

1.3.3 TVs

1.3.3.1 TVs Creation Graph   1.3.3.2 TVs Creation Graph

——— : Composition
——▸ : Version Derivation

Fig. 8. Example of the ambiguous relationships between composite artefact's 1.3.3 TVs

Each designer stores the TVs of the artefacts he(she) designs in the private partition of his(her) database. When a TV is promoted to a WV, a copy of the version is made and stored in the public partition of his(her) database. When a WV is promoted to an RV, no copying takes place but a flag indicating that the specific version is the current RV for the artefact, is set set to true. If this RV is later demoted to a WV this flag is set back to false.

6   Conclusions and Future Work

We presented an Object Versioning System to Support Collaborative Design within a CE context. The initial model of VSSCD was based on a three-level hierarchical partition of the engineering database. An artefact's version could be

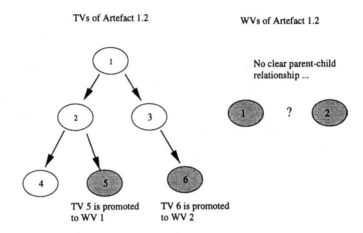

Fig. 9. Example of the ambiguous relationships between artefact's 1.2 WVs

in five predefined states (TV, TWV, WV, WRV and RV). The initial model of VSSCD was tested in an experimental collaborative bridge design. The results showed that the initial model was a good base but it had several deficiencies. This led us to make improvements to VSSCD the most important of which were :

- redefinition of the semantics of TVs, WVs and RVs
- dropping of the TWVs and WRVs as unnecessary
- definition of a new version state, *working–abstraction*, providing for inter-disciplinary communication
- definition of a more flexible engineering database structure

A prototype of VSSCD has been implemented. Our main effort in the near future, will concentrate on completing and testing the implementation of this prototype. It is our intention to enhance VSSCD's functionality with a conflict resolution facility providing for the resolution of conflicts arising when designs of different designers are incompatible. A second experiment is planned, with the use of computers, after the completion of VSSCD's implementation development, in order to test the resulted system.

References

1. Rosenman, M.A. "Dynamic Decomposition Strategies in the Conceptual Modelling of Design Objects". *Concurrent Engineering : Research and Applications*, 1(1):31–38, March 1993.
2. Krishnamurthy, K. and K.H. Law. "A Data Management Model for Design Change Control". *Concurrent Engineering : Research and Applications*, 3(4):329–343, December 1995.

3. Katz, R.H. "Towards a Unifying Framework for Version Modeling in Engineering Databases". *ACM Computing Surveys*, 22(4):376–408, December 1990.

4. Ahmed, S., A. Wong, D. Sriram, and R. Logcher. "Object–Oriented Database Management Systems for Engineering : a Comparison". *Journal of Object Oriented Programming*, pages 27–44, June 1992.

5. Zhang, H.C. and D. Zhang. "Concurrent Engineering : An Overview from Manufacturing Engineering Perspectives". *Concurrent Engineering : Research and Applications*, 3(3):221–236, September 1995.

6. LeBlanc, A.R. and G.M. Fadel. "Design Data Storage and Extraction Using Objects". *Concurrent Engineering : Research and Applications*, 1(1):31–38, March 1993.

7. Katz, R.H. and E. Chang. "Managing Change in a Computer-Aided Design Database". In *Proceedings of the 13th VLDB Conference*, pages 455–462, 1987.

8. Chou, H.T. and W. Kim. " A Unifying Framework for Version Control in a CAD Environment". In *Proceedings of the 12th VLDB Conference*, pages 336–344, 1986.

9. Ecklund, D.J., E.F. Ecklund, Jr., R.O.Eifrig, and F.M.Tonge. "DVSS : A Distributed Version Storage Server for CAD Applications". In *Proceedings of the 13th VLDB Conference*, pages 443–454, 1987.

10. Machura, M. "Managing Information in a Co-operative Object Database System". *Software–Practice and Experience*, 26(5):545–579, May 1996.

11. Cellary, W. and G. Jomier. "Consistency of Versions in Object Oriented Databases". In *Proceedings of the 16th VLDB Conference*, pages 432–441, 1990.

12. Ahmed, R. and S.B. Navathe. "Version Management of Composite Objects in CAD Databases". In *Proceedings of the ACM SIGMOD International Conference on Management of Data*, pages 218–227, 1991.

13. Talens, G., C. Oussalah, and M.F. Colinas. "Versions of Simple and Composite Objects". In *Proceedings of the 19th VLDB Conference*, pages 62–72, 1993.

14. Oxman, R. "Observing the Observers : Research Issues in Analysing Design Activity". *Design Studies*, 16(4):275–283, April 1995.

15. Miles, J.C., C.J. Moore, W.A. Gray, T.W. Carnduff, and I.Santoyridis. "Information Flows Between Designers - An Experimental Study". In *Proceedings of the 3rd Workshop of the European Group for Structural Engineering Applications of Artificial Intelligence*, pages 13–15, Glasgow, UK, August 1996.

16. Santoyridis, I., T.W. Carnduff, W.A. Gray, and J.C. Miles. "A Generic Configurable Versioning System for Cooperative Engineering Design : Conclusions from a Bridge Design Experiment". *Submitted for publication in "Concurrent Engineering : Research and Applications"*, 1996.

17. Object Design, Inc. *"ObjectStore C++ API Reference Release 4"*, June 1995.

18. Object Design, Inc. *"ObjectStore C++ API User Guide Release 4"*, June 1995.

19. Lamb, C., G. Landis, J. Orenstein, and D. Weinreb. "The ObjectStore Database System". *Communications of the ACM*, 34(10):50–63, October 1991.

Schema Integration with Integrity Constraints

Stefan Conrad   Michael Höding   Gunter Saake   Ingo Schmitt   Can Türker

Institut für Technische Informationssysteme
Otto-von-Guericke-Universität Magdeburg
Postfach 4120, D–39016 Magdeburg
E-mail: {conrad|hoeding|saake|schmitt|tuerker}@iti.cs.uni-magdeburg.de

Abstract. In this paper we discuss the use and treatment of integrity constraints in the federated database design process. We consider different situations occurring frequently in the schema transformation and schema integration process. Based on that, general rules are given which describe the correct treatment of integrity constraints. Other proposed integration approaches do not consider integrity constraints at all or are restricted to special kinds of constraints. Therefore, our approach can be used to extend or complete existing integration methodologies.

1   Introduction

Considering the current situation in enterprises we can discover that many different information systems are used in different parts of the enterprise. Furthermore, there is an increasing need to get a uniform access to the heterogeneous databases lying behind those information systems. The aim is to obtain a federated database system in the sense of [13]. Besides a uniform access to data stored in different database systems, migration of applications and data from one database system to another one is an additional motivation for building federated database systems [8].

The integration of heterogeneous databases is a well-known problem. A large number of approaches for integrating the local schemata of such databases have been proposed up to now, e.g. [14, 2, 10, 5]. Unfortunately, most approaches do not take integrity constraints into consideration, or if they respect constraints they only capture certain kinds of constraints [9].

The aim of this paper is to give a survey about the problems arising when integrating schemata and their integrity constraints. Due to the heterogeneity of data models used for local schemata, the first step of schema integration is usually a transformation of the local schemata into schemata expressed in a common data model. Together with the schemata the integrity constraints must be transformed. Obviously, there are often a lot of constraints inherent to the data model used by a local schema. These constraints must be made explicit by the transformation, if such kinds of constraints are not inherent to the common data model.

After having removed the heterogeneity w.r.t. data models, the integration can take place. All proposed methodologies capture the integrity constraints inherent to the common data model used for integration. This is due to the fact that these constraints are already captured by the semantics of the modeling concepts of the common data model. The integration rules given by integration methodologies respect this semantics. If we now consider the constraints explicitly given for the schemata to be integrated, we can see that there are many cases where we can simply transfer the local constraint to the integrated schema. However, we often have to face situations where this is not possible.

In this paper we discuss such cases and point out possible and reasonable solutions. For presentation we use the *Generic Integration Model* GIM [12, 11]. GIM provides an intermediate graphical notation in which the schemata to be integrated can be represented in a normalized way. We extend this notation in a straightforward way for representing integrity constraints.

The remainder of this paper is organized as follows: First, we briefly introduce the concepts of GIM and extend its graphical notation for capturing integrity constraints. In Section 3 we introduce an example which we use in the subsequent sections for discussing the transformation and integration of constraints. Details on schema transformation and integration using GIM can be found in Section 4 and 5. There we especially investigate solutions for integrating conflicting constraints. Finally, we conclude with discussing some important aspects of our approach and with a comparison with related work.

2 Foundations

In this section, we briefly recall the basic steps of the design process of a federated database and introduce the Generic Integration Model GIM which we use as an intermediate representation layer from which object-oriented integrated schemata may be easily derived.

According to [13], the existing local schemata of the different (heterogeneous) component databases represent the starting point for building a federated database. In the first design step the local schemata, which are defined in the data models of the component databases, are transformed into a common data model. After this transformation step the data model heterogeneity is overcome. The following schema integration step itself is very difficult and is further subdivided in several steps: preintegration, comparison, conforming, merging, and restructuring of the schemata to be integrated (for details see [1]). After the schema integration the schema heterogeneity (e.g. naming or structural conflicts) is removed. In the last design step, external schemata which are specific views on a federated schema are derived.

For best support of the integration process we have designed a data model called the Generic Integration Model. In GIM, only schema information which is necessary for the integration process can be expressed. The following list summarizes the basic concepts of GIM:

- *Simple data types*
- *Non-overlapping class extensions*
- *Object identifier*
- *Bidirectional binary references*
- *Integrity constraints similar to SQL2*

GIM is not intended to be used as an interface to global applications. Rather, GIM is an intermediate representation form which is only used for integration purposes. A detailed description of GIM can be found, for instance, in [12, 11]. Here, we introduce only the notation of GIM diagrams which are used to model GIM schemata (cf. Figure 1).

The horizontal dimension of a GIM diagram refers to the extensional aspect of a class whereas the vertical dimension refers to the intensional aspect of a class. A class itself is represented by a rectangle. References between two classes are illustrated by lines connecting the respective reference attributes. The names

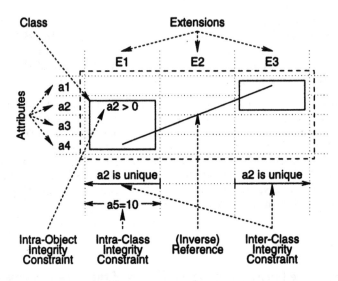

Figure 1: Diagram conventions

of the extensions and the names of the attributes are located on the top and on the left of the diagram, respectively.

In GIM, we distinguish three categories of integrity constraints. The first one, called *intra-object* integrity constraints refers to constraints which may be validated on exactly one object, e.g. the not null condition. This kind of constraints are represented within the respective GIM class and define possible values for a set of attributes of an object. The second category of constraints concern the *intra-class* integrity constraints. These constraints may be only validated by considering the whole extension of a class. The uniqueness condition, for instance, falls in this category. Finally, there are *inter-class* integrity constraints which refer to objects of several classes. Both, intra-class and inter-class integrity constraints are located below the GIM diagram as depicted in Figure 1.

3 A Running Example

In this section, we introduce an example which we use in the following sections to illustrate our approach for the design of federated databases.

We assume that there is a company with two departments, the sales and the construction department. Both departments have their own informations systems which are based on two different database systems. The sales department stores information about the commercial aspects of the products in the sales database. As depicted in Figure 2, this database contains a local schema which consists of a class transport machines (TM). The construction department of the company is responsible for the construction and production of roller conveyors (RC) which are a special kind of transport machines. In consequence, the information system of this department, which relies on the construction database, deals with data concerning the properties of roller conveyors. The local schema of this database consists of two classes RC and DRC, whereas the latter one represents driven roller conveyors which are special roller conveyors.

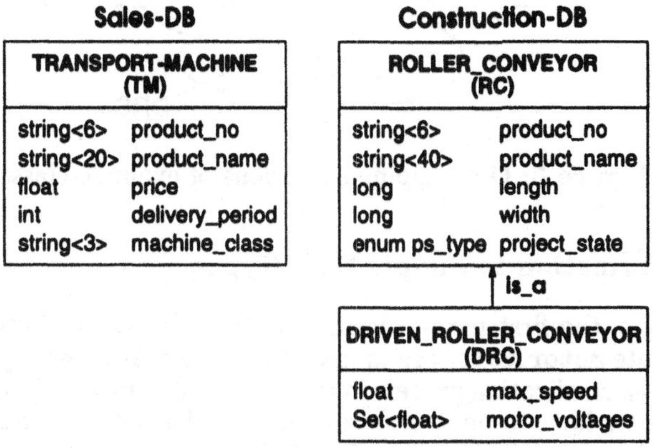

Sales-DB

TRANSPORT-MACHINE (TM)	
string<6>	product_no
string<20>	product_name
float	price
int	delivery_period
string<3>	machine_class

Construction-DB

ROLLER_CONVEYOR (RC)	
string<6>	product_no
string<40>	product_name
long	length
long	width
enum ps_type	project_state

is_a ↑

DRIVEN_ROLLER_CONVEYOR (DRC)	
float	max_speed
Set<float>	motor_voltages

Figure 2: Existing local schemata

Moreover, suppose that there are several integrity constraints defined on these local schemata. Table 1 summarizes all existing constraints.

Attributes	Ext.	Description	Remark
Sales-DB			
product_no	TM	key and not null	intra-class
Construction-DB			
product_no	RC	key	intra-class
length, width	RC	length<15*width	intra-object
project_state	RC	in_design⇒in_construction⇒completed	intra-object

Table 1: Existing local integrity constraints

Finally, let us have a look at the extensions of the local classes. Due to the fact that there are transport machines in the sales database which are also roller conveyors in the construction database, we have to deal with overlapping extensions of classes which are stored in the different databases[1]. However, there are also roller conveyors stored in the construction database which are not contained in the sales database and, vice versa, there are transport machines stored in the sales database which are not contained in the construction database. This situation of partially overlapping extensions is depicted in Figure 3 and will be further considered during the federated database design process described in the following sections.

4 Schema Transformation into GIM

In this section, we briefly present the transformation of the two schemata of our example into the Generic Integration Model. Thereby, we especially focus on the evolution of the integrity constraints during the transformation process.

---

[1] We assume that objects stored in both databases can be identified by equal product numbers.

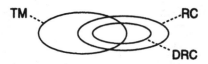

Figure 3: Overlapping extensions of example classes

4.1 Transformation to Simple Data Types

In our example, the first normal form is violated by the definition of the set-valued attribute motor_voltages in class driven_roller_conveyor. Therefore, similar to the normalization process in the relational database design process set-valued attributes have to be transformed into "independent" classes. The result of this normalization step is a new class NV (norm-voltages) which contains the reference attribute drc_ref and the integrity constraint B1 which defines the existential dependency of class NV from class DRC. In order to identify different norm voltages, we have to introduce the constraints B2 and B3 which ensure the primary key condition (cf. Table 2).

Please note that some problems may occur if there is no isomorphic mapping between local data types and GIM data types. In this case, additional integrity constraints must be derived to restrict the domain of a GIM data type, e.g. upper bounds, lower bounds, accuracy bounds or enumerated values. In our example, we have generated the new integrity constraints A1 and B4 in order to restrict the length of the character strings which represent the product names (cf. Table 2).

4.2 Non-overlapping Class Extensions

The requirement that all class extensions should be non-overlapping is contradictory to the specialization concept of object-oriented data models. Even in relational schemata this requirement can be violated although no specialization concept exists in the relational data model. Such a violation can be resolved by extensional decomposition. If the extensions of the classes A and B overlap, then we generate three classes A−B, B−A and A∩B (using the usual set operations − and ∩) which have non-overlapping extensions. The intensions of class A−B and class B−A are the same as of class A and B, respectively. The intension of class A∩B contains all attributes of both classes A and B.

Moreover, after the extensional decomposition has been carried out, the relevant integrity constraints have to be transformed. Intra-object integrity constraints can be adopted directly to the classes which are the result of the extensional decomposition. In contrast, intra-class integrity constraints have to be transformed into inter-class integrity constraints covering all resulting classes. Please note that integrity constraints originally defined on a single class change to a inter-class constraint after the extensional decomposition because the original class is subdivided in several classes.

In our example, the result of the decomposition of the classes roller_conveyor and driven_roller_conveyor are the classes DRC and RCnotDRC. Please notice that the extension of class RCnotDRC contains all roller conveyors which are *not* driven roller conveyors. In contrast, the extension of class DRC contains only the driven roller conveyors. The intension of class RCnotDRC is adopted from the class roller_conveyor whereas the intension of the class DRC contains the attributes from both classes roller_conveyor and `driven_roller_conveyor`. Furthermore, the key constraint of the class `roller_conveyor` is transformed into the inter-class unique constraint B5 and has to be checked against the union of the extensions of classes RCnotDRC and DRC. The transformed schemata are depicted in Figure 4 as GIM diagrams. The integrity constraints for these component schemata are listed in Table 2.

No	Attributes	Extensions	Description	Remark
A1	prod_name	TM	length<20	intra-object
A2	prod_no	TM	unique	intra-class
A3	prod_no	TM	not null	intra-object
B1	drc_ref	NV	card(drc_ref>0)	intra-object
B2	voltage	NV	not null	intra-object
B3	voltage	NV	unique	intra-class
B4	prod_name	RCnotDRC, DRC	length<40	intra-object
B5	prod_no	RCnotDRC ∪ DRC	unique	inter-class
B6	project_state	RCnotDRC, DRC	in_design⇒in_construction⇒completed	intra-object
B7	length, width	RCnotDRC, DRC	length<15*width	intra-object

Table 2: Integrity constraints of the component schemata

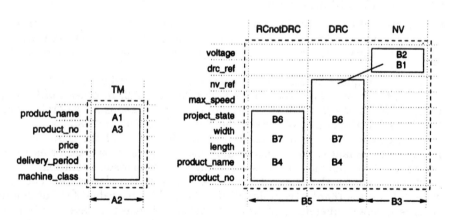

Figure 4: Schemata transformed to GIM

In conclusion, we briefly summarize the basic principles of the evolution of integrity constraints during the transformation process. In the following, we list two important rules which may be helpful for a tool-assisted design process:

Rule 1: Intra-object integrity constraints have to be adopted to the classes resulting from the extensional decomposition process.

Rule 2: Intra-class integrity constraints are always transformed into inter-class integrity constraints of the extensional decomposed classes.

Each transformation of integrity constraints must obey these rules.

5 Schema Integration

After all local schemata have been transformed into the common data model the data model heterogeneity is resolved. In order to overcome the schema heterogeneity the component schemata have to be integrated. Schema integration is a very complex task. Many kinds of conflicts between two schemata to be integrated can occur which have to be resolved. A prerequisite for conflict resolution is that all conflicts can be detected. Such a detection cannot be done automatically, rather it must be assisted by an integration tool. We propose the following steps for the integration process:

1. Resolving meta conflicts
2. Resolving attribute conflicts
3. Resolving intensional conflicts
4. Resolving extensional conflicts
5. Derivation of an object-oriented integrated schema

After having carried out step one to four all conflicts are resolved in the GIM presentation. As result from these four steps we obtain the *normalized* schema which is used to derive an object-oriented integrated schema.

In order to improve the comprehensibility of the complex integration steps we show the results of the homogenizing operations by means of our example. We focus on the aspect how integrity constraints have to be dealt with during the integration steps.

5.1 Resolving Meta Conflicts

A meta conflict exists if objects of a class differ in values of a specific attribute and their corresponding objects of another schema differ in their class assignment. The values of the first schema correspond to classes of the other schema [7].

In our example, the value "roller conveyor" of the attribute machine_class of class TM corresponds to the classes RCnotDRC and DRC. In other words, only transport machines of which the attribute machine_class is set to "roller conveyor" may correspond to objects of the classes RCnotDRC and DRC.

Meta conflicts can be resolved by the transformation of the class being in the attribute variant to the corresponding class variants. This transformation is accompanied by splitting the class according to a comparison operation.

In our example, the class TM has to be split into the classes TMnotRC and TMisRC. The class TMnotRC contains all objects of which the value of the attribute machine_class is different from "roller conveyor" whereas the class TMisRC contains only objects of which the value of the attribute machine_class is "roller conveyor". The intensions of both resulting classes are adopted from the class TM.

If a class is split by a comparison operation then new integrity constraints restricting attribute values are created. In our example, the value of the attribute TMisRC.machine_class is restricted to the fixed value "roller conveyor" (A4). This attribute can be dropped from the intension. The integrity constraint A5 of the class TMnotRC prohibits the value "roller conveyor".

Furthermore, following Rule 1, the integrity constraints A1 and A3 are adopted to the classes. However, following Rule 2, the uniqueness constraint has to be transformed into the inter-class integrity constraint A2. A2 is defined on the union of the extensions of the new classes. The resulting GIM classes of the construction database are depicted in Figure 5.

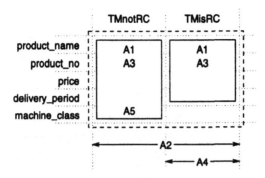

Figure 5: Sales schema after resolving the meta conflict

5.2 Resolving Attribute Conflicts

In order to arrange classes to each other in the intensional dimension, their attributes have to be compared to each other. Two or more attributes are considered as one attribute in the normalized schema if they are semantically equivalent. The semantical equivalence of attributes has to be established by the integration administrator. Attribute conflicts occur if the domains of several attributes, which have been declared as semantically equivalent before, are not compatible (see also [4]). Such conflicts can be resolved by defining value pairs in form of lookup tables or procedural functions in case there is an isomorphic mapping between the corresponding domains. If no isomorphic mapping can be found then sometimes the attribute conflict can be transformed to an integrity constraint conflict by introducing new integrity constraints.

In our example we assume that all attributes, which have same names are semantically equivalent and compatible. An exception concerns the attribute product_name. Since the maximal string length of this attribute is restricted to 20 in the schema of the sales database and to 40 in schema of the construction database they are not compatible and no isomorphic mapping between them can be found. This attribute conflict was transformed to an integrity constraint conflict in Section 4 by introducing the integrity constraints A1 and B4. We will show in Section 5.5 how to deal with conflicting integrity constraints.

Putting the transformed Classes into one Diagram

After having resolved the attribute conflicts, the classes of both schemata can be arranged vertically (intensionally) in one GIM diagram. From the extensional relationships between the local classes (cf. Figure 3) and the restruction operations up to now, the extensional relationships of the restructured classes can be derived automatically. The result is depicted in Figure 6.

We have now reached the point where the classes of both schemata can be put into one diagram (cf. Figure 7). In order to illustrate all extensional overlappings the extension of class RCnotDRC is located to the left and to the right of the extension of class DRC in Figure 7. This graphical decomposition must not be considered as a restructuring of the schema. It is necessary only for illustration purposes.

As we can see in Figure 7, the intensions and extensions of the classes overlap, e.g. classes TMisRC and DRC. However, an extensional overlapping is not allowed

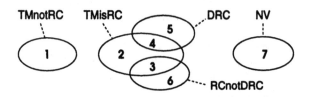

Figure 6: Extensions of the GIM classes

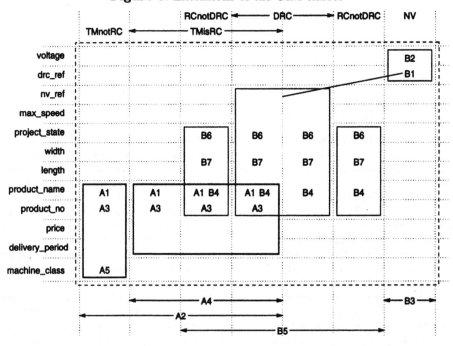

Figure 7: GIM classes in one diagram

in GIM. In the next subsections we show how the intensional and extensional overlappings have to be resolved.

5.3 Resolving Intensional Conflicts

We solve intensional conflict by intensional decomposition. Intensional decomposition means to group attributes in such a way that all attributes of a group are attributes of the same set of classes. Intensional decompositions are represented graphically by horizontal lines (cf. Figure 8). If a class is decomposed intensionally then the extensions of the resulting classes are the same but their intensions are disjoint. The intensional decomposition does not change integrity constraints in our example.

5.4 Resolving Extensional Conflicts

The resolution of extensional conflicts is more complex than the resolution of intensional conflicts due to the different consequences for the integrity constraints.

In order to meet the demand for disjoint or identical class extensions in GIM, we have to decompose extensionally overlapping classes. This process is described in more detail in [12].

The result of this decomposition is illustrated in Figure 8. For example, since the classes TMisRC and DRC (cf. Figure 7) overlap, they are decomposed into the three classes TMisRC, DRCisTM, and DRCnotTM. The resulting class extensions have to be given names. In general, this is a quite difficult task. Therefore, we construct the names by means of set operations ('is' refers to intersection and 'not' refers to difference).

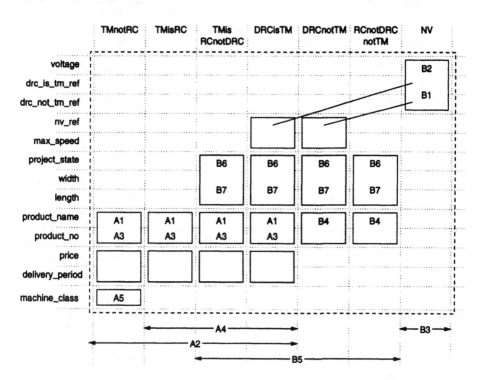

Figure 8: GIM schema after intensional and extensional decomposition

The decomposition of GIM classes causes changes of integrity constraints by applying rule one and two. For example the intra-object constraint B7 of the class DRC is adopted to the classes with the extensions DRCisTM and DRCnotTM.

However, Rule 1 and 2 do not cover all integrity constraint transformations. Each object of the class DRCisTM is an object of the sales database as well as of the construction database. Therefore, for the class DRCisTM the integrity constraints of the classes DRC and TMisRC have to be combined as a logical conjunction.

Rule 3: If the extension of a normalized GIM class is equivalent to the intersection of local class extensions, then the local intra-object and local intra-class integrity constraints must be combined as a logical conjunction.

Applying Rule 3 to the class DRCisTM the intra-object integrity constraints A1, A3, B4, B6, and B7 are combined as a logical conjunction. Due to the fact that A1 is more restrictive than B4, the constraint B4 can be omitted.

The class DRCisTM hides redundancy. The values of the attributes product_no and product_name of this class are stored in both databases. In general, it can happens that the attribute values of the objects are different in both databases. The problem is how to deal with such inconsistencies. We propose to generate new integrity constraints defining equivalence conditions on all attribute values of such kind of objects. Such integrity constraints have to be hidden from global applications. In order to guarantee consistency with regard to these integrity constraints, the autonomy of the component database management systems has to be restricted. If local applications change the state of one database then this change has to be propagated to another database management system which manages information about the same real-world entities. Furthermore, before global applications are allowed to read federated data, all inconsistent data has to be made consistent. In other words the data heterogeneity has to be overcome.

Rule 4: If a global GIM class presents the intensional and extensional intersection of local classes from different databases, then redundancy exists. Such redundancy must be controlled by new integrity constraints which have to be hidden from global applications.

5.5 Derivation of Object-Oriented Integrated Schemata

Now we are able to generate an object-oriented integrated schema. A generation algorithm is described in [12]. Here, we only sketch the generation.

The classes of the object-oriented schema are generated by composing GIM classes to larger ones. There are two different composition operations, the intensional and the extensional composition. Only classes with equal extensions can be composed intensionally. If an inter-class integrity constraint is defined which describes a dependency between attributes of the involved classes then this integrity constraint becomes an intra-class constraint.

The extensional composition is more difficult than the intensional composition. Problems occur when the classes to be composed are restricted by different integrity constraints. We propose to combine such integrity constraints as a logical disjunction. Such composed integrity constraints are weaker than their components. Therefore, all objects of the involved GIM classes can be made available to global applications.

Rule 5: If a class of the object-oriented integrated schema is generated by an extensional composition of different GIM classes, then their integrity constraints must be combined as a logical disjunction.

Larger classes can be constructed not only by extensional compositions but also by intensional compositions.

Since the used object-oriented data model supports the specialization concept, different classes can encompass intensionally and extensionally each other. *A superclass encompasses its subclasses extensionally and a subclass encompasses its superclasses intensionally.* Applying these rules to the integrated schema we are able to derive different inheritance hierarchies (cf. [12]).

In Figure 9 we show, how the GIM classes can be composed to classes of the object-oriented integrated schema. In the GIM diagram each composed class is surrounded by a dashed rectangle and is marked with a character. Following the rules of deriving specialization relations between classes we are able to derive the inheritance hierarchy (cf. Figure 10) from the diagram.

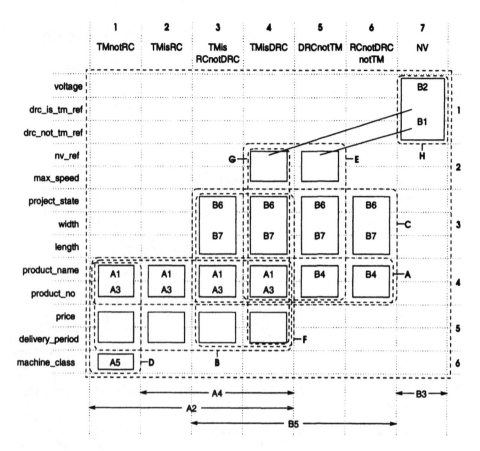

Figure 9: Derivation of an object-oriented integrated schema

	Derived Classes	Extensions	Intensions	Integrity Constraints
A	Product	1,2,3,4,5,6	4	X1
B	TM	1,2,3,4	4,5	X2,X3,X4
C	RC	3,4,5,6	3,4	X1,X5,X6,X7
D	TMnotRC	1	4,5,6	X2,X3,X4,X8
E	DRC	4,5	2,3,4	X1,X5,X6
F	TMisRC	3,4	3,4,5	X2,X3,X5,X6
G	TMisDRC	4	2,3,4,5	X2,X3,X5,X6
H	NV	7	1	X9,X10,X11

Table 3: Derived classes and integrity constraints

Table 3 shows the name, the intension and the extension of each derived class in correspondence to Figure 9.

Table 4 contains the meaning of the new integrity constraints.

The composition to the class G necessitates a further transformation step. The reference attributes **nv_ref** of the GIM classes with the extensional coordinate 4 and 5 are merged to one reference attribute of the composed class. This merging leads to a merging of the inverse reference attributes **drc_is_tm_ref** and **drc_not_tm_ref** of the class NV to the reference attribute **drc_ref**.

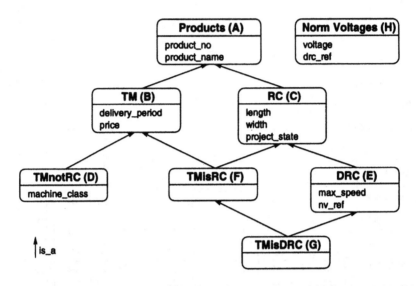

Figure 10: Derived object-oriented integrated schema

No	Attributes	Extensions	Description	Origin	Remark
X1	product_name	Product	length()<40	A1VB4	intra-object
X2	product_name	TM	length()<20	A1	intra-object
X3	product_no	TM	not null	A3	intra-object
X4	product_no	TM	unique	A2	intra-class
X5	project_state	RC	in_design⇒in_construction⇒completed	B6	intra-object
X6	length, width	RC	length<15*width	B7	intra-object
X7	product_no	RC	unique	B5	intra-class
X8	machine_class	TMnotRC	≠'roller conveyor'	A5	intra-object
X9	drc_ref	NV	card()>0	B1	intra-object
X10	voltage	NV	not null	B2	intra-object
X11	voltage	NV	unique	B3	intra-class

Table 4: Integrity constraints of the integrated schema

6 Discussion and Outlook

By means of a running example we have demonstrated basic principles of integrating schemata together with their integrity constraints. Although we have used our own integration model GIM for this purpose, the results can also be transferred to other schema integration approaches. In this way current schema integration approaches can be extended or completed by a comprehensive treatment of integrity constraints during the integration process. Constraints are an important part of database schemata and, therefore, they must be considered with equal rights during the whole integration process. In the following we briefly discuss several aspects of our approach and compare our work with related work. Finally, we give an outlook on ongoing and future work.

Considering integrity constraints during the transformation and integration process we can see that integrity constraints can change their characteristics. For several cases, this behavior is obvious, for instance, certain kinds of constraints being inherent to object-oriented data models must be made explicit when transforming to GIM (or a common data model in other approaches). However, not all model-inherent constraints of local database schemata must be made explicit, because there are also constraints being inherent to GIM (e.g., extensions in GIM are always non-overlapping). A typical behavior of constraints is the change between inter-class and intra-class when we apply extensional and intensional decomposition or composition.

Besides the evolution of pre-existing integrity constraints, we have shown that we usually have to add new global constraints for resolving several kinds of conflicts arising in the federated database design process.

We have found general rules for treating integrity constraints in the schema transformation and schema integration process. These rules mainly refer to decomposition and composition of classes and their corresponding extensions. We have presented the application of the rules by means of an example. It can be proved that the rules are correct. The proof can be based on a formal framework underlying the *Generic Integration Model* GIM. The correctness of our rules is, however, not only restricted to GIM. It is possible to apply these rules in the context of other integration approaches in which classes are decomposed and/or composed during the transformation and integration process.

In comparison with other recent approaches in the area of database integration it can be seen that our approach provides a useful extension which could be adopted by others. For instance, [5] presents an object-oriented integration approach. For resolving conflicts, additional generalization classes have to be introduced into the original class hierarchy. Explicit constraints are not used. In [14] an own object-oriented data model is introduced, and rules are given for the integration. Furthermore, some simple integrity constraints are considered. [6] discusses a large number of conflicts between schemata in great detail, however, the treatment of explicit constraints is not investigated. [15] proposes to consider data integration before schema integration. For data integration several kinds of integrity constraints are considered (for a classification of integrity constraints see e.g. [3]). The integration of constraints is discussed with regard to conflicts for data integration. Another approach coming closer to our ideas is described in [10, 9] where certain kinds of integrity constraints are considered. Our approach extends that one by allowing to deal with more general kinds of integrity constraints. We are considering constraints as first class elements in the integration process. Thereby, we are able to fill some gaps left open by other proposals.

We are currently working on a formalization for the integration of integrity constraints. This formalization is to capture all cases in which the integrated constraints can be derived automatically. In addition, we intend to provide tool support for schema integration with constraints. Several parts of a tool supporting schema integration using GIM have already be implemented. Furthermore, we have developed a prototype of a federated database system for investigating the influence of different kinds of conflict resolution on the dynamic behavior of a federated system. Especially, with regard to integrity constraints and different ways of integrating them we intend to develop criteria which will help in choosing the best way of integrating schemata together with their constraints.

References

1. C. Batini, M. Lenzerini, and S. B. Navathe. A Comparative Analysis of Methodologies for Database Schema Integration. *ACM Computing Surveys*, 18(4):323–364, December 1986.
2. R. Busse, P. Fankhauser, and E. J. Neuhold. Federated Schemata in ODMG. In J. Eder and L. A. Kalinichenko, editors, *East/West Database Workshop, Proc. 2nd Int. Workshop*, pages 356–379, Springer, 1994.
3. R. Cooper and Z. Qin. A Graphical Data Modelling Program with Constraint Specification and Management. In P. M. D. Gray and R. J. Lucas, editors, *Advanced Database Systems, Proc. 10th British National Conf. on Databases, BNCOD 10*, pages 192–208, LNCS 618, Springer, 1992.
4. L. DeMichiel. Resolving Database Incompatibility: An Approach to Performing Relational Operations over Mismatched Domains. *IEEE Transactions on Knowledge and Data Engineering*, 1(4):485–493, December 1989.
5. M. Garcia-Solaco, M. Castellanos, and F. Saltor. A Semantic-Discriminated Approach to Integration in Federated Databases. In S. Laufmann, S. Spaccapietra, and T. Yokoi, editors, *Proc. 3rd Int. Conf. on Cooperative Information Systems (CoopIS'95)*,, pages 19–31, 1995.
6. W. Kim, I. Choi, S. Gala, and M. Scheevel. On Resolving Schematic Heterogeneity in Multidatabase Systems. In W. Kim, editor, *Modern Database Systems*, pages 521–550, ACM Press, 1995.
7. R. Krishnamurthy, W. Litwin, and W. Kent. Interoperability of Heterogeneous Databases with Schematic Discrepancies. In Y. Kambayashi, M. Rusinkiewicz, and A. Sheth, editors, *Proc. 1st Int. Workshop on Interoperability in Multidatabase Systems*, pages 144–151, IEEE Computer Society Press, 1991.
8. E. Radeke and M. H. Scholl. Framework for Object Migration in Federated Database Systems. In *Proc. 3rd Int. Conf. on Parallel and Distributed Database Systems*, IEEE Computer Science Press, 1994.
9. M. P. Reddy, B. E. Prasad, and A. Gupta. Formulating Global Integrity Constraints during Derivation of Global Schema. *Data & Knowledge Engineering*, 16(3):241–268, July 1995.
10. M. P. Reddy, B. E. Prasad, P. G. Reddy, and A. Gupta. A Methodology for Integration of Heterogeneous Databases. *IEEE Transactions on Knowledge & Data Engineering*, 6(6):920–933, December 1994.
11. I. Schmitt and S. Conrad. Restructuring Class Hierarchies for Schema Integration. In R. Topor and K. Tanaka, editors, *Database Systems for Advanced Applications '97, Proc. 5th Int. Conf., DASFAA'97, Melbourne, Australia, April 1-4, 1997*, pages 411–420, World Scientific Publishing, 1997.
12. I. Schmitt and G. Saake. Integration of Inheritance Trees as Part of View Generation for Database Federations. In B. Thalheim, editor, *Conceptual Modelling — ER'96, Proc. 15th Int. Conf.*, pages 195–210, LNCS 1157, Springer, 1996.
13. A. P. Sheth and J. A. Larson. Federated Database Systems for Managing Distributed, Heterogeneous, and Autonomous Databases. *ACM Computing Surveys*, 22(3):183–236, September 1990.
14. S. Spaccapietra, C. Parent, and Y. Dupont. Model Independent Assertions for Integration of Heterogeneous Schemas. *The VLDB Journal*, 1(1):81–126, July 1992.
15. M. W. W. Vermeer and P. M. G. Apers. The Role of Integrity Constraints in Database Interoperation. In T. M. Vijayaraman, A. P. Buchmann, C. Mohan, and N. L. Sarda, editors, *Proc. 22nd Int. Conf. on Very Large Data Bases (VLDB'96), Bombay, India*, pages 425–435, Morgan Kaufmann Publishers, September 1996.

A Method for Integrating Deductive Databases

Lihui Xu and Alexandra Poulovassilis

Department of Computer Science
King's College London
Strand, London WC2R 2LS
{lihui,alex}@dcs.kcl.ac.uk

Abstract. This paper presents an approach for integrating deductive databases. In our approach deductive databases are expressed in a functional database programming language. For integrating the extensional parts of deductive databases, we use a binary relational ER model with subtyping as the common data model and propose a semi-automatic method to perform the integration. For integrating the intentional parts of deductive databases, we formally define identity and containment relationships between derived functions and propose a systematic method for comparing their semantics and integrating them.

1 Introduction

This paper addresses the integration of deductive databases. Deductive databases couple a conventional database (the *extensional database*) with a knowledge base (the *intentional database*). The extensional database is described by a database schema expressed using a particular data model. Rules are commonly expressed as formulae in a logic language such as Datalog [20]. However, following recent work in functional database languages [7, 17, 8], we assume that rules are expressed as equations in a functional language. This language supports sets as first class objects and subsumes Datalog in the sense that any set of Datalog rules can be translated into a set of equations with the same semantics; in fact the language is more expressive than Datalog since set-manipulation functions such as nesting, counting and unnesting can be defined [8]. Integrity constraints are also more expressive than those of logic languages since cardinality and other aggregation constraints can be expressed [11].

In this paper we consider the integration of both the extensional and the intentional parts of a set of component deductive databases. The common data model (CDM) that we use for integrating the extensional parts is a binary relational ER model with subtyping. This model has fewer constructs than general ER models supporting higher-degree relationships, thus simplifying the integration process. There is no loss of expressiveness since an n-ary relationship can be represented as an entity type and n binary relationships.

This paper has two contributions. Firstly, we propose a semi-automatic approach for integrating the component schemas where the DBA needs only declare the relationships between schema constructs and need not specify how the global schema is derived. Secondly, we propose a systematic method of comparing the semantics of rules and integrating them accordingly.

The outline of the paper is as follows. In Section 2 we give an overview of the functional database programming language (DBPL) that we use to define the component and integrated databases, covering only aspects of the language that are prerequisites for this paper; more comprehensive accounts can be found in [17, 7, 8, 11, 4]. In Section 3 we present our deductive database integration method. In Section 4 we compare our method with other related methods; for reasons of space this comparison is brief and a fuller discussion may be found in [21]. Finally, in Section 5 we give our conclusions and indicate directions of further work.

2 The Language

2.1 Types

Our functional DBPL is strongly, statically typed and we use the notation e_1, ..., e_n :: t to indicate that the expressions $e_1, \ldots, e_n$ all have type t. A number of primitive types are supported, such as *Bool*, *Str*, *Num* and *Chr*. Also supported are *function types*, of the form $t_1 \rightarrow t_2$ where t_1, t_2 are arbitrary types, and *structured types* such as polymorphic product, list and set types. In particular, $[t]$ is a list type and $\{t\}$ a set type for any type t, and $(t_1, \ldots, t_n)$ is an n-product type for $n > 1$ and any types $t_1, \ldots, t_n$, The user can declare enumerated types and new constants of such a type. For example, the following declarations declare two enumerated types and two constants of each type:

$$\text{\_type} \quad Person;$$
$$\text{\_type} \quad Male;$$
$$\text{\_value } P1, P2 \;::\; Person;$$
$$\text{\_value } M1, M2 \;::\; Male;$$

Enumerated types play the role of entity types in our CDM and henceforth we use the terms 'enumerated type' and 'entity type' interchangeably. For every enumerated type, T, a system-defined 0-ary function *allT* returns the current extent of T in the form of a set. For example, after the above declarations *allPerson* $= \{P1, P2\}$ and *allMale* $= \{M1, M2\}$. We term the *allT* functions *type-extent functions*.

The user can also declare type synonyms, for example:

$$\text{\_type } Name \;==\; Str;$$
$$\text{\_type } Date \;\;==\; (Num, Num, Num);$$

Subtype relationships between entity types can be specified. For example, the declaration

$$\text{\_type } Male < Person;$$

causes the extent of *Person* to expand to include the extent of *Male*, so that we now have *allPerson* $= \{P1, P2, M1, M2\}$ and *allMale* $= \{M1, M2\}$. We refer the reader to [4] for further details of subtyping in our DBPL and of the type inference algorithm used.

2.2 Data functions

Factual information is stored within updatable, set-valued functions termed *data functions* which correspond to the extensional relations of a logic database. For example, the following data function stores persons and their names:

$$\_datafun\ name :: \{(Person, Name)\};$$

Since we have adopted a binary relational CDM, henceforth we assume that all data functions have a type which is of the form $\{(t_1, t_2)\}$ where each of t_1 and t_2 is either an entity type or a type synonym.

2.3 Intentional functions

These consist of one or more equations which are specified by the user. For example, the following commands specify two equations that define the higher-order *foldr* function and one equation that defines the *sum* function in terms of *foldr* (the notation $(x : xs)$ denotes a list with head x and tail xs):

$$\_define\ foldr\ op\ e\ [] \qquad = e;$$
$$\_define\ foldr\ op\ e\ (x : xs) = op\ x\ (foldr\ op\ exs);$$
$$\_define\ sum\ xs \qquad\qquad = foldr\ (+)\ 0\ xs$$

2.4 Derived functions

Derived functions are a class of intentional functions that correspond to, and generalise, the intentional predicates of logic databases. They also generalise the derived functions of the functional data model [15] in that they are associative as opposed to uni-directional. In order to formally define derived functions, we need to introduce the notion of a *comprehension*, $\{h \mid Q_1; \ldots; Q_m\}$, where h is an expression, and Q_1 to Q_m are *qualifiers*. Each qualifier is either a boolean-valued expression, termed a *filter*, or it is a *generator* of form $p \leftarrow s$, where p is a pattern (i.e. an expression without functions) and s is a set-valued expression. Overall, a comprehension returns a set of type $\{t\}$, where t is the type of h.

Definition 1. A *derived function*, f, is one that is defined by an equation of one of the following two forms:

$$f = g_1 \cup \ldots \cup g_n;$$
$$f = \{h \mid p_1 \leftarrow g_1; \ldots; p_n \leftarrow g_n; Q\};$$

where $n \geq 1$, Q is a, possibly empty, sequence of filters, and each g_i is either the identifier f, or a data function, or another derived function. For the purposes of this paper we assume that derived functions have a type of the form $\{(t_1, \ldots, t_n)\}$ for any $n \geq 1$, where for $n = 1$ the type (t_1) is syntactically equivalent to the type t_1.

Derived functions may be recursively defined. For example, *ancs*, which returns the set of pairs (x, y) such that x is an ancestor of y:

_derived ancs = parents ∪ ancs'
_derived ancs' = {(x, z) | (x, w_1) ← parents; (w_2, z) ← ancs; w_1 == w_2}

We refer the reader to [10] for a more detailed account of derived functions in our language, including a discussion of evaluation and optimisation issues.

2.5 Integrity Constraints

An integrity constraint is a derived function that must always evaluate to the empty set e.g. *uniqueName* ensures that a person has only one name:

$$\_constraint\ uniqueName = \{(x, n, m) \mid (x, n) \leftarrow name;\ (y, m) \leftarrow name;$$
$$x == y;\ n\ !=\ m\}$$

Without loss of generality, we assume that no integrity constraint calls any other integrity constraint, including itself. This has no impact on the expressiveness of integrity constraints but simplifies the database integration process somewhat.

3 The Database Integration Strategy

In Section 3.1 we define the notion of a *component database* and its *stratification*, and discuss how constructs in the component databases are mapped to those of the integrated database. We present our database integration strategy in Sections 3.2 - 3.5.

3.1 Component Databases and Mappings

Following our discussion in Section 2, each component database, and also the integrated database, satisfies the following definition:

Definition 2. A *database* is a quintuple of sets, $\langle Schema, EDB, IDB, CDB, PDB \rangle$, where:

- *Schema* (the schema) consists of the type declarations and the subtype relationships between entity types;
- *EDB* (the extensional database) consists of the data functions and the type-extent functions;
- *IDB* (the intentional database) consists of the derived functions;
- *CDB* (the constraint database) consists of the integrity constraints;
- *PDB* (the procedural database) consists of all other intentional functions.

The members of the sets *Schema*, *EDB*, *IDB*, *CDB* and *PDB* are termed *database constructs*.

For the purposes of our database integration strategy we impose a *stratification* on the data functions, derived functions and integrity constraints of each component database, i.e. on the set $EDB \cup IDB \cup CDB$, which reflects the dependencies between function definitions. Since we have made the assumption that no integrity constraint calls any other integrity constraint, henceforth we assume that all stratifications are of the form

$$EDB, IDB^1, \ldots, IDB^s, CDB^1, \ldots, CDB^t$$

where $IDB^1 \cup \ldots \cup IDB^s$ is a partition of IDB, $CDB^1 \cup \ldots \cup CDB^t$ is a partition of CDB, and each CDB^i contains a single integrity constraint.

Given n component databases, $D_1, \ldots, D_n$, where $D_i = \langle Schema_i, EDB_i, IDB_i, CDB_i, PDB_i \rangle$ we integrate them into a single database:

$$D = \langle Schema, EDB, IDB, CDB, PDB \rangle$$

In doing so, we need to establish mappings between each D_i and D. The *schema-level mappings* define the correspondence between the database constructs of each D_i and those of D while the *instance-level mappings* define the actual values of the database constructs of D in terms of those of $D_1, \ldots, D_n$. From now on we use the notation $D_i.x$ to denote a database construct x of a component database D_i, and $D.x$ to denote a database construct x of the integrated database D.

Definition 3. The *schema-level mapping*, M_i, between D_i and D maps each database construct in D_i to one in D i.e. $M_i : D_i \longrightarrow D$. In particular M_i maps database constructs in $Schema_i$ to those in $Schema$, database constructs in EDB_i to those in EDB, and so forth.

Definition 4. For each type t in D_i there is an *instance-level mapping* $\tau_{D_i.t}$ which maps values of type t in D_i to values in D as follows:

(i) If $D_i.t$ is an entity type or type synonym, then $\tau_{D_i.t}$ maps values of type $D_i.t$ to values of type $M_i(D_i.t)$ according to some semantics specified by the DBA.

(ii) If $D_i.t$ is a primitive type, then $\tau_{D_i.t}$ maps values of type $D_i.t$ to themselves.

(iii) Given values $e_1 :: t_1, \ldots, e_k :: t_k$ in D_i, then $\tau_{D_i.(t_1,\ldots,t_k)}$ maps tuples $(e_1, \ldots, e_k)$ to tuples $(\tau_{D_i.t_1}(e_1), \ldots, \tau_{D_i.t_k}(e_k))$.

(iv) Given values $e_1, \ldots, e_k :: t$ in D_i, then $\tau_{D_i.[t]}$ maps lists $[e_1, \ldots, e_k]$ to lists $[\tau_{D_i.t}(e_1), \ldots, \tau_{D_i.t}(e_k)]$ and $\tau_{D_i.\{t\}}$ maps sets $\{e_1, \ldots, e_k\}$ to sets $\{\tau_{D_i.t}(e_1), \ldots, \tau_{D_i.t}(e_k)\}$.

3.2 Schema and EDB Integration

Given a database $D = \langle Schema, EDB, IDB, CDB, PDB \rangle$, we can represent its *Schema* and *EDB* by means of a directed graph, G, such that each entity type or type synonym $T \in Schema$ is represented by a node labelled T, each subtype relationship $T_i < T_j$ is represented by an *inc-edge*, $T_i \implies T_j$, from T_i to T_j and each data function $f :: \{(T_i, T_j)\}$ is represented by a *rel-edge*, $T_i \longrightarrow T_j$, labelled f from T_i to T_j. We call the subgraph of G induced by the rel-edges its *rel-subgraph* and the subgraph induced by the inc-edges its *inc-subgraph*.

From now we use G_i and G to represent the graphs of a component database D_i and the integrated database D, respectively. The graph representations of two example databases are given in Figures 1 and 2. *ICTRAIN* stores information about inter-city passenger trains and *LOCTRAIN* information about local passenger trains (local trains call at both cities and towns while inter-city trains only travel between cities).

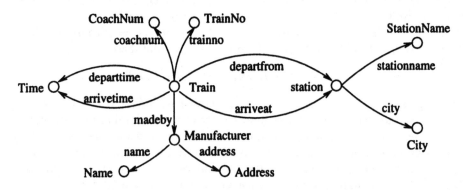

Fig. 1. Graph representation of *ICTRAIN* database

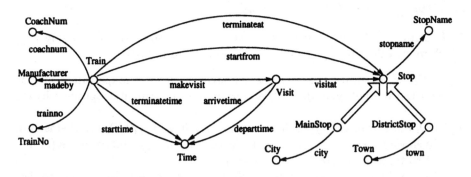

Fig. 2. Graph representation of *LOCTRAIN* database

Our *Schema* and *EDB* integration method relies on the above graph representation of the component schemas. In particular, when integrating *Schema$_i$* and *EDB$_i$* for $i = 1 \ldots n$, we first integrate their nodes, then their inc-subgraphs, and finally their rel-subgraphs:

(a) Integrating Nodes. In order to integrate the nodes of $G_1, \ldots G_n$, the DBA has to provide correspondence statements between them. There are four kinds of correspondence statements:

Definition 5. Given two types $D_i.T_i$ in $Schema_i$ and $D_j.T_j$ in $Schema_j$, a correspondence statement between them can be one of the following: $D_i.T_i$ *is equivalent to* $D_j.T_j$, $D_i.T_i$ *is contained in* $D_j.T_j$, $D_i.T_i$ *is overlapping with* $D_j.T_j$, or $D_i.T_i$ *is disjoint with* $D_j.T_j$.

For example, in order to integrate the example databases $ICTRAIN$ and $LOCTRAIN$ into one database, $TRAIN$, the following correspondence statements may be specified:

- $ICTRAIN.Train$ is equivalent to $LOCTRAIN.Train$
- $ICTRAIN.CoachNum$ is equivalent to $LOCTRAIN.CoachNum$
- $ICTRAIN.TrainNo$ is equivalent to $LOCTRAIN.TrainNo$
- $ICTRAIN.Name$ is equivalent to $LOCTRAIN.Manufacturer$
- $ICTRAIN.Time$ is equivalent to $LOCTRAIN.Time$
- $ICTRAIN.StationName$ is contained in $LOCTRAIN.StopName$
- $ICTRAIN.Station$ is contained in $LOCTRAIN.Stop$
- $ICTRAIN.Station$ is equivalent to $LOCTRAIN.MainStop$
- $ICTRAIN.city$ is equivalent to $LOCTRAIN.city$

We note that the correspondence statement *is-equivalent-to* defines an equivalence relation. The entity types and type synonyms in the integrated $Schema$ are constructed from the equivalence classes of this relation; the names of these types are chosen by the DBA. If an equivalence class consists of the types $D_{i_1}.T_{i_1}, \ldots, D_{i_k}.T_{i_k}$ and its corresponding type in $Schema$ is $D.T_i$, then the schema-level mappings obtained from this correspondence are:

$$M_{i_j}(D_{i_j}.T_{i_j}) = D.T_i, \text{ for } j = 1 \ldots k$$

The instance-level mappings $\tau_{D_{i_j}.T_{i_j}}$ for $j = 1 \ldots k$ need to be specified by the DBA. The extent of $D.T_i$ is then $\bigcup_{j=1}^{k} \{\tau_{D_{i_j}.T_{i_j}}(x) \mid x \in D_{i_j}.allT_{i_j}\}$.

In some cases, for instance if two integrated entity types $D.T_i$ and $D.T_j$ are disjoint or overlapping, the DBA may decide to define a common supertype for them. If so, the DBA can create a supertype $D.T$ of $D.D_i$ and $D.T_j$ such that $D.allT = D.allT_i \cup D.allT_j$. Likewise, if $D.T_i$ and $D.T_j$ are overlapping, the DBA can create a subtype $D.T$ of $D.T_i$ and $D.T_j$ such that $D.allT = D.allT_i \cap D.allT_j$.

After node integration, the entity types and type synonyms in the integrated database $TRAIN$ are as shown in Figure 3.

(b) Integrating Inc-Subgraphs. For any two types $D.T_1$ and $D.T_2$ in $Schema$ if one of the following conditions is satisfied we add an inc-edge from $D.T_1$ to $D.T_2$ into the inc-subgraph of G i.e. add $D.T_1 < D.T_2$ to $Schema$:

(i) $D.T_2$ is an entity type created by the DBA and it is a supertype of $D.T_1$, or $D.T_1$ is an entity type created by the DBA and it is a subtype of $D.T_2$.

(ii) $D.T_1$ and $D.T_2$ are derived from two equivalence classes, C_1 and C_2, and there exist $D_i.T_{i_1} \in C_1$, $D_i.T_{i_2} \in C_2$, and an inc-edge $D_i.T_{i_1} \Longrightarrow D_i.T_{i_2}$.

(iii) $D.T_1$ and $D.T_2$ are derived from two equivalence classes, C_1 and C_2, and there exists $D_i.T_{i_1} \in C_1$ and $D_j.T_{j_2} \in C_2$ $(i \neq j)$ such that the DBA has specified the correspondence statement "$D_i.T_{i_1}$ is contained in $D_j.T_{j_2}$".

(c) **Integrating Rel-Subgraphs.** Integrating the rel-edges of the G_i also needs the DBA to provide correspondence statements between the data functions that form their labels.

Definition 6. Given data functions $D_i.f_i :: \{(D_i.T_{i_1}, D_i.T_{i_2})\}$ in EDB_i and $D_j.f_j :: \{(D_j.T_{j_1}, D_j.T_{j_2})\}$ in EDB_j, and a path of m data functions from $D_j.T_{k_1}$ to $D_j.T_{k_{m+1}}$ in EDB_j, $D_j.f_{k_1} :: \{(D_j.T_{k_1}, D_j.T_{k_2})\}, \ldots, D_j.f_{k_m} :: \{(D_j.T_{k_m}, D_j.T_{k_{m+1}})\}$, where $m \geq 1$, there are four kinds of correspondence statements:

(i) $D_i.f_i$ is equivalent to $D_j.f_j$,

(ii) $D_i.f_i$ is contained in $D_j.f_j$,

(iii) $D_i.f_i$ is generalizable with $D_j.f_j$,

(iv) $D_i.f_i$ is mergeable with the path $D_j.f_{k_1}, \ldots, D_j.f_{k_m}$.

Some prerequisites exist for the correspondences between data functions, which are as follows for each of the above cases respectively:

(i) $D_i.T_{i_1}$ is equivalent to $D_j.T_{j_1}$ and $D_i.T_{i_2}$ is equivalent to $D_j.T_{j_2}$.

(ii) $D_i.T_{i_1}$ is equivalent to or contained in $D_j.T_{j_1}$ and $D_i.T_{i_2}$ is equivalent to or contained in $D_j.T_{j_2}$.

(iii) (a) $D_i.T_{i_1}$ is disjoint with $D_j.T_{j_1}$ and $D_i.T_{i_2}$ is equivalent to or contained in $D_j.T_{j_2}$. Or

(b) $D_i.T_{i_1}$ is equivalent to or contained in $D_j.T_{j_1}$ and $D_i.T_{i_2}$ is disjoint with $D_j.T_{j_2}$. Or

(c) $D_i.T_{i_1}$ is disjoint with $D_j.T_{j_1}$ and $D_i.T_{i_2}$ is disjoint with $D_j.T_{j_2}$.

(iv) $D_i.T_{i_1}$ is equivalent to or contained in $D_j.T_{k_1}$ and $D_i.T_{i_2}$ is equivalent to or contained in $D_j.T_{k_{m+1}}$, or vice versa.

In particular, prerequisite (iii) requires that generalizable data functions store disjoint but similar information, while the prerequisite (iv) requires that if a data function is mergeable with a path of data functions then the information provided by the former and the latter are either equivalent or one contains the other.

For example, the following correspondence statements between the data functions of *ICTRAIN* and *LOCTRAIN* may be specified:

- *ICTRAIN.trainno* is equivalent to *LOCTRAIN.trainno*
- *ICTRAIN.coachnum* is equivalent to *LOCTRAIN.coachnum*
- *ICTRAIN.departtime* is equivalent to *LOCTRAIN.starttime*
- *ICTRAIN.arrivetime* is equivalent to *LOCTRAIN.terminatetime*
- *ICTRAIN.departfrom* is contained in *LOCTRAIN.startfrom*

- *ICTRAIN.arriveat* is contained in *LOCTRAIN.terminateat*
- *ICTRAIN.stationname* is contained in *LOCTRAIN.stopname*
- *LOCTRAIN.madeby* is mergeable with *ICTRAIN.madeby*, *ICTRAIN.name*

Definition 7. If two nodes $D.T_1$ and $D.T_2$ of G are constructed from equivalence classes C_1 and C_2 respectively, and a data function $D_i.f_i :: \{(D_i.T_{i_1}, D_i.T_{i_2})\}$ is a rel-edge of G_i such that $D_i.T_{i_1} \in C_1$ and $D_i.T_{i_2} \in C_2$, then we call the edge $D_i.f_i$ a *component edge* between $D.T_1$ and $D.T_2$.

The construction of the integrated rel-subgraph consists of the integration of equivalent edges, containing edges, generalizable edges and mergeable edges. The integration begins by integrating equivalent component edges. The relationship *is-equivalent-to* between component edges is an equivalence relation which divides the component edges between two nodes $D.T_1$ and $D.T_2$ into equivalence classes. If two equivalence classes F_i and F_j contain edges f_i and f_j respectively such that f_i is contained in f_j, then we integrate these two classes into one class. Two equivalence classes might be further generalized. For example, suppose two generalizable data functions *starttime* :: $\{(Coach, Time)\}$ and *departtime* :: $\{(Train, Time)\}$, where *Coach* and *Train* are disjoint, exist in two different component databases and types *Coach*, *Train* and *Time* have been integrated as *Coach*, *Train* and *Time* in the integrated database. If the DBA has created a supertype *Vehicle* for *Coach* and *Train* in the integrated database, he might also want to integrate *starttime* and *departtime*. He can do so by generalizing *starttime* and *departtime* as *leavetime* :: $\{(Vehicle, Time)\}$. The mergeability of single data function $D_i.f_i$ with a path of data functions $D_j.f_{k_1}$, ..., $D_j.f_{k_m}$ represents a *structural conflict* in the component databases. In this case, by constructing $m - 1$ intermediate nodes, we transform $D_i.f_i$ into a path of k data functions $D_i.f'_{k_1}$, ..., $D_i.f'_{k_m}$ such that $D_i.f'_{k_r}$ and $D_j.f_{k_r}$ $r = 1 \ldots m$ are equivalent or one contains the other.

After performing the above four kinds of integration, the final rel-edge equivalence classes are obtained. The data functions of EDB, are constructed from these classes and their names are chosen by the DBA. If $\{D_{i_1}.f_{i_1}, \ldots, D_{i_k}.f_{i_k}\}$ is such a class and its corresponding integrated data function is $D.f_i$, then the schema-level mappings obtained from this correspondence are:

$$M_{i_j}(D_{i_j}.f_{i_j}) = D.f_i, \; for \; j = 1 \ldots k$$

The value of $D.f_i$ is $\bigcup_{j=1}^{k} \{\tau_{D_{i_j}.t_{i_j}}(x)|x \in D_{i_j}.f_{i_j}\}$ where $\{(D_{i_j}.t_{i_j})\}$ is the type of $D_{i_j}.f_{i_j}$.

To illustrate steps (a)-(c) above, Figure 3 gives the graph representation of the *Schema* and *EDB* of the integrated database *TRAIN*.

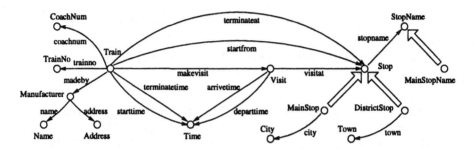

Fig. 3. Graph representation of $TRAIN$ database

3.3 IDB Integration

After integrating $Schema_1, \ldots, Schema_n$ and $EDB_1, \ldots, EDB_n$, the next step is to integrate $IDB_1, \ldots, IDB_n$.

We first transform function definitions into their integrated form before comparing their semantics. We recall that each IDB_i is partitioned into a series of strata, $IDB_i^1, \ldots, IDB_i^{s_i}$. We start by integrating the first set of strata $IDB_1^1, \ldots, IDB_n^1$. We then integrate the second set of strata, and so forth. Thus, when we are integrating the set of strata $IDB_1^j, \ldots, IDB_n^j$, we have already integrated $Schema_i$, EDB_i and $IDB_i^1, \ldots, IDB_i^{j-1}$ for $i = 1 \ldots n$. So transforming the definition of a derived function $D_i.f$ in IDB_i^j into its integrated form consists of translating the database constructs of the so far integrated database in its definition. In particular, each constant $c :: t$ is translated to $\tau_{D_i.t}(c)$, and each function g in $EDB_i \cup IDB_i$ is translated to $M_i(g)$ if $M_i(g) \in IDB$ or otherwise to g.

For two given derived functions, in order to know whether they can be integrated into one function we need compare their semantics. We define containment and identity relationships between two derived functions as follows:

Definition 8. For two derived functions $f, g :: t$, if for any element x in the semantic domain of t, $x \in f$ implies $x \in g$, then we say that g *contains* f or f *is contained by* g, which is expressed as $f \subseteq g$. If $f \subseteq g$ and $g \subseteq f$, then we say that f and g are *identical*, which is represented as $f \equiv g$.

Definition 9. For two sets of derived functions $F = \{f_1, \ldots, f_r\}$ and $G = \{g_1, \ldots, g_r\}$, we say that F and G are *mergeable* if

(i) F and G are two sets of mutual-recursive functions and either $f_m \equiv g_m$ or $f_m \subseteq g_m$, for $m = 1, \ldots, r$. Or
(ii) F and G are two singleton sets of non-recursive functions and $f_1 \equiv g_1$ or $f_1 \subseteq g_1$.

More generally, if k sets of derived functions $F_i = \{D_i.f_{i_1}, \ldots, D_i.f_{i_r}\}$ for $i = 1 \ldots k$ are mergeable, then then we will integrate them into one set of derived functions $F = \{D.f_1, \ldots, D.f_r\}$ such that:

$$M_i(D_i.f_{i_j}) = D.f_j, \text{ for } i = 1 \ldots k \text{ and for } j = 1 \ldots r$$

The value of $D.f_j$ is $\bigcup_{i=1}^{k}\{\tau_{D_i.t_{i_j}}(x)|x \in D_i.f_{i_j}\}$ where $\{(D_i.t_{i_j})\}$ is the type of $D_i.f_{i_j}$.

The overall algorithm for IDB integration is as follows, where n is the number of component databases, each IDB_i is partitioned into s_i strata and s is the number of strata the algorithm has constructed so far for D:

Algorithm Derived Function Integration:
$s := 0$;
for $j := 1$ **to** $max(s_1, \ldots, s_n)$ **do**
   for $i := 1$ **to** n **do**
      if $IDB_i^j \neq \emptyset$ **then**
         transform every function in IDB_i^j into its integrated form;
         $k := 1$;
         while $k \leq s$ **do**
            if IDB_i^j and IDB^k are mergeable **then**
               integrate IDB_i^j into IDB^k;
               break;
            end
            $k := k + 1$;
         end;
         if $k > s$ **then**
            $s := s + 1$;
            $IDB^s := IDB_i^j$;
         end;
      end
   end
end.

When we integrate derived functions using the above algorithm, we must know whether the functions obey an identity or containment relationship. The following propositions provide a way to establish the relationships between derived functions by syntactically comparing their definitions, starting off with information about the identity or containment of data functions and recursively applying the propositions. Derived functions defined by a comprehension may need some syntactic transformation in order to facilitate the syntactical comparison, and a number of equivalences have been proposed in [9] which can utilized for this purpose. Formal proofs of the propositions are beyond the scope of this paper and will appear in a forthcoming technical report.

Proposition 10. Given two non-recursive derived functions f and g such that

$$f = \{e|p_1 \leftarrow f_1; \ldots; p_n \leftarrow f_n; Q\}$$
$$g = \{e|p_1 \leftarrow g_1; \ldots; p_n \leftarrow g_n; Q\}$$

if $f_i \equiv g_i$ for $i = 1 \ldots n$, then $f \equiv g$, otherwise if $f_i \subseteq g_i$ for $i = 1 \ldots n$, then $f \subseteq g$.

Proposition 11. Given two non-recursive derived functions f and g such that

$$f = f_1 \cup \ldots \cup f_m$$
$$g = g_1 \cup \ldots \cup g_n$$

if there is a mapping α from $\{f_1, \ldots, f_m\}$ to $\{g_1, \ldots, g_n\}$ such that for every $f_i \in \{f_1, \ldots, f_m\}$, $f_i \subseteq \alpha(f_i)$ then $f \subseteq g$. If both $f \subseteq g$ and $g \subseteq f$, then $f \equiv g$.

Proposition 12. Given two non-recursive derived functions f and g such that

$$f = \{e | p_1 \leftarrow f_1; \ldots; p_n \leftarrow f_n; Q'\}$$
$$g = \{e | p_1 \leftarrow f_1; \ldots; p_n \leftarrow f_n; Q\}$$

if for all instantiations of free variables, Q is true whenever Q' is true, then $f \subseteq g$.

Proposition 13. Given two sets of mutual recursive derived functions $\{f_1 = e_1, \ldots, f_r = e_r\}$ and $\{g_1 = e'_1, \ldots, g_r = e'_r\}$, if

$$(f_1 \equiv g_1) \& \ldots \& (f_r \equiv g_r) \Rightarrow (e_1 \equiv e'_1) \& \ldots \& (e_r \equiv e'_r)$$

then $f_i \equiv g_i$, for $i = 1 \ldots r$.

Proposition 14. Given two sets of mutual recursive derived functions $\{f_1 = e_1, \ldots, f_r = e_r\}$ and $\{g_1 = e'_1, \ldots, g_r = e'_r\}$, then if

$$(f_1 \subseteq g_1) \& \ldots \& (f_r \subseteq g_r) \Rightarrow (e_1 \subseteq e'_1) \& \ldots \& (e_r \subseteq e'_r)$$

and there is no derived function of the form $f' = \{h | p_1 \leftarrow g'_1; \ldots; p_n \leftarrow g'_n; Q\}$ in above two sets such that some g'_k is empty[1], then $f_i \subseteq g_i$, for $i = 1 \ldots r$.

To illustrate, we list the derived functions of $ICTRAIN$ and $LOCTRAIN$ in Appendices A and B respectively. The following relationships can be established between these derived functions, where $TR[f]$ denotes the translation of a derived function f into its integrated form:

- $TR[ICTRAIN.directreach] \equiv TR[LOCTRAIN.directreach1]$
- $TR[ICTRAIN.reachbyltransfer] \subseteq TR[LOCTRAIN.onetransferreach]$
- $TR[ICTRAIN.easyreach] \subseteq TR[LOCTRAIN.easyreach]$
- $TR[ICTRAIN.idirectreach] \subseteq TR[LOCTRAIN.indirectreach]$
  $TR[ICTRAIN.reachable] \subseteq TR[LOCTRAIN.reachable]$

The resulting IDB is given in Appendix C.

---

[1] This condition guarantees that the proposition can be expressed as an *inclusive predicate* which can be proved by means of *fixed point induction* [14].

3.4 CDB Integration

The next integration step is to integrate $CDB_1, \ldots, CDB_n$ to give CDB. We recall that no integrity constraint calls any other integrity constraint, which means that each integrity constraint is defined in terms of data functions and derived functions only. Before integrating the integrity constraints in the component databases, we transform each of them into their integrated form by translating their definitions into the database constructs of *Schema*, *EDB* and *IDB*.

As with derived function integration, integrity constraint integration is also based on the semantics of the constraints. During the integration, for each component database D_i we compare the semantics of each constraint c_i in D_i with that of each integrity constraint c_j in each D_j, $j \neq i$. In both the following cases, c_i holds in the integrated database and we place it into a new stratum of the CDB: (i) if every D_j contains a constraint c_j such that c_i is contained by or is identical to c_j; (ii) if some D_j contain a constraint c_j such that c_i is contained by or is identical to c_j, but others do not, but if we evaluate c_i with respect to latter databases, either we always get the empty set or there are functions in the definition of c_i which are not defined in these databases. In all other cases we do not transfer c_i to D.

For example, when we compare the constraints in the component databases $ICTRAIN$ and $LOCTRAIN$, given in Appendices A and B, we have that:

- $TR[LOCTRAIN.onlytravelonce] \equiv TR[ICTRAIN.onetrip]$
- $TR[LOCTRAIN.traveltime] \subseteq TR[ICTRAIN.tripduration]$
- $TR[LOCTRAIN.rushhourtrain]$ is not applicable to $LOCTRAIN$.

Thus the integrity constraints obtained for the integrated database $TRAIN$ are as given in Appendix C.

3.5 PDB Integration

The final integration step consists of integrating $PDB_1, \ldots, PDB_n$ to give PDB. For this step, we do not attempt any automatic semantic integration of function definitions. We simply translate the function definitions of $PDB_1, \ldots, PDB_n$ into the database constructs of the so far integrated database and place the resulting definitions into the PDB.

4 Related Work

Since the 1980s a variety of approaches have been proposed for schema integration [6, 5, 12, 18]. Roughly, these approaches can be divided into two categories: *declarative statement* and *procedural statement* approaches. Our methodology for integrating the schema and extensional part of deductive databases falls into the category of declarative statement approaches.

Recently several papers addressing the integration of deductive databases have also appeared in literature [2, 19, 16]. Compared with these approaches, we propose a systematic method to compare the semantics of rules, and we integrate not only non-recursive derived functions but also recursive derived functions.

Some work has recently been done on the integration of integrity constraints [13, 1] and our approach is similar to both of these. All three approaches perform constraint integration in three steps: transformation, comparison of semantics and integration. However, in our approach we have provided a formal basis for comparing semantics and our integrity constraints are more expressive.

5 Conclusion

In this paper we have described a method for integrating deductive databases. For the extensional database integration, we use a binary relational ER model with subtyping as the common data model, and have proposed a semi-automatic method for integrating the component schemas where the DBA needs only declare the relationships between schema constructs and need not specify how the global schema is derived. For the intentional database integration, we integrate rules from different component databases according to their denotational semantics and have proposed a systematic method of comparing the semantics of rules; our method is useful especially in the case of recursive rule integration, which has not been dealt with by previous work. For further work we plan to investigate and formally define the notions of *correctness, completeness* and *minimality* [3] in our context, and to show that our method satisfies them, and to implement an interactive tool that supports our method.

A   The EDB and CDB of the ICTRAIN database

```
_derived directreach = {(from,to)|(train1,station1)<-departfrom;
        (train2,station2)<-arriveat;(station3,from)<-stationname;
        (station4,to)<-stationname; train1==train2;
        station1==station3; station2==station4};
_derived reachby1transfer = {(from,to)|(from, to1)<-directreach;
                            (from2,to)<-directreach; to1==from2};
_derived easyreach = directreach U reachby1transfer;
_derived indirectreach = {(from,to)|(from, to1)<-directreach;
                        (from2,to)<-reachable; to1==from2};
_derived reachable = directreach U indirectreach;
_constraints onetrip = {(train1,dtime1,dtime2)|
        (train1,dtime1)<-departtime; (train2,dtime2)<-departtime;
        train1==train2; dtime1!=dtime2};
_constraints tripduration = {(train,dtime,atime)|
        (train,dtime)<-departtime; (train1,atime)<-arrivetime;
        train==train1; ((fst dtime - fst atime)>12)};
_constraints peaktimetrain = {(train,cnum)|
        (train,stime)<-starttime; (train1,cnum)<-coachnum;
        train==train1; (fst stime)<10; cnum<8};
```

B   The EDB and CDB of the LOCTRAIN database

```
_derived callat = {(train,stname,dtime)|
        (train,visit1)<-makevisit; (visit2,stop2)<-visitat;
        (stop3,stname)<-stopname;(visit4,dtime)<-departtime;
        visit1==visit2; stop2==stop3; visit2==visit4};
_derived directreach1 = {(from,to)|(train1,stop1)<-startfrom;
        (train2,stop2)<-terminateat; (stop3,from)<-stopname;
        (stop4,to)<-stopname; train1==train2; stop1==stop3;
        stop2==stop4};
_derived directreach2 = {(from,to)|(train1,from,dtime1)<-callat;
        (train2,to,dtime2)<-callat; train1==train2;
        dtime1<dtime2};
_derived directreach3 = {(from,to)|(train1,stop1)<-startfrom;
        (train2,to,dtime2)<-callat; (stop3,from)<-stopname;
        train1==train2; stop1==stop3};
_derived directreach4 = {(from,to)|(train1,from,dtime1)<-callat;
        (train2,stop2)<-terminateat; (stop3,to)<-stopname;
        train1==train2; stop2==stop3};
_derived directreach  = directreach1 U directreach2
                        U directreach3 U directreach4;
_derived onetransferreach = {(from,to)|(from,to1)<-directreach;
                            (from2,to)<-directreach; to1==from2};
_derived easyreach = directreach U onetransferreach;
_derived indirectreach = {(from,to)|(from,to1)<-directreach;
                            (from2,to)<-reachable; to1==from2};
_derived reachable = directreach U indirectreach;
_constraints onlytravelonce = {(train1,stime1,stime2)|
        (train1,stime1)<-starttime; (train2,stime2)<-starttime;
        train1==train2; stime1!=stime2};
_constraints traveltime = {(train,stime,ttime)|
        (train,stime)<-starttime;(train1,ttime)<-terminatetime;
        train==train1; ((fst stime-fst ttime)>10)};
_constraints rushhourtrain = {(train,stname)|(train,stop1)<-stop;
        (stop2,stname)<-stopname;(train3,sttime)<-starttime;
        (stop1 in allDistrictStop); stop1==stop2; train==train3;
        (fst stime)<9}
```

C   The EDB and CDB of the TRAIN database

```
_derived callat = {(train,stname,dtime)|(train,visit1)<-makevisit;
        (visit2,stn2)<-visitat; (stn3,stname)<-stationname;
        (visit4,dtime)<-departtime; visit1==visit2; stn2==stn3;
        visit2==visit4};
_derived directreach1 = {(from,to)|(train1,stn1)<-startfrom;
```

```
          (train2,stn2)<-terminateat; (stn3,from)<-stationname;
          (stn4,to)<-stationname; train1==train2; stn1==stn3;
          stn2==stn4};
_derived directreach2 = {(from,to)|(train1,from,dtime1)<-callat;
          (train2,to,dtime2)<-callat;train1==train2;dtime1<dtime2};
_derived directreach3 = {(from,to)|(train1,stn1)<-startfrom;
          (train2,to,dtime2)<-callat; (stn3,from)<-stationname;
          train1==train2; stn1==stn3};
_derived directreach4 = {(from,to)|(train1,from,dtime1)<-callat;
          (train2,stn2)<-terminateat; (stn3,to)<-stationname;
          train1==train2; stn2==stn3};
_derived directreach  = directreach1 U directreach2
                        U directreach3 U directreach4;
_derived onetransferreach = {(from,to)|(from,to1)<-directreach;
                             (from2,to)<-directreach; to1==from2};
_derived easyreach = directreach U onetransferreach;
_derived indirectreach = {(from,to)|(from,to1)<-directreach;
                          (from2,to)<-reachable; to1==from2};
_derived reachable = directreach U indirectreach;
_constraints onlytravelonce = {(train1,stime1,stime2)|
          (train1,stime1)<-starttime; (train2,stime2)<-starttime;
          train1==train2; stime1!=stime2};
_constraints traveltime = {(train,stime,ttime)|
          (train,stime)<-starttime;(train1,ttime)<-terminatetime;
          train==train1;((fst stime - fst ttime) > 12)};
_constraints rushhourtrain = {(train,stname)|(train,stop1)<-stop;
          (stop2,stname)<-stopname; (train3,sttime)<-starttime;
          (stop1 in allDistrictStop);stop1==stop2;
          train==train3; (fst stime)<9}
```

References

1. R.M. Alzahrani, M.A. Qutaisha, N.J. Fiddan and W.A. Gray, "Integrity Merging in an Object-Oriented Federated Database Environment", in Proc. 13th British National Conference on Databases (BNCOD-13), Manchester, 1995. Springer-Verlag LNCS 940.
2. C. Baral, S. Kraus and J. Minker., "Combining Multiple Knowledge Bases", IEEE Trans. on Knowledge and Data Engineering, Vol.3, No.2, June 1991.
3. C. Batini, M. Lenzerini and S. Navathe, "A Comparative Analysis of Methodologies for Database Schema Integration", ACM Computing Surveys, Vol.18, No.4, Dec. 1986.
4. S. Courtenage and A. Poulovassilis, "Combining Inheritance and Parametric Polymorphism in a Functional Database Language", in Proc. 13th British National Conference on Databases (BNCOD-13), Manchester, 1995. Springer-Verlag LNCS 940.
5. J. Koh and A. Chen, "Integration of Heterogeneous Object Schemas," Proc. of Entity-Relationship Approach-ER'93, Arlington, Texas, USA, Dec. 1993.

6. A. Motro, "Superviews: Virtual Integration of Multiple Databases," IEEE Transactions on Software Engineering, Vol.13, No.7, July 1987.

7. A. Poulovassilis and C. Small, "A Functional Programming Approach to Deductive Databases", in Proc. 17th International Conference on Very Large Databases (VLDB), Barcelona, 1991.

8. A. Poulovassilis and C. Small, "A Domain-theoretic Approach to Integrating Functional and Logic Database Languages", in Proc. 19th International Conference on Very Large Databases (VLDB), Dublin, 1993.

9. A. Poulovassilis and C. Small, "Investigation of Algebraic Query Optimisation for Database Programming Languages", in Proc. International Conference on 20th Very Large Databases, Santiago, Chile, 1994.

10. A. Poulovassilis and C. Small, "Optimisation of Derived Functions in Database Programming Languages", Technical Report 96/14, Dept. of Computer Science, King's College London, 1996.

11. S. Reddi, "Integrity Constraint Enforcement in the Functional Database Language PFL", in Proc. 11th British National Conference on Databases (BNCOD-11), Keele, 1993. Springer-Verlag LNCS 696.

12. M. Reddy, B. Prasad, P. Reddy and A. Gupta, "A Methodology for Integration of Heterogeneous Databases", IEEE Transactions on Knowledge and Data Engineering, Vol.6, No.6, Dec. 1994.

13. M. Reddy, B. Prasad and A. Gupta, "Formulating global integrity constraints during derivation of global schema", Knowledge & Data Engineering, 16, 1995.

14. D.A. Schmidt, *Denotational Semantics*, Allyn and Bacon, 1986.

15. D.W. Shipman, "The functional data model and the data language DAPLEX", ACM Trans. on Database Systems, Vol.6, No.1, March 1981.

16. L. Sirounian and W. Grosky, "A Knowledge Model For Unifying Deductive and Non-Deductive Heterogeneous Databases", IEEE Trans. on Knowledge and Data Engineering, Vol.7, No.1, Feb. 1995.

17. C. Small and A. Poulovassilis, "An Overview of PFL", in Proc. 3rd International Workshop on Database Programming Languages, Nafplion, August 1991.

18. S. Spaccapietra and C. Parent, "View Integration: A Step Forward in Solving Structural Conflicts," IEEE Transactions on Knowledge and Data Engineering, Vol.6, No.2, April 1994.

19. V. Subrahmanian, "Amalgamating Knowledge bases", ACM Trans. on Database Systems, Vol.9, No.2, June 1994.

20. J.D. Ullman, *Principles of Database and Knowledge-Base Systems*. Computer Science Press, 1988.

21. L. Xu and A. Poulovassilis, "A Method for Integrating Deductive Databases," Technical Report 97/02, Dept. of Computer Science, King's College London, 1997.

Author Index

Balownew, O., 116
Benford, S., 135
Berti, L., 119
Bode, T., 116
Bratbergsengen, K., 69
Bratsberg, S.E., 23

Carnduff, T.W., 184
Chau, H.L., 139
Conrad, S., 200
Cremers, A.B., 116

Dunlop, A.N., 131

Faulstich, L.C., 169
Ferreira Rezende, F. de, 54
Fiddian, N.J., 129

Gloeckner, A., 54
Gluche, D., 84
Gray, W.A., 129, 184
Grøvlen, Ø., 38
Grust, T., 84
Gupta, H., 121

Haase, O., 123
Härder, T., 54
Henrich, A., 123
Heuer, A., 84
Hey, A.J.G., 131
Höding, M., 200
Hvasshovd, S.-O., 23, 38

Jin, J.J., 126

Kalinski, J., 116
Kambayashi, Y., 137
Kerschberg, L., 1
Knafla, N., 154
Kröger, J., 84

Lam, F.M., 139
Lei, R., 126
Linnemann, V., 169
Lutze, J., 54

Madurapperuma, A.P., 129
McLaren, I., 121
Miles, J.C., 184

Ngu, A.H.H., 126
Nørvåg, K., 69

Papiani, M., 131
Poulovassilis, A., 215

Roberts, S.A., 133
Rollinson, S.R., 133
Rottmann, H., 116

Saake, G., 200
Santoyridis, I., 184
Schmitt, I., 200
Scholl, M.H., 84
Spiliopoulou, M., 169

Taylor, I., 135
Torbjørnsen, Ø., 23, 38
Türker, C., 200

Vella, A., 121

Winiwarter, W., 137
Wolff, J.E., 116
Wong, R.K., 139

Xu, L., 215

Zurek, T., 101

Lecture Notes in Computer Science

For information about Vols. 1–1192

please contact your bookseller or Springer-Verlag

Vol. 1193: J.P. Müller, M.J. Wooldridge, N.R. Jennings (Eds.), Intelligent Agents III. XV, 401 pages. 1997. (Subseries LNAI).

Vol. 1194: M. Sipper, Evolution of Parallel Cellular Machines. XIII, 199 pages. 1997.

Vol. 1195: R. Trappl, P. Petta (Eds.), Creating Personalities for Synthetic Actors. VII, 251 pages. 1997. (Subseries LNAI).

Vol. 1196: L. Vulkov, J. Waśniewski, P. Yalamov (Eds.), Numerical Analysis and Its Applications. Proceedings, 1996. XIII, 608 pages. 1997.

Vol. 1197: F. d'Amore, P.G. Franciosa, A. Marchetti-Spaccamela (Eds.), Graph-Theoretic Concepts in Computer Science. Proceedings, 1996. XI, 410 pages. 1997.

Vol. 1198: H.S. Nwana, N. Azarmi (Eds.), Software Agents and Soft Computing: Towards Enhancing Machine Intelligence. XIV, 298 pages. 1997. (Subseries LNAI).

Vol. 1199: D.K. Panda, C.B. Stunkel (Eds.), Communication and Architectural Support for Network-Based Parallel Computing. Proceedings, 1997. X, 269 pages. 1997.

Vol. 1200: R. Reischuk, M. Morvan (Eds.), STACS 97. Proceedings, 1997. XIII, 614 pages. 1997.

Vol. 1201: O. Maler (Ed.), Hybrid and Real-Time Systems. Proceedings, 1997. IX, 417 pages. 1997.

Vol. 1203: G. Bongiovanni, D.P. Bovet, G. Di Battista (Eds.), Algorithms and Complexity. Proceedings, 1997. VIII, 311 pages. 1997.

Vol. 1204: H. Mössenböck (Ed.), Modular Programming Languages. Proceedings, 1997. X, 379 pages. 1997.

Vol. 1205: J. Troccaz, E. Grimson, R. Mösges (Eds.), CVRMed-MRCAS'97. Proceedings, 1997. XIX, 834 pages. 1997.

Vol. 1206: J. Bigün, G. Chollet, G. Borgefors (Eds.), Audio- and Video-based Biometric Person Authentication. Proceedings, 1997. XII, 450 pages. 1997.

Vol. 1207: J. Gallagher (Ed.), Logic Program Synthesis and Transformation. Proceedings, 1996. VII, 325 pages. 1997.

Vol. 1208: S. Ben-David (Ed.), Computational Learning Theory. Proceedings, 1997. VIII, 331 pages. 1997. (Subseries LNAI).

Vol. 1209: L. Cavedon, A. Rao, W. Wobcke (Eds.), Intelligent Agent Systems. Proceedings, 1996. IX, 188 pages. 1997. (Subseries LNAI).

Vol. 1210: P. de Groote, J.R. Hindley (Eds.), Typed Lambda Calculi and Applications. Proceedings, 1997. VIII, 405 pages. 1997.

Vol. 1211: E. Keravnou, C. Garbay, R. Baud, J. Wyatt (Eds.), Artificial Intelligence in Medicine. Proceedings, 1997. XIII, 526 pages. 1997. (Subseries LNAI).

Vol. 1212: J. P. Bowen, M.G. Hinchey, D. Till (Eds.), ZUM '97: The Z Formal Specification Notation. Proceedings, 1997. X, 435 pages. 1997.

Vol. 1213: P. J. Angeline, R. G. Reynolds, J. R. McDonnell, R. Eberhart (Eds.), Evolutionary Programming VI. Proceedings, 1997. X, 457 pages. 1997.

Vol. 1214: M. Bidoit, M. Dauchet (Eds.), TAPSOFT '97: Theory and Practice of Software Development. Proceedings, 1997. XV, 884 pages. 1997.

Vol. 1215: J. M. L. M. Palma, J. Dongarra (Eds.), Vector and Parallel Processing – VECPAR'96. Proceedings, 1996. XI, 471 pages. 1997.

Vol. 1216: J. Dix, L. Moniz Pereira, T.C. Przymusinski (Eds.), Non-Monotonic Extensions of Logic Programming. Proceedings, 1996. XI, 224 pages. 1997. (Subseries LNAI).

Vol. 1217: E. Brinksma (Ed.), Tools and Algorithms for the Construction and Analysis of Systems. Proceedings, 1997. X, 433 pages. 1997.

Vol. 1218: G. Păun, A. Salomaa (Eds.), New Trends in Formal Languages. IX, 465 pages. 1997.

Vol. 1219: K. Rothermel, R. Popescu-Zeletin (Eds.), Mobile Agents. Proceedings, 1997. VIII, 223 pages. 1997.

Vol. 1220: P. Brezany, Input/Output Intensive Massively Parallel Computing. XIV, 288 pages. 1997.

Vol. 1221: G. Weiß (Ed.), Distributed Artificial Intelligence Meets Machine Learning. Proceedings, 1996. X, 294 pages. 1997. (Subseries LNAI).

Vol. 1222: J. Vitek, C. Tschudin (Eds.), Mobile Object Systems. Proceedings, 1996. X, 319 pages. 1997.

Vol. 1223: M. Pelillo, E.R. Hancock (Eds.), Energy Minimization Methods in Computer Vision and Pattern Recognition. Proceedings, 1997. XII, 549 pages. 1997.

Vol. 1224: M. van Someren, G. Widmer (Eds.), Machine Learning: ECML-97. Proceedings, 1997. XI, 361 pages. 1997. (Subseries LNAI).

Vol. 1225: B. Hertzberger, P. Sloot (Eds.), High-Performance Computing and Networking. Proceedings, 1997. XXI, 1066 pages. 1997.

Vol. 1226: B. Reusch (Ed.), Computational Intelligence. Proceedings, 1997. XIII, 609 pages. 1997.

Vol. 1227: D. Galmiche (Ed.), Automated Reasoning with Analytic Tableaux and Related Methods. Proceedings, 1997. XI, 373 pages. 1997. (Subseries LNAI).

Vol. 1228: S.-H. Nienhuys-Cheng, R. de Wolf, Foundations of Inductive Logic Programming. XVII, 404 pages. 1997. (Subseries LNAI).